Paving the empire road

MANCHESTER
1824

Manchester University Press

Paving the empire road

BBC television and Black Britons

Darrell M. Newton

MANCHESTER UNIVERSITY PRESS
Manchester and New York

*distributed in the United States exclusively
by Palgrave Macmillan*

The right of Darrell M. Newton to be identified as the author of this work has been asserted by him in accordance with the Copyright, Designs and Patents Act 1988.

Published by Manchester University Press
Oxford Road, Manchester M13 9NR, UK
and Room 400, 175 Fifth Avenue, New York, NY 10010, USA
www.manchesteruniversitypress.co.uk

Distributed in the United States exclusively by
Palgrave Macmillan, 175 Fifth Avenue, New York,
NY 10010, USA

Distributed in Canada exclusively by
UBC Press, University of British Columbia, 2029 West Mall,
Vancouver, BC, Canada V6T 1Z2

British Library Cataloguing-in-Publication Data
A catalogue record for this book is available from the British Library

Library of Congress Cataloging-in-Publication Data applied for

ISBN   978 0 7190 8167 5 hardback

First published 2011

The publisher has no responsibility for the persistence or accuracy of URLs for any external or third-party internet websites referred to in this book, and does not guarantee that any content on such websites is, or will remain, accurate or appropriate.

Typeset in Minion and Optima
by Action Publishing Technology Ltd, Gloucester
Printed in Great Britain
by the MPG Books Group, UK

For Mamarama, my Pickle and the Bean

Contents

Illustrations

All illustrations courtesy of British Pathé.

Acknowledgements

First, my heartfelt respect goes out to John Fiske, advisor and friend. Thanks are due to the marvellous Stuart Hall, who gave me hours of time as we discussed the nexus of race and class on British television, and his favourite shows. I will never forget the kindness, and fortitude, of Michele Hilmes.

The marvellous Stephen Bourne and Jim Pines have been tremendous inspirations to me, as have Helen Wheatley, Horace Newcomb, Jason Jacobs, Paddy Scannell, Lez Cooke, Jonathan Bignell, Sarita Malik, and Wendy Webster. Thank you to all of the scholars, especially Christine Geraghty, who kindly listened to the many papers I've given at conferences throughout England, Wales, and the United States.

Rachel Lawson, Jeff Walden, and Jacqueline Kavanagh of the BBC Archives and Vicky Mitchell of BBC Vision have demonstrated an appreciation for scholarship time and again. The members of the Black and Asian Studies Association (BASA), notably Arthur Torrington and Marika Sherwood, keep my curiosity refreshed with each new e-mail; as do Marie Gillespie, Anthony McNicholas, and members of IAMHIST.

I will never be able to repay the kind support shown by Jan Oliver, Neema Kambona, Treva Etienne, Michael McMillan, Cyril Husbands, Kadija George-Sesay, Brenda Emmanus, Michael Abbensetts, Jack Gold, Peter Ansorge, Graeme Stephenson, and others I've met or contacted while researching this project.

My partner Tabitha continues to listen patiently to my banter, as my mother Grace smiles down upon me even now.

Finally, MUP believed in me, and felt this study was far from being 'too specialised' for publication, particularly since it affects each of us as children of media, no matter our gender or ethnic identity.

Portions of this work were previously published as 'Shifting sentiments: West Indian immigrants, the BBC and cultural production', in Helen Wheatley, ed., *Re-viewing Television History: Critical Issues in Television Historiography*, London: I.B. Tauris, 2007; 'The last great white hope: Dyke and diversity', *Sable Literature Magazine* (March 2008): and 'Calling the West

Indies: the BBC World Service and Caribbean voices', *The Historical Journal of Film, Radio and Television Special Issue: BBC World Service, 1932–2007* (December 2008).

Abbreviations

ABC	American Broadcasting Company
ABC TV	African Broadcasting Corporation
ACC	Afro-Caribbean Channel
ATV	Associated TeleVision
BBC	British Broadcasting Corporation
BBF	BBC Black Forum
BAFTA	British Academy of Film and Television Arts
BET	Black Entertainment Television
BskyB	British Sky Broadcasting
BWI	British West Indies
CBS	Columbia Broadcasting System
CO	Colonial Office
CPU	Community Programme Unit
CUKC	Citizen of the United Kingdom and Colonies
EM	Ethnic minorities
ENSA	Entertainment's National Service Association
GMTV	Good Morning Television
HBO	Home Box Office
IDTV	Identity Television
ITA	Independent Television Authority
ITC	Independent Television Commission
ITN	Independent Television News
ITV	Independent Television
LCRE	Leicester Campaign for Racial Equality
LWT	London Weekend Television
MOI	Ministry of Information
MP	Member of Parliament
MTV	Music Television
NBC	National Broadcasting Company
TGWU	Transport and General Workers Union
TUC	Trades Union Congress

UM   Union Movement
UPN   United Paramount Network
WAC   Written Archive Centre

Introduction

A multitude of publications on British television history have both hailed and deconstructed the policies and influences of the British Broadcasting Corporation (BBC). Since 1922, the organisation has attempted to serve audiences with an intention to inform and acculturate them on every subject deemed acceptable. Within its development, a public service agenda was an essential part of programming practices, influenced greatly by Sir John Reith, who, despite his extreme dislike for both politicians and television, later served as the Director-General of the organisation during its first sixteen years of service. As an educational tool, Reith saw the BBC as a 'mighty instrument to instruct and fashion public opinion; to banish ignorance and misery; to contribute richly and in many ways to the sum total of human well being'.[1] Prior to his departure in 1938, the first public demonstration of the Baird Television System took place, and within years programmes produced under the first Director of Television Gerald Cock offered *televisual* constructs of what England and Britain represented for generations to come. Audiences soon had a choice of musical variety programmes, and a host of dramatic teleplays and informational talks, each demonstrating the ability of television to hopefully do what BBC radio had done for nearly fifteen years: entertain and inform a variety of publics on current, global, and national events.

One such event occurred on 22 June 1948, as the troop transport *Empire Windrush* arrived at Tilbury Docks with West Indian immigrants eagerly searching for a better life within the British Isles. The group of 492, comprising mainly young Jamaican men, came to England on a one-time-only passageway, thereby changing post-war England and notions of Britishness forever. Economic conditions in their homelands had not improved during the war, and in some cases became worse, forcing many African-Caribbeans to return to England seeking work or extended military service. In some cases, newspapers reported the arrival of the settlers innocuously, as 'Jamaicans' seeking work, including 'singers, students, pianists, boxers and a complete dance band',[2] while the letters to the editor page warned of civil unrest as these men sought employment. One writer explained that, knowing of the scarcity of labour in the United Kingdom, settlers would wonder why Central Europeans received preferential treatment, now that the threat of war had passed. The letter further discussed a near riot in Jamaica that took place years after the colonial riots of 1936–38. When a recruiting office could not offer any more jobs, angry applicants caused the police to dispense the crowd with tear gas.[3] Minister of Labour George Issacs, formerly Member of Parliament (MP) for Southwark, had already voiced concerns over the lack of organised arrangements for the Jamaicans' arrival and subsequent employment. Furthermore, he expressed hope that 'no encouragement' be given to 'others to follow them'.[4]

Meetings held at the Home Office on 18 February 1949 addressed what action the Colonial Office could take. In addition, the Ministries of Labour, Health, and Transport and the National Assistance Board each hoped to diminish the flow of immigrants by communicating to the West Indies that finding accommodation and employment in the United Kingdom was highly difficult. In the report from the Working Party on the Employment in the UK of Surplus Colonial Labour, a measure called for a group of representatives from varying government departments to tackle the problem of 'colonials' 'already here by dispersal', and by arranging for 'voluntary repatriation of the misfits'. The Colonial Office had determined that multiple industries – including agriculture, tin plate, sheet steel, cotton, and others – held no interest in hiring colonials or offering training programmes, yet, by the end of 1948, 300 positions were held for European volunteer workers and Poles. Coal mining was considered unlikely to support the absorption of West Indian labourers, unless in 'one and twos', and had support from a union that would not allow such measures.[5] The Home Department also took stronger actions to control immigration due in large part to public concerns over housing. Besides a measure calling for colonials to be segregated into hostels,[6] the Ministry of Labour and the Colonial Office offered no solutions, and to affect general housing would cause dismay and resentment among what was called 'the older Dominions'.[7]

Despite these challenges, of particular importance to this study was the *visual* impact of this imagined incursion via the advent of post-war television. The Tilbury disembarkation, as filmed by British Pathé newsreel crews, appeared on BBC's *Television Newsreel* programme (BBC 1948–54) under the item 'Jamaican Emigrants arrive'.[8] Though the event was televised to only a modest portion of the population, given that fewer than 50,000 combined radio and television licences were held in 1948, this could not be ignored, particularly when considering news coverage of their arrival, and the growing presence of television within the domestic space. Portions of the segment teemed with paternalism and patronage, as voiceovers reminded audiences that these immigrants should be welcomed as 'citizens of the Empire sailing to the Mother country with good intent'.[9] This provided one of the first occasions in which audiences outside of the movie theatres witnessed their arrival as a *mediated* event, despite a presence of Black people in England since the fifteenth century. As the technological advances of television continued, content drew from other events realised as historically significant, such as the coronation of Queen Elizabeth II, as broadcast over BBC television and radio on 2 June 1953. When considering the importance placed upon proceedings deemed important to the populace, *Television Newsreel*'s coverage at Tilbury brought these hopeful citizens onto the private screens, and into the homes, of White Britons.

Images of West Indians were surely not foreign to White British audiences. Newsreels such as *The Empire Marches* (1941), *War comes to Africa* (1942), and *Defenders of India* (1941) had already featured African-Caribbeans and other soldiers of colour during World War Two, urging their allegiance to Mother England in her time of need. The film *West Indies Calling* (1943), also sponsored by the Ministry of Information (MOI), featured a discussion of the war effort by radio producer Una Marson, cricketer-turned-statesman Learie Constantine, and RAF officer Ulric Cross. Shown were West Indian soldiers in London, as they made their way toward Broadcasting House to do an edition of the BBC radio programme *Calling the West Indies*.[10] The MOI focused upon morale-boosting efforts in the film, which also features a multiracial array of West Indian men and women serving in various military capacities. The film concludes with a dance in which Black West Indian men and White women politely twirl about the floor. These smiling and seemingly pleasant people engage in warm conversations, as crooner Archie Lewis sings *Goodbye Little Girl*, an anthem of sentiment for those West Indian troops assigned to the war effort abroad, and perhaps seeking new opportunities for post-war employment. The narrative attempts to demonstrate how, at a time when American troops stationed in England engaged in open bigotry, the Corporation helped to frame Britain as a far more tolerant nation, yet, as Webster recognises, 'studiously avoids any mention of racism'.[11]

These images were not to be confused with the Black entertainers seen on the BBC before the war, and shortly after, treating audiences to dance routines and song. These performers were primarily African-American, and their popularity originated with earlier film, stage, and sound appearances. The budding BBC television production staff, who saw themselves as professionals in visual communication, came largely from the theatre, film, and sound industries. It is reasonable to assume that the technical and aesthetic influences that moulded their creative endeavours included an appreciation of these established musicians and entertainers. Concurrently, the exposure of these Black Americans to British audiences partially disrupted attempts at resistance to the Americanisation of British entertainment. Though Basil Nicholls, Controller of Programmes at the BBC in 1943, had insisted that the Home Service, Light Programme, and Arts Programmes should be 'firmly British in character', the reliance upon African-American artists demonstrated their entertainment value within British culture. An early example was the American duo of Ford 'Buck' Washington and John 'Bubbles' Stublett, who appeared on one of the first BBC television broadcasts on 2 November 1936.[12] Draped in eveningwear, as shown by BBC cameras at Alexandra Palace, songstresses like Nina Mae McKinney and Adelaide Hall drew upon the popularity earned on radio and the stage. Also featured in these early television specials was immensely popular singer/actor Elisabeth Welch, who had performed numerous times on the radio. The exotic images of these crooners and dancers and many others were very different from those of West Indian settlers streaming from ships, seeking employment and housing.

As public opinion, the government, and the dominant press continued to highlight immigration from the Caribbean, West Indians were increasingly linked to crime, unemployment, and housing shortages. Despite the liberal attitudes expressed among some BBC managers as discussed in this study, the BBC Television Service and Pathé began to label their arrival as 'Our Jamaican Problem' in their segments, despite a reasonably positive report on their arrival (Figure 1).[13] As immigration to the UK increased, early architects of the BBC Television Service planned and approved television programmes that examined the impact of racial relations upon traditional Englishness. Soon after these decisions, the BBC transmitted more programmes on immigration and other related issues, but with reactions from audiences that were sometimes positive, often negative.

Within *Paving the Empire Road: BBC Television and Black Britons*, an institutional case study of the BBC Television Service occurs, as it undertook the responsibility of creating programmes that addressed the impact of Black Britons, their attempts to establish citizenship within England, and subsequent issues of race relations and colour prejudice. Beginning in the 1930s and into the twenty-first century, I provide a historical analysis of policies invoked and practices undertaken as the Service attempted to assist White Britons in understanding the impact of African-Caribbeans, and their assimilation into constructs of Britishness. Management soon approved talks and scientific studies as a means of examining racial tensions, though not in Britain itself.[14] As ITV challenged the discourses of British broadcasting, and BBC2 began broadcasting in 1964, more issues of racial relations appeared on the screens of viewers, each reflecting sometimes comedic, somewhat dystopic, often problematic circumstances of interculturalism. In

Figure 1 While images of the Windrush arrival on the BBC first offered a more welcoming narrative (1a), immigration increases led to segments labelled 'Our Jamaican Problem'. Reporter John Parsons talks with an unknown West Indian man (1b).

the years that followed however, social tensions led to transmissions that included a series of news specials on Britain's colour bar, and docudramas such as *A Man from the Sun* (BBC, 11 June 1956) that attempted to frame the immigrant experience for British television audiences, but from the West Indian point of view.

Despite these efforts, many West Indians making the transition toward citizenship continued to feel isolated from mainstream British society. As the BBC moved further into television broadcasting, the organisation and its managers drew from ideologies of nationalism that continued to place the African-Caribbean settler in a position marginalised from the imagined mainstream of English culture. As evidenced by the work of Stephen Bourne and Jim Pines, various actors of African-Caribbean origin have chronicled their struggles within British television. However, the concerns of 'typical coloured folk', as the League of Coloured Peoples called them,[15] eventually came to the attention of management through a series of community meetings. These assemblies brought management together with these new citizens to determine what they were experiencing and how best to help them, and to define their lives and experiences in England. As an example, BBC's Director-General Hugh Greene called upon leaders of London's West Indian, Pakistani, and Indian communities in 1965 to discuss ways the Television Service could better serve their needs as new citizens. These 'public conferences' created possibilities within a social and institutional environment that had been foreshadowed by social tensions, some of which were examined by programming; yet seldom from the perspective of West Indians themselves. After gauging the opinions of these groups, management, with support from the Director-General, could hypothetically develop better policies, and programmes, that addressed the transitions and challenges undertaken by these peoples. Though sources carefully discuss the development of the BBC and its massive influence, there are seldom discussions about how ethnicity as a focus of management practices shaped television programming and policy-making before the turbulent 1960s. This study therefore discusses how the BBC ultimately drew upon various African-Caribbean organisations to serve as advisors and coordinators in these efforts, helping, in large part, to shape the future of British television. This includes portions of discussions, transcripts, and programming notes in the words of participants and Black Britons themselves. Subsequent chapters include a more extensive analysis of television and radio programming, along with personal interviews. Topics include representations of race and ethnicity as related to immigrant cultures in England following World War Two, the future of British television, and multiethnic audiences. This also includes the contemporary efforts of Black Britons recently working within the British media as employees of the BBC, writers, producers, and actors.

Historically, what concerns did West Indian organisations express, and what suggestions were made as the BBC continued to shape its programming choices in relation to race and immigration? How did the political climate of the time affect internal decisions made by BBC management when considering the subject of race relations within its programming decisions? How could the voices of these new citizens be heard and their desires for social enhancement known? What effect does the absence of these voices have upon a historical study of BBC television, representations of race, and the canonical formation of programming texts?

Despite the importance of each of these questions and many others, the documents examined at the BBC Written Archive Centre (WAC) also provided a record, evidence of how broadcast policies concerning racial issues often vacillated and changed, depending upon a range of issues. As images of race and West Indian culture appeared on television, limited social relations between White and Coloured people held these discursive subjects in place, in part because of the BBC's own authoritarian, sociological, and ideological influences. The initiation of procedures aimed at racial fairness and social responsibility were dependent largely upon the whims and directives of department heads, producers, and their assistants. Memoranda, letters, and corresponding policy decisions each provide a useful indicator for the social environment of the day, as do original radio and television scripts addressing issues as diverse as Calypso routines for variety shows and the riots at Notting Hill. Archived viewer research reports were invaluable as historical narratives demonstrating the cultural saliency of the service and its efforts to address the contemporary presence of Black Britons during the 1950s and beyond. These reports often drove programming decisions made during the years in question, underscoring the importance of these documents as resources. These documents and others in the study never completely and irrefutably reflect actual attitudes held by the viewing public or management in the years collated, but they do provide an indication. It would also be difficult to reconstruct this programming critically using mere transcripts and synopses; however, this study examines some of this material and highly important decisions undertaken by management about such programming. Additional research methodology includes the textual analysis of multiple BBC television programmes beginning in the 1950s until beyond 2000, including dramas, sitcoms, documentaries, and news magazines. Whilst this method of research also requires semiotic analysis of representations cast by BBC producers and writers, written documents provide an insight into the underscoring of difference and subjectivity that resulted when programming analysed the impact of West Indian immigration.

Other research conducted on immigrants groups in Stepney, Easton, and London in post-war Britain indicated that a strong amount of disorganisation existed among first-generation Coloured immigrants and their political aims, particularly when compared to Asian communities.[16] Studies cite the extent to which some 'European influences ... disrupted the culture of the country of origin', and these affections related 'closely to the attitudes adopted by immigrants after arrival'.[17] Despite these findings, research in *Paving* demonstrates that many West Indian organisations displayed a strong sense of solidarity against the racialism they experienced in England, and despite multiple indigenous origins. As suggested by Michael McMillan, the term 'West Indian' became a reference to how, during the Civil Rights Movement, Caribbean migrants began to see themselves as such when arriving to England and meeting other people from the region, reinforcing 'a sense of solidarity under the auspices of a heterogeneous black community'.[18] The integration of Coloured people into England's urban areas and workplaces provided rich opportunities for citizens of colour to thrive among each other, and create possibilities for group empowerment. By 1950, the corporation identified twenty-one immigrant organisations of colour working toward social welfare, cross-cultural association and integration. Lists of societies and organisations recognised by the BBC, complied anonymously with a commentary, included:

- the Malay Society of Great Britain 'tend to be rather exclusive', but specialised in questions on the East;
- the West Indian Students Union, St Martins in the Fields, considered an active overseas committee that held tea parties for 100 guests from Africa, Asia, the West Indies, America, and Europe;
- the Stepney League of Coloured Peoples, whose secretary, Mr Roy Nelson, hoped to organise an all-Coloured West Indian variety show for the West End;
- the Asian Film Society;
- the League of Coloured Peoples, whose executive committee were mostly also members of the Caribbean Labour Congress;
- the West African Students' Union, Nigeria Union, whose members held a summer school session for others;
- the Women's Nigerian League, whose female students held Christmas tea parties and national dances 'in native garb' – also affiliated with the British Commonwealth League, a group chaired by Mrs Alexander Society of St Francis, whose Father Neville ran an 'eight bed hostel and school for coloured people';
- the All Nations Social Club, whose members rented a room from the YMCA near Baker Street station for dancing and socials;
- the 77 Cultural and Social Club, known for their 'gigantic coloured

children's Christmas Parties';
- the Afro-West Indian Services, a group that held dances and were 'recently visited by the Governor of Jamaica';
- the Anglo-Caribbean Club, Racial Unity Executive Committee;
- Mr and Mrs Azu Mate, who travelled about the country looking after Coloured students, and who were also members of the Racial Unity Executive Committee; and
- Dr S.D. Cudjoe, president of the African Arts Club.[19]

The roster of West Indian organisations recognised by the BBC also included churches and missionary societies, the Student Christian Movement, the Victoria League, the East and West Friendship Council, and others, each of which aimed to promote friendship between British people and overseas students.[20] As racial relations became a focus of programming narratives, the creation of some programmes drew upon these groups as advisors, providing a chronology of efforts undertaken by management to quell racial tensions. Feedback and suggestions from many West Indian groups and community activists provided important background information, as did hand-written responses and anecdotal after-thoughts.

The study, which draws from a larger academic project, also focuses upon the BBC as a *non*-commercial network considered free of pressures thought to be innate to commercial advertising and sponsorship, supposedly freeing the service to engage in selected practices of its choosing. While this study does not intend to draw the reader into a highly theoretical discussion of these matters, it does acknowledge the research of many others who provided guidance and historical insight.

The Black presence in the United Kingdom is clearly documented,[21] yet this study is concerned with the post-war immigration patterns after *Windrush*, and the coincidence of television in the home. Media historians have chronicled the development of the corporation and its vast ideological construction of a nation.[22] The organisation's origins, intent, and onus have been discussed,[23] as have dystopic forecasts of commercial influences upon British audiences, but with little regard to multiethnic perspectives during the formative years of the 1930s until the early 1960s. Social influences of the BBC during this period, and its ultimate responsibilities to nationhood, have been deconstructed,[24] as have the many contemporary discussions of race in media and within *Englishness*.[25] To understand the historic significance of West Indian immigration, particularly after World War Two, is to understand the effort undertaken by the BBC through its public service and educational agenda on radio and television.[26] The aesthetic value of Caribbean writers and the BBC's efforts to expose them to larger audiences provides a liberal framework to examine specific policies relating to postcolonial culture and literary values.[27] Also of particular importance have been texts dedicated to a chronology of West Indian actors within BBC programming as a whole[28] and on British television generally.[29] However, studies of West Indian ethnicity and immigrant cultures are essential to the framing of West Indian culture by the dominant.[30] Yet hybrid identities[31] and postcolonial theory[32] are essential in addressing notions of diasporic formations and resistance within the imperial centre.

While networks such as ITV, Channel 4, and others surely featured Black people and race-related matters within selected programming, this study examines the BBC as a forerunner of these endeavours. No matter what the circumstances, or challenges to BBC management, television would play a highly significant role in how millions would perceive these hopeful citizens.

Within Chapter 1, this study outlines the influence of radio upon the BBC Television Service, management directives, and pre-war programming. Discussions include the contributions, concerns, and discussions of West Indian producers like Una Marson and Kenneth Ablack, as they helped to shape the BBC's approach when addressing African-Caribbean audiences and related issues. Beginning in 1939, the programme *Calling the West Indies* featured West Indians troops on active service reading letters on air to their families back home in the Islands. The programme later became *Caribbean Voices* (1943–58) and highlighted West Indian writers who read and discussed literary works on the World Service. Among other issues are the corporation's concerns over racial prejudice, the *Colour Bar* radio series (1943), and audience reception during and after the war. Ultimately, portions of these shows shifted focus and began to offer personal views of the African-Caribbean experience in the UK. During the programming segments *We See Britain* (1949) and *West Indian Diary* (1949), service members, teachers, and others who visited or lived in England discussed their personal experiences for the benefit of those considering immigration. These programmes offered rare opportunities for West Indians to discuss their perspectives on life among white Britons and subsequent social issues. Plans to address racialism led to the first 'Coloured Conference', in which the BBC called upon members of the West Indian community and students to assist them in planning programmes related to racial understanding. After World War Two, the service began to increase its attention toward racial issues and immigration. The usage of Pathé Newsreels on BBC television led to early news and public affairs programming that often featured stories related to the challenges of West Indian immigration.

Chapter 2 includes an analysis of race and BBC television policy with a discussion of early Black images on BBC television, and the decisions that led to their appearances. This includes icons such as African-Americans Elisabeth Welch and Adelaide Hall, as compared to West Indian performers

Edric Connor, Boscoe Holder, and others. Efforts undertaken by the service to further educate audiences on racial issues as a social concern included the first television talks regarding the scientific origins of race, and subsequent audience surveys. Heading the effort were former radio producers Grace Wyndham Goldie and Mary Adams. In turn, Goldie, serving as Assistant Head of Talks, helped to develop the first television programme of its kind, *Race and Colour: A Scientific Introduction to the Problem of Racial Relations* (BBC, 9 November 1952). Despite this controversial issue and subsequent discussions, surveys completed after the programme led to disappointing results. Participants were unconcerned about anthropological origins, and instead wanted to learn what citizens could do to avoid racial problems where West Indians had settled. In an effort to examine these issues, BBC producer Anthony de Lotbiniere began researching a series of *Special Enquiry* news shows in 1955 that would highlight the impact of newly arrived West Indians upon Birmingham, principally entitled *Has Britain a Colour Bar?* Within a year, the docudramatic teleplay *A Man from the Sun* (BBC, 11 June 1956) was produced. The teleplay examined the experiences of newly arrived West Indian immigrants from 'their' perspectives (though written by White Briton John Elliot), but was transmitted to mixed reviews, this time from West Indian audiences. As the BBC continued to consider how television could assist West Indian communities in their efforts to assimilate, the service began to document the appearance of African-Caribbeans within BBC programming, a response to criticisms about stereotyping and limited portrayals.

Chapter 3 begins with an examination of the 1960s, and heightened concerns about urban unrest following the riots at Notting Hill and in Nottingham. Each event created further concerns for White Britons, who nervously studied the increasing racial tensions on city streets, yet encouraged West Indians to speak out even more about programming issues and hiring practices within the BBC. Soon after, the Second Coloured Conference at Broadcasting House allowed management to meet with African-Caribbean community leaders (and Indian and Pakistani leaders) about planned television programmes and their potential impact. Also distributed at the meeting was the *Going to Britain* booklet, a cryptic primer on life in the UK for relatives of West Indian immigrants considering relocation.

Critical analyses of racially themed BBC television programming in the 1960s and 1970s includes *Till Death Us Do Part* (BBC, 1965–68, 1972–75), *Rainbow City* (BBC, 1967) and the iconic *Empire Road* (BBC, 1978–79), one of the first BBC 'soaps' to feature a first- and second-generation Black British family attempting to navigate life in an English urban setting. Also included is *Fable* (BBC, 20 January 1965), a drama that reverses an apartheid-like situation in which Blacks had come to oppress Whites, but in the UK. Concerns of its impact upon White audiences were so disturbing to BBC management that the service delayed its transmission until after a by-election. By comparison are *The Fosters* (ITV, 1976–77), *Love Thy Neighbour* (1972–76), and *Mixed Blessings* (1978–80), as a sampling of programmes that emphasised West Indian characters and their comedic representations on British television during this turbulent era. The Community Relations Commission was important in providing a voice for West Indians, included recruitment efforts at the BBC for African-Caribbean employees, much to the dismay of the dominant press. Their participation led to cultural affairs programming such as the self-referential *Open Door* documentary series (BBC, 1973–76), *Skin* (BBC, 1979), the *Black and White Media Show* (BBC, 1986) and the *Black Britain* news-magazine series (BBC, 1995–2000). Also discussed are critical perspectives from both the mainstream and minority presses, and various contemporary university studies on race and television as they relate to efforts by the BBC and other terrestrial channels. Also discussed is the remit of Channel 4 as an avenue for minority programming.

In Chapter 4, interviews feature the contemporary perspectives of Black Britons working within the London television market. Issues for discussion with the interviewees included representations of race and class, programming and opportunities for minorities, empowerment and opportunity, Americanisation as an influence, the birth of Black-owned Identity Television, presence, diversity, and the future of Black Britons on BBC television. Subjects include recent BBC Director of Multicultural Programming Jan Oliver, cultural critic Stuart Hall, actor Treva Etienne, journalist Neema Kambona, BBC presenter Brenda Emmanus, journalist Kadija George-Sesay, and BBC Diversity Manager Cyril Husbands. Follow-up interviews years later (highlighted in Chapter 5) continue these discussions of, among other issues, newer programmes, current representations, and future possibilities for diverse programming. By comparison, their concerns exemplify the challenges still facing these professionals of colour when dealing with the hegemony and patronage of the BBC and the British television industry. Through a series of open-ended questions, media professionals comment on, among other things, the BBC and its broadcast policies. These discussions occur within the 1990s, considered a turning point by some for racial representations on British television. Each question and subsequent response reflects decades of personal experiences with the Service.

Chapter 5 highlights the BBC under Director-General Greg Dyke, a leader thought to represent the best chance for diversity within the corporation. Dyke's first meeting with the BBC Black Forum (BBF) organisation, a group of Black and Asian employees seeking diversity within the corporation, highlighted this dilemma as the Director-General attempted to effect change, but with unexpected results. Following Dyke's sudden departure was what one African-Caribbean manager at the BBC called 'the Great Redundancy', as many efforts at placing African-Caribbeans before and behind the camera were lost in a wave of budget-related terminations. The chapter also includes recent perspectives on BBC programming that attempts to highlight African-Caribbean issues (*Babyfather*, 2001; *Shoot the Messenger*, 2006; *Small Island*, 2009) with actor/director Treva Etienne, and recent BBC managers Jan Oliver and Cyril Husbands.

Notes

1 John Charles Walsham Reith, *Into the Wind*. London: Hodder and Stoughton, 1949: 103.
2 *The Times*, 23 June 1948: 2.
3 Paul B. Rich, *Race and Empire in British Politics*. Cambridge: Cambridge University Press, 1986: 149.
4 Mike Phillips and Trevor Phillips, *Windrush: The Irresistible Rise of Multi-Racial Britain*. London: Harper Collins, 1998: 59.
5 Kew, CO/318/13 and 318/478/3.
6 *Ibid.*
7 Kew, CAB 129/78.
8 BBC Programme as Broadcast Record, *Television Newsreel* programme number 50, 25 June 1948.
9 *Ibid.*
10 *Calling the West Indies*. Dir. John Page. Prod. Donald Alexander for Paul Rotha Productions, 1942–43.
11 Wendy Webster, *Englishness and Empire 1939–1965*. Oxford: Oxford University Press, 2005: 42.
12 BBC Programming records, 1937, volume 8, part 1, p. 282.
13 BBC Programme as Broadcast Record, *BBC and Pathé News*, 17 January 1955.
14 To Goldie from James Bredin on the Africa Series: Scientific Programme, *The Scientists look at Race*, 15 October 1952, T32/209/3, BBC WAC.
15 Rendall to ACOS, 28 December 1943, R34/305/1.
16 David Pearson, *Race, Class and Political Activism: A Study of West Indians in Britain*. Westmead, Farnborough: Gower, 1981.
17 Michael Banton, *White and Coloured: The Behaviour of British People towards Coloured Immigrants*. Brunswick, NJ: Rutgers University Press, 1960: 214.
18 Michael McMillan, e-mail interview, 13 June 1907.
19 R99/3/1, BBC WAC.
20 David Clover, *Dispersed or Destroyed: Archives, The West Indian Students' Union and Public Memory*. SCS conference, University of Newcastle, July 2005.
21 K.L. Little, *Negroes in Britain: A Study in Race Relations in English Society*. London: Kegan Paul, 1947; Anthony Richmond, *Colour Prejudice in Britain: A Study of West Indian Workers in Liverpool*. London: Routledge, 1954; Banton,

White and Coloured).

22 Asa Briggs, *The History of Broadcasting in the United Kingdom, Volume 4: Sound and Vision*. Oxford: Oxford University Press, 1979; Anthony Smith, *British Broadcasting*. Plymouth: David and Charles, 1974; Paddy Scannel and David Cardiff, *A Social History of British Broadcasting: Volume One 1922–1939 Serving the Nation*. Oxford: Basil Blackwell, 1991; Humphrey Carpenter, *The Envy of the World: Fifty Years of the BBC Third Programme and Radio Three*. London: Weidenfeld and Nicolson, 1996; Andrew Crisell, *An Introductory History of British Broadcasting*. New York: Routledge, 1997.

23 Baron John Charles Walsham Reith, *Broadcast Over Britain*. London: Hodder and Stoughton, 1924; Andrew Boyle, *Only the Wind Will Listen: Reith of the BBC*. London: Hutchinson and Company, 1972; Grace Wyndham Goldie, *Facing the Nation: Television and Politics, 1936–1976*. London: Bodley Head, 1977.

24 Burton Paulu, *British Broadcasting in Transition*. Minneapolis: University of Minnesota Press, 1961.

25 Rich, *Race and Empire in British Politics*; Webster, *Englishness and Empire*.

26 Burton Paulu, *British Broadcasting: Radio and Television in the United Kingdom*. Minneapolis: University of Minnesota Press, 1956; William A. Belson, *The Impact of Television: Methods and Findings in Program Research*. London: Crosby Lockwood and Son, 1967.

27 A. Walmsley, *The Caribbean Artists Movement, 1966–72*. London: New Beacon Books, 1992; Cyril Dabydeen, 'Where doth the berbice run', *World Literature Today*, 68 (1994): 451–6; Alison Donnell, ed., *Companion to Contemporary Black British Culture*. London: Routledge, 2002; D. Balderston, M. Gonzalez, and A. Lopez, eds, *Encyclopedia of Contemporary Latin American and Caribbean Cultures*. London: Routledge, 2000.

28 Stephen Bourne, *Black in the British Frame: Black People in British Film and Television 1896–1996*. London: Cassell, 1998; Sarita Malik, *Representing Black Britain: Black and Asian Images on Television*. London: Sage, 2002.

29 Jim Pines, ed., *Black and White in Colour: Black People in British Television since 1936*. London: British Film Institute, 1992; Therese Daniels and Jane Gerson, eds, *The Colour Black*. London: BFI, 1989.

30 Robert Barry Davidson, *Black British: Immigrants to England*. London: Oxford, 1966; Susan Benson, *Ambiguous Ethnicity: Interracial Families in London*. Cambridge: Cambridge University Press, 1981; Margaret Byron, *Post-War Caribbean Migration to Britain: The Unfinished Cycle*. Aldershot: Avebury, 1994; Phillips and Phillips, *Windrush*; Harry Goulbourne, *Caribbean Transnational Experience*. London: Pluto Press, 2002.

31 Homi Bhabha, *The Location of Culture*. London: Routledge, 1994; Marie Gillespie, *Television, Ethnicity and Cultural Change*. London: Routledge, 1995; Avtar Brah, *Cartographies of Diaspora: Contesting Identities*. New York: Routledge, 1996; Patrick D. Murphy and Marwan M. Kraidy, eds, *Global Media Studies: Ethnographic Perspectives*. New York: Routledge, 2003.

32 Albert Memmi, *The Colonizer and the Colonized*. Boston: Beacon Press, 1967; Stuart Hall, 'The Whites of their Eyes: Racist Ideologies and the Media', *The*

Media Reader. London: BFI, 1990; Stuart Hall, *Cultural Dialogues in Cultural Studies*. London: Routledge, 1996; Paul Gilroy, *The Black Atlantic-Modernity and Double Consciousness*. Cambridge, MA: Harvard University Press, 1993; Paul Gilroy, *Against Race: Imagining Political Culture beyond the Color Line*. Cambridge, MA: The Benknap Press of Harvard University Press, 2002; Paul Gilroy, *Postcolonial Melancholia*. New York: Columbia University Press, 2006; Robert J.C. Young, *Colonial Desire: Hybridity in Theory, Culture and Race*. London: Routledge, 1995; Kwesi Owusu, ed., *Black British Culture and Society*. London: Routledge, 2000; Michael McMillin, *The Front Room: Migrant Aesthetics in the Home*. London: Black Dog, 2007.

1

Radio, race, and the Television Service

Well one thing I think that will interest West Indians is what is the attitude – of the English people as a whole, – how do they take to strangers. After all West Indians are coming over here in increasing numbers, and they'd like to know what sort of person they're going to meet, and how they're going to be treated.

(West Indian humorist and Government Public Relations officer for Jamaica, A.E.T. Henry, on the BBC radio programme *We See Britain*, 1 June 1949)[1]

When considering the sentiments of Henry as he spoke to audiences over the BBC's Caribbean Services, it is likely that this opinion reflected the concerns of many West Indian immigrants at the time. Much like John Elliot's teleplay *A Man from the Sun* (BBC, 1956) attempted to highlight the post-war immigration issue from the fictional perspective of actor Errol John's character Cleve, BBC radio programmes, and the broadcast policies that supported them, occasionally provided actual opportunities for actual perspectives on Britain. Whether guests were students, famed authors, cricketers, or settlers seeking employment, these hopeful citizens, beginning in the 1930s until the reappearance of BBC television after the war, offered their intentions and concerns to radio listeners. This included analyses of social issues such as the colour bar, in a country where one did not supposedly exist.

This chapter examines how BBC radio and its practices created possibilities for the recognition of these African-Caribbean voices, as they discussed life in England years before the *Windrush* arrival, and just before television re-emerged as a cultural force. It also examines how programmes created for West Indian audiences changed foci, and began to offer varied, personal perspectives on life for African-Caribbean immigrants. Whilst this portion of the study does not seek to research exhaustively the BBC's influence within the Caribbean, it does attempt to provide a framework for how broadcast policies from radio, and onward to television, engaged the presence of African-Caribbean subjects. West-Indian-themed programmes broadcast from 1941 until 1945 also provided platforms for rallying cries during World War Two, as the empire called out to its colonial peoples to assist in the good fight, and what Webster called the 'people's war'. Communities, supposedly bound by duty, helped to reinforce the imperial presence in most intertextual manner, as West Indians Una Marson, Sir Learie Constantine, and Ulric Cross broadcast messages of involvement and commitment over BBC radio and newsreels.[2] While race and subsequent social relations were never a principle consideration within these early BBC directives, the mere participation and presence of West Indians and other Colonials made it inevitable.

The Empire Service and West Indies broadcasting

The British Broadcasting Corporation began as a *company* serving the public with an intention to acculturate audiences on every subject deemed acceptable. By November of 1932, the BBC had over 5,000,000 licence holders and by 1938, 98 per cent of the populace could listen to programmes at their convenience.[3] As radio garnered more attention, the public service agenda that was a staple of the BBC's overall directives emerged as a principle part of its programmes and their production. Sir John Reith believed that radio touched those of every social class as audiences listened in even the most inaccessible and remote regions of the nation.[4] It is also apparent that the BBC's incorporation by royal charter rather than Parliamentary statute still could not mask the high degree of government control. The issuance of a broadcasting licence by the appointment of governors, the amount of the licence fee, the right to veto broadcasts of specific programmes were all issues mandated by the very politicians Reith acknowledged, yet did not like.[5] The corporation's policy with regard to programme structure, founded upon a balanced programme service, hoped to meet the needs of all segments of the public, with reference to minority as well as majority tastes, through broadcasting musical and dramatic repertoire at regular intervals. Furthermore, as suggested by the Beveridge Commission, broadcasting would serve the general social interest, with an educational impulse maintained.[6] Issues of censorship and social control were evident, as the government eventually insisted that neither communists nor fascists be given access to BBC wireless or television for their campaigns, and an unofficial news blackout guaranteed that little attention be given to the political programmes of Oswald Mosley's British Union of Fascists or the right-wing Union Movement.[7]

The importance of the BBC reached a level of international significance in 1932 when the Corporation began its Empire Service, which, for all purposes, was the early version of the BBC World Service. It was Christmas Day of that year when King George V gave the first royal broadcast to subjects living in the UK and some of its colonies; the message was scripted by Rudyard Kipling, author of 'The White Man's Burden', a poem that directed the British to engage in colonial practices and ethnic subjugation. By the mid-1930s, the BBC reached audiences in Australia, India, South Africa, West Africa, and Canada, with extended foreign-language services beginning in 1938. Within a decade, the BBC Empire Service began broadcasting English language programmes to nearly all of the colonies. Within the British West Indies (BWI), the four most populated islands of Jamaica, Trinidad, Guiana, and the Windward Islands reportedly had 93,000 radio receiver sets according to a report from the United States Information Agency. After considering this data, the organisation determined that these listed radio sets represented a sizable audience of nearly three million citizens, which was worth consideration.[8] Efforts toward an expansion of West Indian broadcasts followed discussions in 1936 aimed at supporting a broadcasting service within the colonies. A report filed with the Colonial Office (CO) detailed the feasibility of such an endeavour and its benefits. In a memo to E.B. Bowyer, J.B. Clark, then Director of Empire Service, provided brief biographical notes on those authoring the report, people with whom the BBC had contact regarding broadcasting in the West Indies. Clark mentioned Frank E. Lyons, whom he called 'distinctly Empire-minded', as an executive with 'wireless and newspaper interests' involved in the promotion of a Jamaica/New York/London telephone service. In addition, Briton Kenneth Skelton ran a commercial radio station in Tampa, Florida and wanted to transfer activities to a British territory, and thus applied for a licence to operate a station in Jamaica. Clark further noted that these men had visited England within the previous three years, inferring a sense of allegiance, if not personal knowledge, to what he referred to as 'home'.[9] In that next year, the group completed an *Interim Report on a Committee on Broadcasting Services in the Colonies* for the CO.

The report, as filed with Ormsby Gore, MP, who served as Secretary of State for the Colonies, acknowledged that the Empire short-wave service from Daventry had already generated a loyal audience. The operation had the endorsement of the Ullswater Committee, including issues of constitutionality, control, and finance of broadcasting service in the BWI. The importance of the BBC's influence in the region was noted as going far beyond financial aspects, as the committee cited how the popular broadcasts of King George V and the Jubilee celebrations were examples of the value of linking the Empire through broadcasting. The report suggests that invaluable opportunities for community and patriotism existed as groups assembled to listen and 'take part' in similar occasions called psychologically favourable, for a more vivid realisation of their connection with the Empire. The committee also envisaged the development of colonial broadcasting, not only as an instrument of what they called entertainment for Europeans, but also as an instrument for the 'enlightenment and education of the more backward sections of the population' including instruction in public health and agriculture.[10]

As research and feasibility studies continued to examine the region, concerns arose over a small radio operation that began without the support or knowledge of the BBC. In a letter from 21 October 1938, J.C.S. Macgregor as Empire Services Director expressed concern over a station identifying itself as the West Indian Broadcasting Company, Jamaica. A World Radio correspondent reported hearing a broadcast that requested feedback on its reception.[11] In response to a letter from Malcolm MacDonald MP, Governor of Jamaica Arthur Richards explained that a young Haitian named Bourke-Denise had begun transmitting from Port au Prince on 24 July 1938 via HH2S. His intention was to develop programmes sponsored by Jamaica merchants, and to provide a daily programme for the benefit of listeners in Jamaica and the other West Indian islands, commencing at 8.30 p.m. each evening. The broadcasts included reports on sporting and other topical events cabled to Haiti for announcement, but mostly reproduced programmes through gramophone records. Technically, the station was poor, with faulty modulation, and service considered deficient in good operating practices. The Governor's office also reported that an 'inspector' had personally listened to the station on a few occasions, and determined the programmes 'purely commercial', with no 'political or propaganda' broadcasts.[12] In this instance, however, the commercial intentions of Bourke-Denise superseded efforts by the Empire Service. Besides planned educational broadcasts on agriculture and health, as earmarked for West Africa by the Ullswater Committee,[13] few programmes addressed indigenous West Indian audiences before World War Two, as Bourke-Denise hoped to.

Marson, Madden and *Calling the West Indies*

According to reports filed in 1939, after Britain declared war on Germany 10,000 West Indian men, primarily from Jamaica, volunteered to fight. The BBC Caribbean Service, which was now operational, served as a recruitment tool for African-Caribbeans who soon travelled to the UK to assist in the war effort.[14] After 1941, specific programming featured, among other things, West Indians troops on active service reading letters on air to their families back home in the islands. Through the launch of radio programme *Calling the West Indies*, a variety of segments revolved around West Indian culture, not as a singular aesthetic, but instead as a host of different, yet familiar forms of island music, dialect, and those individuals heralded by the BBC as worthy of association. The development of radio programmes for audiences of colour now moved beyond cricket matches, and often included pro-Empire propaganda and implications of racial tolerance. These efforts included Una Marson's involvement through subsequent programming efforts. After Marson had travelled to Britain in the 1930s, Cecil Madden, as a co-creator of the popular *Picture Page* (BBC, 1936–39; 1946–52), gave her the opportunity to do freelance work on the pre-war television show, working closely with 'coloured visitors and interviewees'. The show, which followed a magazine format with interviews from well-known personalities of film and radio, was transmitted live from Alexandra Palace, with the first episode broadcast weeks before the official opening of the service on 2 November, as part of ongoing test transmissions. Madden found that, during a summer internship at Alexandra Palace, Marson consistently worked to a high standard.[15] As Madden attempted to improve the West Indian Service, he called upon Marson to assist him in overseeing the content of radio programmes for the region. From the start, Marson suggested that programmes address West Indian audiences specifically, which Madden roundly supported. He suggested in a 1940 memo written to Sir Alan Burns, Mr Beckett, and Mr N.J.B. Sabine of the CO, that Marson's suggestions for the programmes and material for the West Indies was inter-esting and promising. The Director of Empire Services, R.A. Rendall, also expressed support of Marson's involvement, and suggested to Madden that she work with J. Grenfell Williams, then African Services Director, to plan and execute specific shows that continued to target West Indian audiences.[16] Marson was encouraged to work closely with Lady Davson and the West India Committee to include names of West Indian soldiers and sailors to feature on the air. Despite a common goal, Marson expressed displeasure as Davson and the committee attempted to become the sole organisation representing West Indians living in the British Isles. She also considered the committee as self-promoting, as they requested that scripts mention the West India Committee specifically.[17] Marson worked closely, albeit more satisfactorily, with Joan Gilbert, who, as an Assistant in the Overseas Entertainments Unit for the Variety Department, worked with Madden as well.

By 1 April of that year, Marson decided to plan what she considered a fixed scheme of two weekly 20-minute programmes, *Calling the West Indies*. However, as discussed in a memo from Gilbert to Madden, Marson indicated that *Calling* would be a variety programme that alternated between the party broadcasts, orchestral offerings, and recorded operas.[18] A schedule from Marson listed Tuesdays as the best days for the *West Indian Party* show, with monthly messages to family and friends in the islands. On Thursdays, the programme featured choirs from various locations, sometimes hosted by Madden. In an effort to create exciting yet varied programming, the report *West Indies Programmes of 1940* featured proposals for different themes each week. Featured were interviews with jazz musician Reggie Forsyth, and the programme featured Ken 'Snakehips' Johnson's classical interpretations. On 26 December, the recurring theme of the West Indian party celebrated Christmas with a festive musical background and a host of guests, including more West Indian soldiers and sailors sending greetings back home to the islands.[19] In a further attempt to support Marson, Madden asked for the assistance of Scottish producer and broadcaster Moultrie Kelsall. With copies to the Director and Deputy Director of Eastern Services, Madden asks Kelsall to participate in a broadcast from the Glasgow studios on 3 and 4 June 1941. Though the programme was mainly broadcast from London, Madden considered using students in Glasgow for it because of their willingness to participate and for a 'change all around' from previous fare.[20] He further explains that the programme would be hosted by Marson and would consist of messages from West Indian students. Gilbert notes at the bottom of the correspondence, 'I imagine you would like me to cope with this from now on', sealing her involvement with the programme.[21] Days later, in a memo to Kelsall, Gilbert thanks him for agreeing to look after the show, noting that the programme would be a single-studio show that will take the form of a party. Gilbert also expressed concern over the potential for embarrassing commentary. In writing to Kelsall, she explains that the producer concerned should 'vet this carefully and would act as a censor for all the messages'.[22]

Despite Marson's efforts to provide diverse programming for West Indian audiences, there were concerns regarding the offerings and their origins. In a cable from Port of Spain in May 1941, there were complaints over the rebroadcast of *Calling*, and according to the Overseas Programme Director, interest in the programme was 'practically nil' because listeners felt ignored in favour of Jamaica. Audiences wanted more talks by those from other islands and more messages for Trinidad, British Guiana, and Barbados.[23] In an effort to underscore the efforts of all West Indians in the conflict, Marson provided lists of West Indian servicemen to Madden and Gilbert, men that hailed from a variety of islands, not only Jamaica, and requested that soldiers be allowed to attend rehearsals for programmes. Marson requested:

> I already have seven messages, students and ambulance people, etc. I think we could do with four soldiers and two airmen, and I think it would be a good idea to try and get these from the different islands … Here is the name and address of a Jamaican soldier in a Canadian regiment who has not been able to send a message yet. I [also] enclose a list of some of the service men here sent to us from Barbados. You could ask for one of these.[24]

Gilbert wrote to Major Turner of the War Office's public relations department for soldiers, Captain Baxter of the Admiralty for sailors, and Squadron

Leader Pollock for the Air Ministry, requesting that service members see Gilbert and Marson at the Criterion Theatre for inclusion in the broadcast.[25] Rosters of possible participants for the June 1941 broadcast came from the Voluntary War Workers association, and a list of medical students and nurses from Barbados. Broadasters A.D. Mackie and Moultrie Kelsall also participated in the recording of the *Close-up* programme, over a two-night period.[26] Noting complaints about a strong Jamaican presence on the show, Marson requested that participants come from different islands, including Barbados, the British Honduras, British Guiana, and Jamaica, offering a mixture of African-Caribbean cultures. Later, a special series of programmes featured a group of Black woodcutters from the Honduras in East Linton, Scotland. Yet four of the men, named Murray, Macdonald, Christie, and MacIssac, informed Scottish Programme Director Andrew Stewart that they had returned to their native land, an obvious reference to their heritages as Scotsmen who were also West Indian.[27] Weeks later, Marson and Kelsall planned a programme that highlighted the men specifically, including a talk on life in Scotland.[28] He forwarded the information to Marson, who created the *Things that Endure* programme featuring the men, and with contributions from poets, writers, singers, and most branches of artistic endeavour[29] Programmes from both Glasgow and Edinburgh continued through the year, including more talks that highlighted the lives of West Indian students living in the region. Madden suggested in a memo to the Assistant Scottish Programme Director in May of that year that Marson be given near autonomy in designing future *Calling* programmes and segments, and the schedule of programmes for July was drawn up entirely on the strength of Marson's suggestions to Madden. He also expressed interested in the new war-time programmes offered by Marson.[30]

By July of 1942, Ena Quade, Programme Executive for the Glasgow office, noted that Marson had developed an amended schedule under the *Calling* banner, and proposed *In Scotland Now*, a talk by Scottish author George Blake, from the Glasgow studios. The next week, more messages came during the late hour of twelve midnight until 12:15 a.m. This group included the foresters, students, service members, and West Indian artists living in Edinburgh and Glasgow.[31] In August of the same year, Marson requested that the Criterion Office book artists for the Message Parties. Acts included singer Gregori Tcherniak with Gerald Sisley, the eclectically classical Albert Sandler Trio, swing singer Harry Parry with Jamaican jazz pianist Yorke de Souza, the Ike Patch Swing Quartet, and the beautifully gifted Elisabeth Welch accompanied by pianist Evel Burns, a musician who later became famous after multiple appearances on *Picture Page*.[32] Each segment offered not only a diverse group of musicians for programmes, but also a mix of musical stylings.

A *coloured* conference

In an effort to continue addressing concerns from both West Indian and West African audiences, the Edinburgh Representative George Burnett sent a letter to the Director of Publicity at the Home Office in January of 1942. Burnett stated that his office had taken advantage of Miss Una Marson's visit to Scotland to have two tea meetings – one in Glasgow and one in Edinburgh – with West Indians and West Africans. Burnett called both meetings unexpectedly successful, with citizens engaging in frank and lively discussions. Marson planned to pass on suggestions for the improvement of both the West Indian and West African services, to those concerned when she returned to London. The discussion prompted Burnett to note that some primary issues discussed by the group included that a

> strong exception was taken to the use of the word 'nigger' in any type of broadcast programmes. It was alleged that the word was used in the last music hall programme. I understand SD [Scottish Director] is taking this matter up himself, We have, I think, a rule against using the word 'nigger', and I strongly recommend that that rule be rigidly enforced – particularly because the use of the word encourages young people – particularly children – to refer to West Indians and West Africans by the opprobrious epithet.[33]

Also noted was considerable criticism of broadcasts to schools, described as inaccurate, childish, and partisan. One speaker in particular condemned the use of missionaries, whom he considered natural propagandists for their faith without complete knowledge of the country about which they were speaking.[34] Burnett, who now served as Publicity Officer for the Edinburgh office, was appreciative of the comments, yet considered the group to be critical of broadcasting in general.[35]

Another meeting held with BBC management regarding issues of race in broadcasting occurred on 15 December 1943 with a liaison from what the Assistant Controller (Overseas Services) identified as the Coloured Committee. At the request of the CO, Barnes, Williams, and Assistant Controller R.A. Rendall met with Mr Betts, who had suggestions and criticisms to make to the BBC. As committee representative and liaison officer with the Colonial Office, Betts had worked closely with the West African Student Union and the League of Coloured Peoples. One of the main objects of the committee was to enlighten the British public about coloured colonial peoples, particularly those from Africa and the West Indies, and to watch for cases of colour discrimination in the newspapers, the theatre and broadcasting. An additional effort was to organise campaigns to counter colour prejudice though lectures to schools and other organisations with suitable broadcasts on the subject. The committee recognised that the BBC was already making some efforts at addressing racialism, but was critical of talks and features that used words considered derogatory to coloured people. Rendall explained that the BBC was always on the lookout to prevent the usage of these kinds of terms, yet he thought the Committee, Betts, and others, should not be concerned with phrases such as 'Black Sambo, or Nigger Minstrels or Ten Little Nigger Boys'. Rendall felt these terms did not arouse an 'anti-colour feeling' in British audiences; that they were traditional music hall phrases, which had no harmful effect,[36] a perspective in opposition to that of most Black people. Betts also felt that the usage of Sir Learie Constantine as a spokesperson for race and colonial issues showed an apologetic attitude that reflected a notion of inferiority. The committee felt that the use of Constantine was not as valuable as the use of a 'typical coloured man'. They also felt that the committee should have a hand in broadcasts that touched on the colour question, and have the right to nominate – or object to – speakers to express its point of view. Barnes and Rendall reminded Betts that Constantine's name was a big draw to listeners, and explained that the BBC was anxious to help break down colour prejudice in the United Kingdom and overseas. Radio could do more to help the effort than it had done in the past, yet felt it was far from clear how the problem could best he tackled.[37] The committee also thought that the BBC should provide a Home Service programme to be organised entirely by the organisation. Rendall quickly pointed out that the BBC could not hand the responsibility for any of its programmes to any outside person or body, and it must reserve the right to choose speakers. However, he added that the organisation was glad to have criticisms and suggestions for programmes, which would receive careful and sympathetic consideration.[38] In closing, Betts suggested that, among the programmes offered, *Children's Hour* could do more to help in the matter of breaking down colour prejudice, and suggested that young audiences also hear African fairy stories and legends. Rendall said that the Schools Department had already done a great deal in the way of programmes about the colonies, and that the African Services Director (ASD) John Grenfell Williams would send scripts to Betts for review.[39] Meanwhile, Marson continued to use the *Calling* programme as a vehicle for issues affecting the African-Caribbean community in the UK and the islands. In a memo to Williams, she suggested a new series on social welfare starting on 11 May 1944. The segments would address the issue of children, and the establishment of a National Society for the Prevention of Cruelty. In support, she planned a talk by Mr Edward Fuller, Deputation Secretary of the Save the Children Fund to speak in the first programme.[40]

Caribbean Voices

Marson, as a writer, also longed to have her work and that of other West Indian writers exposed. In late 1942, the BBC broadcast *Voice*, a six-part poetry programme, in which she worked alongside George Orwell, who served as editor. The programme provided an opportunity for Marson to read her works over the airwaves, along with other West Indian authors. A second *Voice* programme was to be broadcast the next year, and Marson began to develop the idea for a project in which West Indian authors like herself would have a venue for which to demonstrate their creative abilities and, in turn, share perspectives on love, hardship, colonial life, and racialism. The World Service began broadcasting the radio programme *Caribbean Voices* (1943–1958) in March 1943. The BBC recorded the twenty-minute show in London, broadcasting to the Caribbean Isles each Sunday via the BBC's General Overseas Service. The organisation had upgraded radio services in the Caribbean region technically, and similar programmes had already established a strong following under Marson. In an interview to the *Sunday Gleaner* in 1942, she acknowledged that she introduced the programme and invited all West Indian writers to contribute. BBC standards were high, she reminded authors, but the programme could provide an inspiring outlet for their writings.

However, Henry Swanzy, often credited as the originator of *Caribbean Voices*, later changed this practice. Originally using only published works, he had joined the BBC as News Talks Assistant for the Empire Department and Overseas Division in 1941, and later became an editor and producer for the literary programme. Despite using different criteria, Swanzy expanded the works used for the programme, with the assistance of Cedric and Gladys Lindo. The couple forwarded the best contributions from writers eager to hear their work over the airwaves, including the works of established West Indian authors like George Lamming, Gloria Escoffery, Samuel Selvon, and V.S. Naipaul (*The Middle Passage*, 1962) who also served as editor from 1954 until 1956. Other famed writers featured on the programme as guests, and sometimes hosts, included Andrew Salkey (*A Quality of Violence*, 1959), Edgar Mittelholzer (*Children of Kaywana*, 1952), Michael Anthony (*The Games were Coming*, 1963), Edward Kamau Brathwaite (*Odale's Choice*, 1967), and producer Una Marson (*Tropic Reveries*, 1930). Other segments of the programme included *Travellers' Tales*, in which poetry addressed life in the UK for students and scholars, and *Serenade in Sepia* (BBC, 1944) featuring West Indian folk singer Edric Connor, who had also served as a guest and host on *Calling the West Indies*. These same authors and many others ultimately encouraged the formation of a creative network of writers based in the Caribbean Isles and in London. The Caribbean Artists

Movement – established in 1966 by Brathwaite, West Indian activist John La Rose, and Salkey – was a direct result of the collaborations made possible by the programme.[41]

According to a series of letters to budding African Caribbean writers, Swanzy also served as ombudsman for writers concerned over rejected pieces. They included well-known authors such as Samuel Selvon, who despite having his work featured on *Voices* also had specific pieces rejected. In one instance, the BBC had to omit the short story *Steel Bands Clash* weeks after protests over the broadcast of *Behind the Hummingbird*. The story, set in Trinidad in the 1940s, surrounds the efforts of a young Indo-Trinidadian man to escape an arranged marriage. He ultimately falls in love with a young woman, who, he later finds, is the very same woman his parents wanted him to wed. The story, told in dialect, featured sexual content and, as scholar Gautam Premnath suggests, featured scenes of 'low life', in that the story-teller is sexually promiscuous and serves as a 'procurer working in the sex trade … [serving] American GIs in Trinidad during the Second World War'. Premnath also explained that the story, as broadcast on the *Voices* programme, prompted several complaints, some by the staff working at *Caribbean Voices* in London itself, and some from audiences in the West Indies. Many came from Barbados, prompting the manager of the Barbados Rediffusion station to send an irate letter 'threatening to cancel future broadcasts of the show if anything similar was broadcast again'.[42] Premnath further explained that, since the programme was still finding its audience, there was an imagined need to conform to concerns over subject matter, conventional narrative forms, and the use of Standard English. Dialect as poetic licence was likely to have provided a voice of authenticity for author Selvon, but the infusion of sexual content made literary contributors and audiences uncomfortable as the region was potentially shown 'in a bad light', and reflected a 'comedown from middle-class respectability'.[43] Swanzy's response to Selvon was apologetic, but suggested that a great many protests were noted by his office, and, as 'responsible parties, producers had to apologize not on literary grounds, but on purely a social grounds'. He further explained that the trouble in conducting a programme like *Caribbean Voices* is that one's values tend to be entirely literary, while the radio is really a social medium. Swanzy very much hoped that Selvon would continue sending in material, yet wanted the writer to remember that the BBC could not allow 'artistic integrity as much as licence – as in that fatal broadcast!'[44]

The *Colour Bar* radio project

Due in part to continued concerns over issues of racial prejudice, as expressed by West Indians like Marson, various authors, and student groups, management began plans in June of 1943 for the creation of a talk programme addressing racial prejudice in Britain tentatively called *The Colour Bar*. There had been attempts to dispel racist attitudes and practices by management, as occasional memoranda between producers demonstrated. Two years before, an issue had arisen regarding a radio skit on the Light Programme in which a character 'marries a darkie'. The comment was criticised by producer Alick Hayes for not raising 'a laugh among African audiences, black or white'.[45] A similar issue arose in 1943 when Assistant Controller R.A. Rendall addressed a directive given at a policy meeting. The Empire Division and the CO had mentioned complaints from coloured people about an Entertainments National Service Association (ENSA) programme in which an image of a Black man was held up to scare White children.[46] The memo, sent to all producers from the Assistant Director, read:

> It appears that coloured people are very sensitive about such a habit of mind on the part of European parents as it tends to bring up some white children to be afraid of, and therefore hostile to, coloured people. I told them that I would mention the matter but that it was impossible to certificate every joke in every programme as being inoffensive to all nationalities and races. As suggested at Programme Policy meeting yesterday, perhaps you could remind producers that there are a lot of coloured people in the country now – Africans, West Indians and Americans – and that there is therefore particularly good reason to be careful not to say anything which might be interpreted as showing colour prejudice.[47]

The actual draft announcement for the *Colour Bar* programme, planned for 21 June 1943, was decidedly more poignant, when asking the listener to consider:

> [The] Colour Bar – there are more coloured people in Britain now than ever before. Thousands of them are British subjects from our Colonial Empire, [but] many of them came here voluntarily, and often at their own expense, to take up war jobs, others have been brought over by Government Departments to do work they are specially qualified for. Most of them are living and mixing in a purely white society for first time, and many are finding that their colour excites prejudice against them – [but] in what ways?[48]

Both messages were seemingly indicative of the BBC's efforts to inhibit stereotypic constructs over the radio airwaves. In one particular case, a concern with jokes heard on international radio programming directly preceded a change of policy on the Television Service.[49]

When addressing issues of race within the *Colour Bar* programme, guests of 'Negro' descent would openly address their perceptions of racialism in England with well-known host anthropologist Kenneth Little. The three included Aduke Alakija, a West African woman studying Social Science at Cambridge; Dr Harold Moody, a West Indian lobbyist and member of the League of Coloured Peoples; and Robert Adams, a teacher, actor, and musician from British Guiana. In addition, also included was Claude Graham, listed as a British businessman trading in cloth. Of particular importance to the programme's narrative were discussions about the mistreatment many Black and West Indian immigrants received when arriving in the UK. All three agreed, and cited getting a place to live as the biggest difficulty. Discussed were examples of how a landlady will often explain that no rooms were available even when they were (Figure 2). Alakija explained,

> Landladies usually tell you that the room's been taken, even when it's obvious that it hasn't – card's still in the window, or you've only just got the address from an agency. Sometimes they just look you up and down and then shut the door. D'you know what that sort of experience feels like when it happens over and over again? You get to a state where you can't bring yourself to go up to another door and ask for lodgings. All you want to do is to escape from the curiosity and the stares and the indifference.[50]

Graham, the British executive, responded by asking if 'some of your people [are] – well – hypersensitive? People stare at you for all sorts of irrelevant reasons'. Robert Adams reemphasised that colour prejudice is obvious in England because 'for some reason people seem to be on the impression is because you're coloured something was wrong with you'. Little chimed in with an answer he received from eight out of eleven hotels and boarding houses when was trying to fix up some students with housing: we must consider our boarders. He further explained that one hotel had broken its usual practice and had taken in coloured people, only to have their ordinary clientele telling others that the rooms have been 'contaminated'.[51] Alakija adds:

> The point is we coloured people are ordinary human beings like you, and we expect to be treated as such. This is the Mother Country of an Empire in which 5 out of 7 people are coloured – surely, you ought to be getting used to the idea by now. We Colonials come over here expecting to find the ideals – democracy and all that we've been told about at home. Can you wonder if some of us go back very disillusioned?

After Adams and Moody agreed, Graham suggests that colour isn't a factor, asking, 'isn't the attitude largely the same here with any foreigner – whether they're black from Jamaica or white from say, Greece? They're all foreigners.'

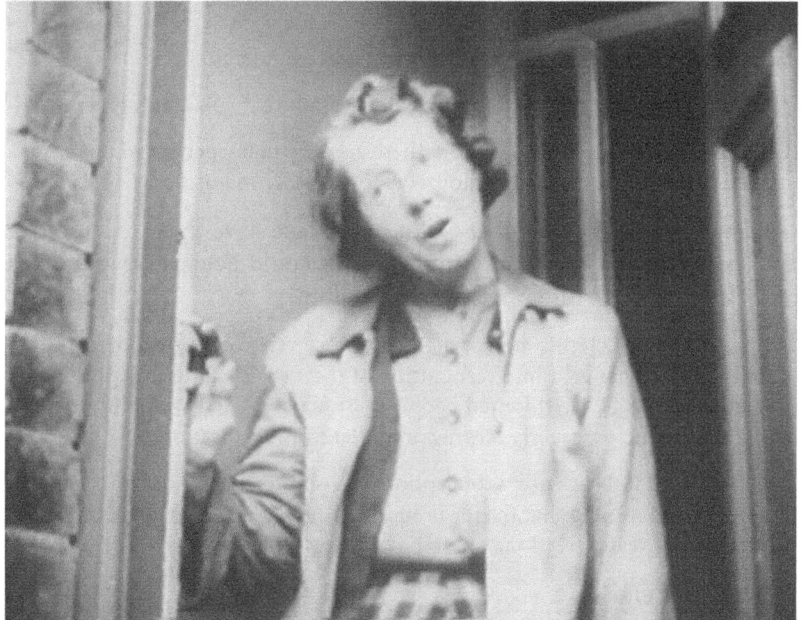

Figure 2 The ubiquitous landlady (2a), who so often refused coloured tenants, appears repeatedly in BBC programmes addressing West Indian immigration (2b). From *The Promised Land? A Question of Colour*

Little responds by discussing a poll taken of 700 private families who took in paying guests. He noted that upwards of 60 per cent of them, perfectly willing to take in white Europeans, specifically refused people of colour. Participants in the poll agreed that a loss of status in one's community was a principle reason behind a refusal, indicating that social position is lost if a Coloured man lived at their dwelling. Other related issues included life within the university for coloured immigrants, the colour bar in hiring, racial differences, and employment.

When considering the amount of positions available in post-war England, there were discussions over a shortage of jobs in the West Indies, and qualified help. Adams asked of Graham:

> [The lack of hiring coloured workers] isn't only an economic problem either. Mr Graham, you are a businessman. Supposing a coloured man presented himself to you for a job, his qualifications were what you required. Would you employ him?

> GRAHAM: Do you want me to try something, which I consider to be a failure before it starts?

> ADAMS: Why not? Aren't you hedging? You don't know the coloured person will be a failure – you're prejudiced against him, and therefore you say he will be a failure.

> GRAHAM: No, no, I'm not personally prejudiced, Adams.

> ADAMS: Then how do you know he will be a failure if you aren't prejudiced?

> GRAHAM: Because, in my opinion, there are very many people who are prejudiced and will not mix with coloured people either in business or socially.

In closing, Adams suggests that Coloured people have the same abilities as White, and if given the same opportunities could achieve very much the same results as the White people. Little responds,

> We need to correct this stereotyped, preconceived conception of coloured people: and to change it into recognition of their social status and prestige … to recognise that in the coloured people there is potentially a vast cultural and social field, which is eagerly seeking an outlet for its aspirations.

> MOODY: And if these wrong conceptions of coloured people are not changed, are we then to assume that the ideas and the benefits of a new world, a greater justice and a greater freedom, are to be only for some?[52]

The transcript ends.

Barnes, colour, and the Colonial Office

After the recording was completed, Director of Talks G.R. Barnes forwarded a memo to the Controller of the Home Service addressing the planned programme, and recommended an evening broadcast time, yet suggested the programme not run at the peak listening time of 9.20 p.m. for fear of exacerbating an already heated issue. He noted that listeners should consider the programme a conversation between friends, and the announcement preceding the broadcast should state that the programme was 'not an attempt to get to the root of the matter, rather a ventilation of widely held views'. There was some trepidation of the subject in that Barnes agreed that although many West Indians would welcome an open discussion of race, other Coloured people such as Chinese and Indians might resent the implications of such a discussion. Barnes then requested a meeting to discuss the matter.[53] During a CO meeting that followed four days later, Mrs Elspeth Huxley, BBC Liaison Officer to the CO, explained that, after discussion of the script, participants of the meeting were strongly in favour of the programme. The CO, which held the position that no official colour bar existed, had received an increasing amount of complaints from Coloured people in general about prejudice and discrimination in urban England. Huxley further detailed how, from the CO's point of view, it would be very helpful to bring 'the whole subject [of race] out into the light of day'. When reflecting on the transcript of the meetings, she felt that such a discussion between Coloured and White people would have a good effect, as colonials 'feel there is a tendency to push the whole subject out of sight'.[54] Huxley stated that West Indians and other immigrants might not object to a frank discussion of difficulties, but they might criticise the hypocrisy surrounding the 'attitude of official non-discrimination and unofficial prejudice'. Huxley was also considered the CO's concerns that an important issue like this one must not be trivialised, and should be analysed on a 'higher level, and [with] a more weighty nature', a likely reference to more intellectual discussions from scholars and perhaps social scientists. However, she felt that a discussion of that nature would deal in generalities and abstract questions beyond ordinary men and women in the UK. She noted that the participants felt that colour prejudice among educated people was less likely, and educated folk would be the ones a weighty talk would address, thereby 'preaching to the converted'. Huxley noted that prejudice was strongest among the 'less educated, the sort of people with whom Colonials find themselves working in factories, and among landladies to whom they apply for rooms'. She suggested that these were the people the talk should reach on the issue of colour prejudice, and that they would be more likely to follow a script that brought the subject 'down to their own level – to the question of what they would do themselves if a black man presented himself asking for a room or a meal'.[55]

Despite the positive reactions by Huxley and the CO, Barnes was concerned and gave no definite recommendation. He did suggest that the biographies of the participants be shared, making it clear to listeners that the discussion was primarily concerned with the feelings of West Africans and West Indians.[56] However, after reviewing the transcript, Sir Richard Maconachie replied most unfavourably, writing:

> Having spent 26 years of my life – on and off – with coloured people, and being still unable to analyse accurately what are the basic reasons for colour prejudice either in myself or anyone else, I find this script pitifully inadequate, and nothing in Mrs Huxley's minute makes me change that view. The basic reasons are difficult and lie deep, and this script admittedly gets nowhere near them. I do not believe that it would do anything whatever – even as a preliminary step – towards changing the attitude of British people (e.g. the digs landlady) towards coloured people. From this point of view, therefore, I should regard the broadcast as – at best – a waste of time.[57]

One week later Barnes recommended that the Home Service not broadcast the programme. He explained that he regretted the decision, and insisted that the speakers receive payment for their efforts. He also suggested keeping the script on file for possible usage later, and requested that Huxley inform the CO of the decision.[58]

In another potential conflict, differences over the programme reflected concerns over the participation of the CO in the content of BBC programming as it related to colonials. In a note to the Controller, Overseas Services from the Controller's Office regarding Huxley, there was a desire to reaffirm her relationship with the BBC as sound, despite concerns that the CO might be seeking the right to see, in advance, anything broadcast about the Colonies. The Controller's Office considered the issue essential when it came to the autonomy guaranteed by Reithian notions, and subsequent practices. Further, he considered it an important principle for the future of broadcasting, asking 'is this safeguarded?'[59] This was apparent when considering Rendall's correspondence to Huxley regarding the CO's desire for the BBC Home Service to broadcast a newsletter modelled after the Dominion's newsletter on the Forces programme. Huxley expressed doubt that the Home Service would agree to this kind of programming and expressed concerns that the material would not be interesting to audiences. Huxley noted that Sabine would look into the numbers of potential audiences and would report back to her and Rendall. Huxley also suggested that an experimental programme could involve the ASD, with help from the CO, collecting available material from government sources or from a BBC representative. She also noted that if the programme were devoted to the West Indies, Marson could deliver it.[60]

However, within days Rendall reported that Sabine had found that only 12,000 men from the Colonies were in the UK at that time. He suggested that, in view of the very small audience, his office would drop the proposal for the colonial newsletter. In this same memo regarding points from the meeting of 7 May, Rendall asked Huxley to report directly to Clark about how things were going at the CO, especially in regard to the Director-General's policies on relations with government departments. In regard to information from the CO, Rendall explained that T.I.K. Lloyd of the department's Middle East section would arrange for Huxley to see all the incoming telegrams from the Colonies, except for defence materials, which would then enable her to see the publicity before the 'Colonial Office machine gets to work on it'.[61] Rendall also expressed interest in the Ministry of Information's plans for colonial publicity in the UK, particularly in the schools. He suggested that as soon as the campaign began, it would be useful to report elements of it back to the Colonies as evidence of increased colonial interest in the country. He asked that Huxley get hold of copies of *50 Facts about the Colonies* as soon as they were ready, and have the ASD distribute them to the Empire Services.[62]

By July of that year, concerns over the BBC's autonomy in broadcasting about the Colonies became paramount. The CO had already become involved in how the BBC handled these delicate matters as related to racialism. Rendall was concerned about a series of points raised at the recent programme policy meeting, and from a letter he considered 'a little long winded', he noted the following concerns by Lloyd:

1) That the Colonial Office should be given advance warning at the earliest possible moment of the BBC's intentions to put on a broadcast concerning colonial affairs.

2) The BBC should attempt to give them a longer period to examine scripts which are sent to them with a request for suggestions and comments.

3) It should be known if the Corporation addressed anything touching on

a. the Middle East

b. colour discrimination and colour prejudice.[63]

Rendall felt that their points should be agreed to, and in projects for talks or programmes Mrs Huxley would serve as the BBC's liaison to the CO. To this end, Huxley kept a record of four weeks of scripts, telephone calls, and letters received from both sources. In the following weeks Scottish social critic W.M. Macmillan provided information including telephone requests from the BBC on the new Governor of Jamaica, the *London Calling* programme, and a talk on the West Indies. However, for the week of 28 June to 3 July, Home Talks requested a script on colour prejudice in the UK for use in a *Travellers' Tales* segment, and received BBC scripts of Learie Constantine discussing the West Indies.[64]

West Indian Diary

An additional concern arose in January 1944, when the CO expressed concern over the reporting of parliamentary questions to the West Indies. The government of Jamaica had pointed out that in some cases the BBC, by reporting such questions, had given publicity to allegations about the British administration, and that the information supplied to audiences was often considered anti-British, if not seditious. The BBC made it clear that the practice of including this information during the weekly *West Indian Diary* programming segment had gone on for some time. It was made clear by T.I.K. Lloyd that the CO 'would not think of attempting to muzzle the BBC', and Rendall pointed out the responsibility of reporting any news or information considered important to the colonies. He also expressed concerns that the organisation should not act as a publicity agent for extreme or irresponsible allegations against British colonial policy.[65] Days later, Rendall wrote to Lloyd expressing a reaffirmation of the BBC's duty to report parliamentary news, again suggesting that the main purpose of *West Indian Diary* and other programmes was to keep the colonies informed of matters of special interest, particularly those related to a growing interest in the UK. Rendall further assured Lloyd that the BBC would continue to exercise judgement in accordance with these aims, while stressing events and ideas that 'unite the Empire and promote the war effort'.[66]

Despite these emphases and intentions, after the war *Diary* shifted focus to examine the lives of West Indians visiting the UK. A programme broadcast over the Colonial Services in January of 1949 began with an interview of a West Indian veteran of World War One discussing life after demobilisation, followed by Ulric Cross interviewing school inspector Ilva LaForest from Trinidad who spent a large portion of her holiday visiting various schools in England. She noted the disparity between financial resources available in England as compared to the West Indies, yet found a great deal of kindness from the English people. These reactions came not only from people in various communities, but from the CO and the Ministry of Education, both of which provided access to facilities. She also suggested to Cross that she was surprised at the ignorance of people, including teachers, not only of the conditions in the West Indies, but where they are situated, causing her 'to do an awful lot of teaching'.[67]

There also existed concerns over the way some of these broadcasts would be perceived by the American Forces, especially when considering racial relations in the USA. Plans made by the Religious Broadcasting Department and the Dean of Westminster featured a performance by an 'unidentified American Negro Choir'. In a memo from Overseas Assistant Francis House, Music Director for BBC Overseas Services, James Steuart Wilson expressed enthusiasm over the live broadcast on the General Forces Programme. This decision would also guide the Dean in his negotiations about the day and hour of broadcast with the American Public Relations office. However, in a memo to Wilson and the Labour MP for Enfield, Ernest Davies, the programme was said to be postponed indefinitely by the Public Relations office, who feared that the American Forces might misunderstand a public concert by a 'Negro' choir. It was determined that the General Forces Programme would not use the programme, later given to the African Services.[68] In 1946, when discussions began again on a *Colour Bar* radio programme, there were further concerns expressed over the perceptions of American Armed Forces Radio management. In a memo from Rendall to Assistant Director of Talks N.G. Luker, he suggested that the North American Service Director's views on this question be determined, since there was concern over the impact of the programme on American opinion. He reminded Luker that, during the last years of the war, the corporation on several occasions refrained from dealing with the subject of race relations out of consideration for Americans living in the UK. Rendall also felt the BBC should express willingness to deal with the subject if the Americans were willing to, but felt it unwise to pressure American collaborators to include the subject if they were unwilling to do so. However, Rendall explained that the BBC should not regard the question of a colour bar as being too delicate for discussion, as far as its 'domestic audience' was concerned. He explained that it was not desirable for the BBC to take the initiative in defining racial relations as a 'difficult matter in England'. However, Rendall felt that if 'the Americans' raised the subject of India or colonial problems, the BBC should not avoid dealing with these matters.[69] Later that year, in yet another effort to track participation by colonial troops in BBC programmes, a memo from Williams listed shows on the Home, Light, African, Pacific, General Overseas, and All Overseas Services. This included programmes as diverse as *Children's Hour*, a pageant to celebrate Empire Day, BBC television's *Picture Page*, and the propaganda-based *We March Tomorrow* feature programme.[70]

We see Britain

In a continued effort to provide further personal views about life in the UK, the *Calling the West Indies* programme featured the segment *We See Britain* on 6 January 1949. A programme presented by former Trinidadian cricketer, and West Indies programme assistant, Kenneth Ablack replaced the regular Thursday night broadcasts on occasion, and featured guests who gave everyday perspectives on life in the UK. Introduced by Ablack was English playwright Anthony Brown, along with cultural critic and author John Metcalf. Brown and Ablack had previously co-produced a programme about the West Indies for BBC's European Service, but for *We See Britain* both men had the opportunity to speak about Britain's economic, political, and educational attachment to the West Indies.[71] Perhaps the most provocative guest on the programme was West Indian author and humorist A.E.T. Henry, who had worked on the *Calling the Caribbean* programme previously with poet Louise Bennett. She and Henry served as the compères for the series, and provided what the programming log called 'recitations of Jamaican dialect rhyme'.[72] As an active participant in the planning of her own appearances, Bennett provided specific examples of dialogue and poetry indigenous to the region. Producer Ablack also invited Bennett and Henry to another segment, *West Indian Guest Night*, on the Overseas (Regional) Programme in 1950, and both appealed to West Indian audiences who appreciated their use of patois and Caribbean dialect.[73]

Within *We See Britain*, the three men discussed how to learn about the country by, as Brown suggested, 'finding a guide who will really show you around, and introduces you to the kind of people who live there now'. As suggested by Ablack at the beginning of the broadcast in 1949, 'we start [the series] with the people of Britain because the British are part of our life and we cannot escape that'. Brown avoided discussions about national monuments and tourist attractions, and mentioned that statistics about British industry and commerce would not educate West Indian listeners on the British people. Henry addressed a question from Ablack about West Indian curiosity and the British. He explained that the average West Indian sees the British as 'so official, so stiff and so aloof. [West Indians] would like to hear what they are like when they're at home.' Metcalf reminds Henry that as the 'old saying goes: the English take their pleasures seriously'. In a statement of intent that addressed the overall focus of the programme, Ablack also included an involvement in every facet of civic government and participation. He stated:

> In the West Indies we are rather inclined to drop down to first names very quickly, in Britain, except on the cricket field, the use of a person's first name is an indication of a real friendship and the English do not easily make friends … The development of institutions, which A.E.T. mentioned – the British pride and interest in his local affairs, and taking it from local to national affairs – the British person realises that loyalty means first being loyal to himself, to his home, and from it goes to the street in which he lives and from his street it

becomes the village, from the village it becomes the town or the country, from the country. He goes step by step. And that is the only way in which you be able to really understand and see British institutions and the British – to go step-by-step with ... and that is how we hope to cover this programme.[74]

When asked to sum up his impressions as a West Indian listener to the programme, Henry responded,

Well, Ken, on the assumption that I was a typical radio listener before I left the West Indies, let me try to interpret the West Indian point of view, by asking myself this question. In those aspects of life in Britain, was I most interested before coming to this country? And in answering that question we have to remember that our educational system is British – the broad contour of our the political system are British – our social and cultural background is British, what might be described as our way of life is fundamentally British. Unlike India or Pakistan or Ceylon or Burma or Africa, West Indians as a people are a very mixed people racially – have never had a separate language or literature or separate traditions. These have all been borrowed from metropolitan Britain, and blended, shall we say, with tropical ingredients to form what is now emerging as a West Indian culture.[75]

The first programme closes with another point raised by Ablack that sums up the overall intent of the programme, not a call to arms against racialism or repatriation, but the need to gain a better understanding of the British ideological construct by discussing the importance of West Indian informality versus a Briton's likeliness to 'stand on formality' as a normal part of social behaviour. With a clear message to West Indian listeners, Henry states,

Well one thing I think that will interest West Indians is what is the attitude – of the English people as a whole, – how do they take to strangers. The degree of tolerance one finds here on the buses, or in the tubes, and that sort of thing. After all West Indians are coming over here in increasing numbers, and they'd like to know what sort of person they're going to meet, and how they're going to be treated.

By comparison, the next broadcast, on 19 January 1949, featured Irish author Harry Craig. In this episode, the directive is clear: perspectives on life in the UK would come from other colonials, namely Irish. Ken Ablack begins the broadcast with:

Good evening, West Indies. This evening we are going to discuss the British. Who are the British? Who do we mean when we say, the British? Tony Brown has gone to Wales to find out whether the Welsh are British and we have included in the programme an Irishman – Harry Craig – who is no stranger to West Indian listeners, as he sometimes reads poetry in *Caribbean Voices*.

Craig continues by discussing his preference for the term 'Irishman', a

seemingly unusual and perhaps seditious point to discuss with primarily
West Indian listeners. Craig states that

> And I am an Irishman and when you refer to me as British I resent it … For
> there is in the character of all Irishmen, even the most flamboyant northern
> unionist, a love of Ireland, independent of his liking of, or his hostility against,
> the English – independent even of his religion.[76]

Metcalf further criticises nationalism noting that, when staying at hotels, he
found that someone would write the term 'British' in the nationality
column, and all the others would have written *ditto*, yet he always took the
trouble to write the word 'English', because he hated the term '"British" – it's
a sort of Imperialistic word. I am really an Englishman, and an English
nationalist'.[77] Metcalf continues by discussing the cartoon stereotypes of
other UK nations found in English papers. He suggests that readers often see
the Scotsmen as 'fly fishing, playing bagpipes, dressed in a kilt and living on
oatmeal and neat whiskey'. He describes the representation of the Irish as
usually 'Paddy O' something, who lives on potatoes, Guinness and illicit
whiskey brewed in a mountain still. Metcalf describes the Welshman to
listeners as 'stark, short, sturdy, and spends most of this time underground
digging coal' or 'above ground refusing to do so'. When asked to describe his
own people by Henry, Metcalf sarcastically replies that the English are 'fine
people, tall, blond, blue-eyed, generous [and] chivalrous to a fault – the
natural leaders of the world for centuries past and to come, honest in all of
their dealings, feared and respected by the enemies and loved and cherished
by their friends'. Ablack responds, 'that's the sort of picture Hollywood
would have us believe'. He then asks Craig to describe the English, which he
places into three categories, 'the scraggy type' with 'long, fawn moustaches,
and says "Tally-ho", and "Good Show, old Chap"'; the 'mild, bowler-hatted
individual', who washes the dishes while his wife 'lies in bed'; and the type of
Englishman 'as Dickens knew him, fat, heavy, waist coated … seen best with
a lump of roast beef in his mouth and gravy on his chin'.

   Henry then responds by discussing advances the West Indies have made
as a postcolonial entity, stating that the region was 'more advanced today –
than the English, Scots and the Welsh and the Irish were when the union
took place in 1707'. He explains that the islands may not have the separate
cultures which the Scots, Irish, and Welsh had, but they did have the
advantage of British political institutions, a better educational system, and a
better understanding between the separate units of the West Indies today. He
adds there are 'far fewer differences between' the cultures of the Caribbeans
and the British 'than there were between the four units which united in
1707'.[78] The programme and its guests provided personal perspectives on the
life of West Indians in the UK, yet avoids a singular perspective. Views of

other White participants allowed for yet another diverse record of ethnicity and nationalism, shared by British colonials with Caribbeans. There was a marked difference in this form of programming during the early 1950s as compared to broadcasts carried by the BBC long after immigration from the West Indies had increased to nearly 100,000 a year between 1950 and 1959.

Also in 1949, more discussions began about the colour bar, as the BBC's efforts to address this issue continued. In a meeting with Radio Talks Producer B.C. Horton, discussions began again about talks programmes, and what she learned when having to deal with racialism 'in a colour bar country'. Following this point, and noted in handwriting by Controller of Talks R.A. Rendall, was 'US!' in reference to American racial relations. Horton, much like those West Indian and West African students of colour, expressed concerns over the treatment of the colour bar as an accepted matter. The working-class Briton, Horton wrote, often 'owes his colour feeling to his own position at home, which makes him want to boss somebody elsewhere. He also may owe it to lack of education (which makes him think of Negroes as niggers)'. She suggested that officials were often worried by the contacts between non-officials and Africans or West Indians, and 'the taboos which the non-official white imposes' upon others. Horton considered the colour question to be a largely passé issue, but found it being 'recreated, just as it was ceasing to exist, to serve a political end'. In the UK, she considered outbreaks of racial bigotry to be a reflection of such post-colonial, self-governing efforts such as Nigerian Nnamdi Azikiwe's Zikism. She suggested that these reactions have little to do with the reality of the situation, for the colour bar is an easy target for the 'subversive or frustrated'. Horton continued, suggesting that resentment may occur when sufficiently trained Africans or West Indians are unavailable to carry out responsible work, and that 'any passing over of native talent is naturally ascribed to colour'. She compared these notions to those of White Southern Americans, who find Blacks distasteful, despite their upbringing at the hands of Black nurses and being 'served by negroes'. She asked 'can the revulsion be overcome and how? It should be remembered that many coloured people also have revulsion to whites'. Aggrey's notions of *Black and White Keys* as grounds for specialisation among the races, prompted Horton to write that the competition for similar tasks among Whites and Blacks may be the primary reason for bias, noting that 'the African … excels at tasks which are different from those, which we excel at'. However, when competing 'on our own ground (whatever this may be) he will always appear inferior', leading to a colour bar.[79]

For the new programme, Horton suggested the involvement of White Britons with knowledge of life in the BWI, including Kenneth Bradley, editor of *Corona*, the new Colonial Service periodical subsidised by the Colonial

Development and Welfare Fund. John Dodds (ex-planter and legislative council, British Guinea) was suggested as a contributor, as was W.E.P. Ward, who was on the staff of the colonial *Achimoto* newspaper, who knew Ghanaian intellectual and racial activist J.E.K. Aggrey well, and who was now Editor of Overseas Education at the CO.[80] However, J. Grenfell Williams, now Head of the Colonial Service, suggested that a series on the *Colour Bar* wouldn't get the service anywhere, and that it would be far better to 'take one great question like the problem of human relations in Africa, and thrash that out'. Ultimately, the Third Programme approved the *Colour Bar* talk, but it focused upon racialism in parts of South Africa, not the experiences of White people in the Caribbean or West Indian immigrants in England. A memo outlined the *Talks on Africa* series, in which Williams suggested that producers choose a different group of coloured participants, 'who crop up again and again'. He then suggested a roster of tentative participants, including a professor of anthropology, who would 'return from Africa in the autumn, full of fresh ideas'; an Australian scientist who worked in East Africa researching social and economic problems, David Nicol, called a highly intelligent African able to 'express himself'; and others including two authors on books related to missionaries and the church in Africa, and Dr Arthur Lewis, Chair of Economics at Manchester University.[81]

Harman Grisewood, controller of the Third Programme in 1950, discussed the possibility of yet another *Colour Bar* series for radio broadcast. In a memo to the Director of the Spoken Word, he provided a list of participants, indicating producer Prudence Smith, and he felt encouraged that the talks would prove unusually interesting, yet the aim was not advocacy. The speakers would not conceal what they believe, but make clear that they were not 'setting out to persuade but to inform'.[82] The series of four talks included the shows *What is a Colour Bar?* featuring Ken Little, who provided and analysis of what the issue means in different nations, and *Origins of the Colour Bar*, with tropic disease expert Dr R.B. Wellesley Cole, one week later. On 9 June at 7.30 p.m., *Why are there Colour Bars Today?* featured an informal symposium hosted by Learie Constantine, as well as the BBC's Elspeth Huxley discussing how a colour bar was often a necessary working arrangement in 'backward countries', E.J. Dingwall on the psychology of race attitudes, and Professor C.S. Penrose on biological differences of race, mixed marriages, and racial purity. The final programme, scheduled for 14 June, was on race policies and politics, with Professor W.I. Macmillan, Director of Colonial Studies at the University of St Andrews, who would give the talk alone due to enormous and varied experience of the problems in nearly every colour-bar country. According to Smith – who worked in conjunction with Audrey Richards, Reader in Social Anthropology of the London School of Economics, and with the Director of Colonial Services –

speakers suggested were chosen based upon their perceived broadcastability as well as authority and suitability. Rounding out the group was John Figaroa, Jamaican writer; Australian sociologist Dr W.E.M. Stanner; and J.H. Huizinga, Dutch journalist, who had recently published articles on immigration policies in the Netherlands.[83] As the final scheme for the *Colour Bar* series was passed by the Third Programme, Smith and others expressed a strong desire to include a pro-apartheid South African Nationalist to speak in favour of the policy, which she felt would 'ensure against any protest by the South African Government'. Her further suggestion was to approach the South African Government to recommend someone. Another idea was to have a guet read one of South African segregationist Dr Eiselen's papers on the dangers of miscegenation, as a 'separate talk', to provide balance to the discussions.[84]

The programme ultimately became one of thirty-one programmes broadcast on the colour bar during 1952, including five on the Light Programme, eleven on the Home Service, and fifteen on the Third Programme. Of the programmes, most dealt specifically with race relations in part of Africa, yet five programmes analysed race relations in the UK, sometimes in comparison to Africans and Black Americans. These programmes included *The Last Freedom* on the Third Programme (18 February 1952), noted as a 'personal statement on racial attitudes among the coloured people', hosted by Black South African writer Peter Abrahams, and *The Conflict of Culture: Racial Misunderstanding and Prejudice* (24 February 1952), noted as a discussion with African journalist Helen Nontando Jabavu, Sierra Leonean poet Abioseh Davidson Nicol, and Peter Abrahams. The Light Programme offered *Any Questions? The Problem of the Colour Bar* (9 May 1952) listed as a discussion, but without guests, and *Wynford Vaughan Thomas reporting on the Colour Bar in Britain* (7 June 1952). The Third Programme also broadcast *Race and Recognition: Growing Colour Problem in Britain* [which is] *Contrasting Position with that in the USA* (20 October 1952) with American cultural anthropologist Ruth Landes.[85]

Of importance was the broadcast of 23 April 1952, when the *Calling the West Indies* programme specifically addressed the input of students and their experiences in the UK. As with broadcasts from the Belfast studios in 1950 and later, the show provided another opportunity for students to specifically discuss their lives living and working in Britain. A producer in the West Indies section, R. Edmett, wrote to the Belfast office in support of West Indian students on the programme, noting that

> The broadcast can take the form of a newsletter and postscript or an interview or O.B. recording or anything that the producer on the spot considers justified. The only maxims to be observed are that it must be Britain through West Indian eyes, news about West Indians in the Region, or something observed by

someone – reporter or otherwise – referring to an item of news which affects the West Indies.[86]

Planned as the first of a series of six broadcasts called *Expatriates*, the subjects discussed the situation of how they and other colonial groups in the country fared. The narrator began by explaining that, at a recent debate in the House of Lords, members discussed the problem of trying to house colonial students. During the debate in April 1952, Lord Chorley had remarked that

> Many of the men and women, who, in the future, will be leaders of their people throughout the Commonwealth and Empire, were now students in the universities and technical colleges in Britain. The impressions they would take home with them depended on what was going on in the British Homes and institutions, and on whether these overseas students were being treated as equals in the citizenship of the commonwealth. Upon those impressions depend future Commonwealth relations.[87]

Lord Chorley suggested that the simplest way to do this was to find some common meeting ground where the people from 'this country and the people from outside the country can meet and talk'. The narrator then explained how the matter was being discussed at various locations, such as a church in Bridlington, Yorkshire, where a local debating society, headed by Major Freemantle, was taking the opportunity to host a group of colonial students from nearby Hull University college. An audience of 350 local men and women listened as students from Kenya, Nigeria, the Gold Coast, Pakistan, Malaya, and the island of Mauritius answered a series of questions about how colonial practices had affected them as citizens and students. After an introduction and warm-up, someone from the audience asked if the occupation of these various countries by the British had improved their lives, their culture and 'their outlook in every way'. None could say that the British had done so. The narrator stated that, 'neither in Malaya, nor in Kenya … had the British brought only good – and their opinions were supported by their team mates from Mauritius, Nigeria and the Gold Coast'. When Freemantle raised the issue of how the British had put a stop to the slave trade on the East African Coast, one African student praised the effort, but doubted whether their motives had been entirely humanitarian or philanthropic. Following this issue, the question arose as to whether the students had experienced colour prejudice in Britain. The indication from the script was that each student felt that a colour bar did exist, and that there were misunderstandings about their intention as Coloured students by White Britons. The programme concluded with rhetorical questions about the existence of a colour bar in the future, as the narrator then indicated that the five students were given an unusual opportunity to speak frankly to a small group of Englishmen and women. He continued by noting that 'whether the answers given by the team were right or wrong, it is important that they were the opinions of university students who may be assumed to have given some thought to these fundamental problems'. The narrator indicated that in future programmes they hoped to introduce sociologists who had worked in the field, and further explore the topic of how colonials fared in Britain's largest cities.[88]

Despite a forum in which these students could express concerns, J. Grenfell Williams preferred limiting their involvement in programming practices. In partial response to these concerns (and for record-keeping purposes), management developed a roster of West Indians who had already broadcast to the home islands for servicemen, nurses, doctors, and students. These included participants from Barbados, nineteen from Jamaica, thirteen from Trinidad, four from British Guiana, and two each from Granada, St Kitts, St Lucia, and the Virgin Islands. Each group included large numbers of service personnel.[89] By November, the *Roundabout* portion of the *Calling* programme also featured personal messages to British Guiana, Antigua, St Vincent, Granada, Trinidad, Aruba, and Cuba, demonstrating an incorporation of concerns expressed over an overabundance of messages to and about Jamaica. Ten years before, the BBC suggested providing accessibility to the Standing Advisory Committee, comprising West African and West Indian students, who commented on programming and provided suggestions. However, in a memo to Miss M. Somerville, Controller, Talks for Home Service, Williams expressed concerns over this commitment by management, and recommended that the BBC not have an observer attending meetings. He noted that, with the best intentions, members of the Committee thought representation implied some commitment by the BBC to do something about any 'particularly urgent problem' which arose. He did indicate that if the corporation planned a programme on coloured students in Britain, there would be 'no harm and perhaps some advantage in a producer attending one or two meetings', but nothing more. Williams reaffirmed intent, when writing that the corporation did 'a considerable amount of broadcasting to the Colonies on the topic mainly with the object of preventing young people from coming to England irresponsibly' and considered himself well aware of most of the problems.[90]

Race and pre-war BBC television policy

The cultural influence of the British Broadcasting Company's Television Service occurred with the initiation of BBC TV in November of 1936. BBC television began standardising its broadcasting with daily programmes broadcasted from the Alexandra Palace facility in London. These shows continued until the start of World War Two forced the service off the air on 1 September 1939. The organisational principles which the Sykes and Crawford committees helped to establish passed directly from radio to television as a public-service monopoly, funded by licence fees and regulated by the Board of Governors. Initially considered less serious than radio's offerings, television programmes were thought to be far more frivolous, and relied upon light entertainment. However, after the Coronation ceremony in 1953, the potential to provide documentary footage and commentary on social events further established the medium.[91]

Before the war, Reith's dislike of television threatened its development under his watch. Yet this medium's time was approaching quickly, despite his sentiments. Grace Wyndham Goldie noted in her memoirs that Reith was 'frightened of television … because he believed that communication by means of vision would be an evil which would be damaging to the country and to the world'. Given Reith's high distrust for politicians, the government's role in broadcasting, and the imminent control it represented, in November 1937 Reith tendered his resignation as Director-General of the BBC, which became official in June 1938. However, it was apparent that Reith was in a position to influence television greatly, just as he had radio. As stated by Goldie, 'the standards which he had set for the British Broadcasting Corporation were to have their effect in later years upon the television services of the world'.[92]

The concerns of an impending war with Germany overshadowed the development of television, which provided two distinct yet overlapping issues. Few people held licences during the era before World War Two, and, since the BBC was otherwise preoccupied with war, television producers worked with near autonomy in the two television studios available. Used in one was the Baird system, in the other, Marconi/EMI. By February 1937, the BBC dropped the Baird system, which was considered less effective. Soon construction of the Alexandra Palace studios for television programming began in North London. Eventual hours of transmission varied, but were approximately from 8.30 p.m. to 10 p.m., creating the first regular television service in the world. A typical evening's viewing consisted of a play transmitted live, Gaumont-British or Movietone newsreels, and a Walt Disney cartoon film. The enthusiasm was overwhelming. Goldie notes:

> Week after week between 1936 and 1939 the main efforts of the new television service, of producers and designers, lighting men and studio managers, costume and make-up departments, as well as money and energy, went into the production of studio plays, mostly stage plays adapted, effectively or otherwise, for television … But the main preoccupation was with drama. This was partly due to the practical circumstances of television. With limited studio

space, money and effort, it was convenient to be able to fill an hour or more of television with a single production.[93]

BBC television production staff, who saw themselves as professionals in visual communication, came largely from the theatre and from films, with a few from sound radio. Goldie noted how the staff generally arrived with attitudes 'which had been shaped by their previous experiences. Both the theatre and the cinema were visual media, sound broadcasting was not.'[94] Goldie implied that the men from cinema and theatre seemed, and indeed felt themselves to be, superior in shaping the future of the new medium.

Of particular delight to BBC audiences were variety programmes featuring African-American entertainers. An early example was the American duo of Buck and Bubbles, appearing during BBC's first public broadcasting day of 2 November 1936.[95] They had been known to do a stick and staircase dance routine that had entertained American audiences previously. The presence of the duo also provided a basis for the first representation of Black people on BBC television. Also featured in these early television specials were Black artists such as singer/actor Elisabeth Welch, who had performed numerous times on the radio. In 1934, Welch had her own BBC radio series entitled *Soft Lights and Sweet Music*, and she notes:

> We were on the air more or less every week for quite a while, so we became known. There was a small group of musicians, four or five in number and I was the singing voice. As a result, I became a name up and down the country without people ever knowing what I looked like.[96]

Within a year, Welch was appearing in the musical programmes beginning in October of 1937 from Alexandra Palace. Welch, who had thus become a favourite of audiences on BBC radio years before, continued to provide entertainment to television audiences, as did other Black performers such as Winifred Atwell, Paul Robeson, and Adelaide Hall. Nina Mae McKinney and Josephine Baker also appeared on the medium Welch called 'radio with pictures' in 1933 as part of Baird's experimental broadcasts.[97] Audiences loved her, and she was in many ways safe within her confines as an African-American entertainer. Welch's heritage (once identified) was met with a great degree of acceptability to most White viewers, particularly when compared to the problematic aspects of the West Indian immigrant. Despite the early present of Welch on the BBC, the visual coding of race on early monochromatic broadcasts was unapparent. Welch spoke of how audiences were unaware of her actual appearance, noting how 'at Alexandra Palace … you didn't need make up. Everybody was white, white, white – you only had eyes and black lips'.[98] Though many audiences knew of her film work with Robeson (*Song of Freedom*, 1936, and *Big Fella* from 1937), there were, as Welch indicates, many members of the radio audience that never actually saw her until the first television broadcasts from Alexandra Palace. Welch's explanation of the BBC's cameras and lack of make-up suggests the image of her as a Black woman evacuated of racial coding, in that everyone appeared as White. As one of England's favourite performers, the polished Welch, visually exposed to television audiences following her work on the radio, found her image as a Black woman altered and eradicated by the very nature of the medium and its technical limitations.

However, African-American Adelaide Hall, unlike Welch, had openly accused the BBC of racist practices in a letter written to the Programme Contracts Director. The letter indicated that a colour bar existed within the BBC due to the show's producer not hiring her to perform in an episode of the *Starlight* musical show in 1943. A letter of response sent to then producer Cecil Madden regarding the matter from the Programmes Contracts Director, W.L. Streeton, read:

> I have no doubt that both Adelaide Hall and her husband will pursue this matter, partly because of their unfortunate impression that there is some colour bar so far as *Starlight* is concerned ... I suggest that if you agree, you might consider putting forward a revised list including Adelaide Hall's name, for reconsideration by the Empire Programme Planners.[99]

Responding to Hall's complaints, Madden wrote,

> Thank you for your confidential memo of the 4th of May and for your intervention in the matter. I think now it is possible to include Adelaide Hall in the *Starlight* series and that, if so, we shall hear no more in the matter from Adelaide Hall or her husband.[100]

In a memo written from Madden to Hall's agent Jack Fallon, she is 'fixed up' for a few future engagements. However, Hall's exposure to television audiences was severely limited, perhaps due to her insistence upon fair treatment. Memos written on following dates showed Hall performing in Glasgow for BBC Radio Scotland in 1946,[101] yet she did not appear on the musical television programme *Close Up* until January 1947.[102] Hall was to appear in the show *Harlem Nocturne* in May of 1947 with the Harlem Octet, but the show was cancelled by the producer, who felt that it did not reach the level of acceptability for broadcast, probably due to lack of rehearsal.[103]

Yet Cecil Madden, in anticipation of increased production of television series, prepared a Television Censorship Code years before that, among other issues, addressed race and colour. The 'file for producers' served as 'only a temporary one' and Madden had the document 'compiled from various sources, some of which need not apply to Television'. Maurice Gorham, appointed Controller of Television in 1945, received the memo and roster of questionable material. The eventual Television Policy Censorship Code served as a guideline for producers, who, when in doubt, contacted the Television Production Officer or Special Projects Manager. Producers were to avoid colour references (yellow, nigger, black, etc.), or 'cracks about Indians such as "Indians in India wear sheets", and 'anything derogatory about coloured people'.[104] It is apparent from the suggestions that among concerns over racialism within the development of programming, with television now being a consideration, there remains the aforementioned concerns over consistency of policy concerning these efforts.

As documents throughout this chapter indicate, there were obvious attempts on the part of BBC management to acknowledge the transcultural effects of West Indians and other colonials, their presence and their intent. Student discussions of racist practices on the part of property owners highlighted problems in assimilation, yet the BBC did offer a liberal approach to exposing these malpractices. However, inconsistencies remain apparent with broader issues of race and culture. Decisions allowed for programmes examining the difficulties of Coloured students in England, yet cancelled the broadcasts, and shunted concerns over racialism to locales such as America, and South and West Africa, instead of Brixton, underscoring a sense of duplicity when addressing social values through public service and education.

Throughout British history, these farmers, loggers, servants, drivers, nurses, and sailors supported and helped build the UK as underclass labour. With their involvement came an engagement with opportunities to approach cautiously the possibilities of cultural assimilation. Even if not fully acknowledged by these dominant producers, imperialism had to engage with these subjects through postcolonialism, nationalism, or subjectivity. Simultaneously, discourses of West Indian cultures resonated within Britishness. The arrival of these new immigrants on the *Empire Windrush* at Tilbury after the war replaced them into the heartland of Britain. Whereas Black Americans as soldiers or entertainers were merely guests, the African-Caribbean immigrant, via the mod con of BBC television, found their very presence as citizens amplified, as the following chapter examines.

Notes

1 From *We See Britain*, 23 April 1952, scripts held in hard copy, West Indian Script Section. All references are BBC WAC unless otherwise noted.
2 Webster, *Englishness and Empire*: 20.
4 Reith, *Broadcast Over Britain*: 78.
5 Boyle, *Only the Wind Will Listen*: 153–4.
6 Paulu, *British Broadcasting in Transition*: 22.
7 Richard Thurlow *Fascism in Britain: A History, 1918–1985*. Oxford: Basil Blackwell, 1987: 245.

8 E3/981, 1 July 1954.
9 Clark to Bowyer, 1 December 1936, E1/1301.
10 Colonial Office No. 139, E1/1301.
11 Macgregor to Bowyer, E1/1301, 21 October 1938.
12 Richards to MacDonald, E1/1301, 31 October 1938.
13 Colonial Office No. 139, E1/1301.
14 *West Indies Calling*. Dir. John Page, Prod. Donald Alexander for the BBC, 1943.
15 Delia Jarrett-Macauley, *The Life of Una Marson, 1905–65*. Kingston, Jamaica: Ian Randle, 1998: 144–6.
16 Madden to Burns, Beckett, and Sabine, E1/1301, 23 July 1940.
17 Jarrett-Macauley, *Life of Una Marson*: 151–2.
18 Gilbert to Madden, 13 May 1941, R46/92.
19 A roster of programmes – 1940 and 1941, R46/92.
20 Madden to Kelsall, 9 May 1941, SC19/28.
21 Kelsall to Madden and Gilbert, 12 May 1941, R46/92.
22 Gilbert to Kelsall and Madden, 15 May 1941, R46/92.
23 Cable to Madden, Marson and DDES, 19 May 1941, R/46/92.
24 Marson to Gilbert, 16 June 1941, R46/92.
25 Gilbert to Turner et al., 25 June 1941 R46/92.
26 Memo from Kelsall, 18 July 1941, SC19/28.
27 Stewart to ASPD and OB assistant ed., 10 September 1941, SC19/28.
28 Marson to Kelsall, 22 September 1941, SC19/28.
29 Empire Music Supervisor to Quade and Marson, 11 September 1941, SC19/28.
30 Madden to ASPD and Gilbert, 15 May 1941, R/46/92.
31 Quade to Scottish Programme Executive, 16 July 1942, SC19/28.
32 Marson to Brown, 28 August 1942, R46/92.
33 Burnett to the Director of Publicity, 14 January 1942, SC19/28.
34 *Ibid.*
35 From Burnett to the SSA Glasgow, 27 January 1942, SC19/28.
36 Notes from 15 December 1943, with Betts, DT, ASD, Even, and Thomas of the CO, R34/305/1.
37 Rendall to ACOS, 28 December 1943, R34/305/1.
38 *Ibid.*
39 ACOS to COS, 28 December 1943, and Notes of a meeting held 15 December 1943, R34/305/1.
40 Marson to ASD, 31 March 1944, R/46/92.
41 A. Walmsley, *The Caribbean Artists Movement, 1966–72*. London: New Beacon Books, 1992.
42 Gautam Premnath, e-mail correspondence, 4–6 November 2009.
43 *Ibid.*
44 Swanzy to Selvon, 29 October 1948, reproduced by Special Collections, University of Birmingham.
45 COS to Hayes, 25 June 1941, R34/306.
46 ACOS to Controller Programmes, 1 May 1943, R51/92.
47 ADOS forwarded by CP, 26 July 1943, R34/306.

48 Barnes to Bucknall, 21 June 1943, R51/324/1.
49 The BBC variety programmes *Policy Guide for Writers and Producers* was for use by radio and television staff. Released in 1948, the guide covered issues of vulgarity, the mention of charitable organisations, the usage of the terms 'British' and 'English', popular music, special considerations for overseas broadcasting, and miscellaneous points which addressed references to racial groups. The BBC had already expressed some sensitivity to these issues before this release.
50 From the *Colour Prejudice* transcript, R51/324/1.
51 Recorded June 1943, R51/324/1.
52 *Ibid.*
53 Barnes to the CHS, 21 June 1943, R51/324/1.
54 Huxley to CHS, 26 June 1943. R51/324/1.
55 *Ibid.*
56 Barnes to CH, 26 June 1943, R51/324/1.
57 CH to the DG, 28 June 1943, R51/324/1.
58 Barnes to Bucknall, 30 June 1943, R51/324/1.
59 CN to COS, 27 July 1943, R34/305/1.
60 ACOS to Huxley, 1 May 1943, R34/305/1.
61 ACOS to Huxley, 10 May 1943, R34/305/1.
62 *Ibid.*
63 ACOS to COS, 22 July 1943.
64 Huxley to Rendall, 24 July 1943, R34/365.
65 ACOS to COS, 10 January 1944, R34/305/1.
66 Rendall to Lloyd, 14 January 1944, R34/305/1.
67 Script of programme, 21 January 1949, R34/305/1.
68 House to Wilson, Spicer, and Davies, 1 and 15 June 1944, R51/92/1.
69 Rendall to the ADT and COS, 31 May 1946, R51/324/1.
70 Williams to Evans, 20 June 1946, R34/305/1.
71 *We See Britain*, 6 January 1949, R51/92.
72 *Ibid.*
73 Bennett's booking forms signed by Ablack and Swanzy, *West Indian Guest Night*, 24 October 1950 to 20 June 1951, RCont1.
74 Ibid.
75 *We See Britain*, 6 January 1949, West Indian Script Section.
76 *Ibid.*
77 *We See Britain*, 20 January 1949.
78 *Ibid.*
79 Horton to Williams, 8 February 1949, R/51/324/1.
80 *Ibid.*
81 Williams to CT, 15 March 1949, R51/92.
82 CTP to DSW, 26 May 1950, R/51/92/1.
83 Smith to ACT, CTP and Rendall, 20 May 1950, R/51/92/1
84 Smith to DCS, 27 January 1952, R/51/92/1.
85 Programmes on the colour bar for 1952, 12 March 1953, R51/92/1.

86 Edmett to Thomas, 9 December 1952, N/54/1.

87 *We See Britain*, 23 April 1952, scripts in hard copy, West Indian Script Section.

88 *Ibid.*

89 List of West Indians, no date, R/46/92.

90 From HCS Williams to CT, Home, 9 July 1953, R/51/92/1.

91 Bob Franklin, ed., *Social Policy: The Media and Misrepresentation*. London: Routledge, 1999; Bob Franklin, ed., *British Television Policy: A Reader*. London: Routledge, 2001.

92 Goldie, *Facing the Nation*: 32.

93 *Ibid.*: 33.

94 *Ibid.*

95 BBC programming records, 1937, volume 8, part 1, p. 282.

96 Pines, *Black and White in Colour*: 22.

97 Stephen Bourne, *Elisabeth Welch: Soft Lights and Sweet Music*. Lanham, MD: Scarecrow, 2005: 37.

98 Pines, *Black and White in Colour*: 23–4; Bourne, *Elisabeth Welch*: 38.

99 Streeton to Madden, 4 May 1943, R34/306/1.

100 Madden to Streeton: Adelaide Hall, 5 May 1943, R34/306/1.

101 Quade to Lipscombe, 16 August 1946, R/49/1095.

102 From the Variety Booking Manager, 4 June 1947, R/49/1095.

103 Brown to Variety Booking Manager, 4 June 1947, R34/306/1.

104 Madden to Gorham, 20 January 1947, T16/162/1.

2

Television programming and social impact

Without question, we should have avoided the coloured man's songs to the white girl. There have been a number of letters complaining about this point, even though some of the correspondents are badly confused by the lightness of some of the coloured artists. It is not too much to say that the production of Black Magic lowered the whole standard of the Service.

(Controller, Television, Norman Collins, 1 February 1950)[1]

As the post-war Television Service worked to establish itself as a viable part of the corporation, examinations of race and ethnicity became part of its commitment to public service, yet negative reactions to imagined sexual miscegenation by viewers evoked a stern reaction from Collins. Now that nationality and belonging were a part of visual programming texts, ideologies that served as a foundation for management to shape this stepchild of radio were subject to reevaluation. It was apparent that these constructs were, in part, only as certain as audience responses and management decisions allowed.

Tight government control of capital expenditures restricted the building of new transmitters and retarded the full nationwide coverage of the BBC's television signal for several years. There were only 14,560 television licences in 1946, but this number rose slowly to 45,564 the following year. By 1948, there were 128,567 registered throughout the UK. In 1949, the government approved a plan by the BBC to make television available to 80 per cent of the total population, expanding television coverage to nearly forty million people over the next five years.[2] By the 1950s, the budget for television was only half that of the Home Service; prompting the resignation of two television controllers; the first in 1947, and in 1950 Norman Collins, who complained of the neglect of television.[3]

After the suspension of television during World War Two, broadcasts recommenced from Alexandra Palace on 7 June 1946. Despite the lapse in service, BBC management reminded the Beveridge Committee that broadcasting must continue to be in the general social interest, and the educational impulse maintained. A major concern for management at Broadcasting House was the desire for the Television Service to develop some degree of autonomy, yet abide by the BBCs exacting standards. Grace Wyndham Goldie, who worked rather closely with Norman Collins, felt a great degree of support from him as television began to flourish, yet Collins was also deeply involved with a bitter battle between his office and BBC management for more freedom and financial resources. Both he and Goldie were also concerned with making television far more topical. One result was that between 1947 and 1950, the year Collins abruptly resigned, the merger of political thought and television as a medium sparked a growth of journalism. This was evident in reporting of results for the general election of 1950. Another primary consideration was the advent of the programme *Foreign Correspondent*, which began in 1949. Originally, the programme did not report on political issues around Europe as originally intended, but instead tried to demonstrate how the Marshall plan and its aid affected the rebirth of Europe following World War Two. On occasion, when experts invited to the studio attempted to discuss these issues, the commentary provided seemed strained and awkward.[4] However, the programme did provide an avenue for continued efforts toward topical programming. After *Foreign Correspondent* was *International Commentary* (BBC, 1951–55), *Race Relations in Africa, India's Challenge, Panorama* (1953–), and *Twenty-Four Hours* (1965–72), several programmes Goldie considered truly current affairs.

As the service attempted to address issues of race in later documentaries and teleplays, these matters became more controversial as viewers witnessed West Indian immigrants arriving on the *Empire Windrush*; an event televised to only a modest portion of the population given that fewer than 130,000 licences were held in 1948. There was no way to ignore this phenomenon, however, particularly when considering newspaper coverage and cinematic newsreels.[5] A major component of this televised imagery was footage shot by the British Pathé Film Company that made its way from motion picture theatres into the homes of licence holders. Unlike before the war, programmers at the BBC during the 1950s did not have access to commercial films or filmed newsreels; a policy established the Newsreel Association of Great Britain and other film companies on Wardour Street in London. In response to this decision, the BBC television film unit in association with British Pathé began formulating a television newsreel section. These individuals were recruited from around the Commonwealth and trained on modern equipment purchased from American and foreign commercial filmmakers. In an exchange agreement with National Broadcasting Company (NBC) in America (later abandoned so that the BBC could use other sources such as Columbia Broadcasting System (CBS) and Telenews), other freelance camera operators were signed on to work under close supervision. The relationship between the BBC included a film exchange deal with NBC, in which film reports of topical news events were traded between the two, and shown to audiences in both nations; primarily on *Newsreel Review of the Week* with Edward Halliday (BBC, 1951).

Management also insisted on establishing a different content and production quality from that of commercial cinema newsreels. The post-war average was 1–2 minutes within an 8.5-minute commercial newsreel, yet BBC crews created stories that were 10–15 minutes, often shooting significantly more footage that addressed one news event only.[6] Careful planning went into the placement of cameras as well, using techniques learned before the war. Unlike the quick edits used in the motion picture newsreels at theatres, these films used longer takes with more close-ups. Viewers had often found it too difficult to keep reorienting themselves if a producer cut from camera to camera too often, or too quickly.[7] With this longer treatment of events, television viewers could better enjoy stories about the Royal Family, visiting dignitaries and movie stars or any other stories deemed significant by the production staff of the BBC film unit. This included the Victory Parade in June 1946 and the royal wedding of Princess Elizabeth and the Duke of Edinburgh in November of 1947. Subsequently the BBC transmitted the first edition of a biweekly 15-minute programme called *Television Newsreel* (BBC, 1948–54) on 5 January. The programme began in part due to the BBC's decision to start producing its own newsreels. An expansion of the film department took place, and more editors and scriptwriters were recruited, resulting in the newsreel programme. The arrival of West Indian immigrants aboard the *Empire Windrush* in 1948 became a landmark event, particularly when shown under the item 'Jamaican Emigrants arrive', using a generous 143 feet of film and shown directly before an innocuous piece on the ninetieth birthday of King Gustav of Sweden. Swedish Newsreel and the French film company Les Actualités Françaises supplied footage for other newsreel stories, yet BBC film crews were on hand at Tilbury Docks to shoot the arrival of the *Windrush* themselves. The segment was transmitted on the evening of Friday, 25 June, three days after the arrival of the vessel. Briefly discussed was the arrival itself and the hopes of these settlers, including short interviews with three West Indian men about their intentions.[8] One wanted a 'good job, any job, with good pay', and another planned to rejoin the RAF. Another man loved Scotland, where he learned case-making during the war, but wanted to earn money and return to Jamaica to help his Mother.

It was also in 1948 that a West Indian actor, Edric Connor, first appeared on the service in a BBC variety show entitled *Music Makers* (BBC, 22 June 1948), ironically, the same date as the arrival of the *Empire Windrush* at Tilbury Docks. West Indian performers were later featured on the variety programme *Bal Creole* (BBC, 1950), which included Trinidadian performer

Boscoe Holder and his wife Sheila Clarke. His group, the West African Rhythm Brothers, was the subject of a 1951 memo from the BBC Controller of Television, Cecil McGiven, to producer Bill Ward. The memo suggested that the group be included on upcoming broadcast of the show *Caribbean Cabaret* and that the performance be as 'loud and savage' as possible for viewers.[9] In a memo from the television controller to the head of live television entertainment in 1951, the West African Rhythm Brothers were to be included within a broadcast somehow, despite a limited schedule. He stated that the network 'seldom got that type of excitement and virility from the half-starved British Isles'.[10]

Audience surveys

To assure that specific programmes reached audiences and served their purposes, the BBC attempted to gauge reactions to various shows. Placing emphasis upon the importance of feedback through the usage of surveys was Maurice Gorham, the first post-war Head of Television, who had worked as Head of Light Programmes. He strongly believed in polling television audiences on viewing habits and tastes just as they had been doing with radio audiences since the 1930s. Though, nine months after the war, fewer than 15,000 households had the combined sound and television licence required, Gorham believed that, as in America, television would rapidly increase in popularity (by 1950, there were a reported 350,000 combined radio and television licences). With the growth of these audiences, a series of *ad hoc* studies were organised, the first in 1948, second in 1950, and a third in 1954. The important determinations were what kind of people were watching television, how much were they watching, and how were leisure hours – and radio listening habits – being directly affected. According to the General Post Office, there was a ten-fold increase in the first two years and the number of licences had reached six million by 1956, which indicated that many citizens no longer considered television a luxury, but a necessity.

Continuous audience research for television began in December 1949 when Robert Silvey, Head of BBC Audience Research, encouraged the formation of panels that would supply feedback on a consistent basis for the BBC. Later that year, he went on radio and later television to appeal for cooperation from viewers. Shortly afterwards, over 24,000 families responded to his request to help establish viewing panels that would answer predetermined questions about those programmes they watched and preferred. Programming categories were established indicating programmes audiences liked very much or moderately, that they were neutral about, they 'don't much like', or they strongly disliked. The discovery of specific tastes in audiences revealed that, of those responding, 88 per cent preferred plays in the television studio, yet 84 per cent enjoyed newsreel films. These preferences also included strong similarities between men and women with the exception of musical comedies, ballet, and magazine programmes, which women preferred. By the end of 1951, the daily interview survey had already become the Survey of Listening *and* Viewing. By October to December of 1952, samples indicated that television had reached 14 per cent of the population and that they viewed an average of just over one hour each evening. By 1953, this audience had grown to 22 per cent, and it increased to 31 per cent a year later.

In a further effort to determine the ultimate reactions of audiences to the race relations programme specifically, Silvey conducted a pre-broadcast survey designed to measure attitudes of viewers toward race. In the Viewer Research Report of 28 November 1952, methodology and results were, after consultation with Goldie, tested for perceived hostility toward the subject. Subjects consisted of viewers recently interviewed through the standard Survey of Listening and Viewing offered by Silvey's group. The 230 audience members participating in the survey represented a cross-section of ages and occupational levels, called 'slightly higher in intelligence than the television public'. Of major importance was a measure of attitudes toward the subject of the series, and what audiences thought about the participation of coloured people in the programme. Viewers also received different statements in answer to questions about this issue and other related matters. After reading and considering these statements, they were to mark statements which they agreed with, and cross statements with which they disagreed. If they had no opinion about a statement, they could indicate this and go on to the next issue.

As an example, Silvey's staff offered the statement, *It's a mistake to try to educate Black people*, to which participants responded:

1) Strongly agree – 0 per cent
2) Agree – 3 per cent
3) No opinion – 6 per cent
4) Disagree – 57 per cent, and
5) Strongly disagree – 34 per cent

This allowed for a partial measurement of the group's attitude. Opinions and attitudes on racism in Africa were queried in a similar fashion, as fifteen statements about the characteristics of Black people were offered, including a general attitude toward Black people, along with twenty-nine statements about Black–White issues in Africa, including land, equality, and interracial marriage. A checklist of responses was also included to help researchers determine the most important problems in Africa, with other issues included as distracters. Those issues directly related to race were offered:

a) There are bad race relations in Africa,
b) There is a colour bar, and
c) There are racial disturbances

and responses were limited to three choices:

1) Not a problem in Africa,
2) A problem in Africa, and
3) Very important problem in Africa.

These responses resulted in a 55 per cent response to (a) as very important; 71 per cent to (b) and 53 per cent to (c).

When viewers were asked more about examining or hearing about race relations in Africa, a series of possible answers were provided with a choice of responses (i.e. agree strongly, agree, disagree, disagree strongly, and no opinion). Under the statement *I would like to hear about the relations of Blacks and Whites in Africa*, 92 per cent expressed an agreement, and 86 per cent wanted to hear more about the way Black people and White people mix in everyday life. However, 78 per cent disagreed when given the statement *To be quite frank, we here in Britain have enough troubles of our own without bothering about the problems of Black people in Africa.*

On attitudes toward seeing coloured people on television expressing their opinions on race relations, 78 per cent disagreed with the statement *Personally, I dislike the idea.* A list of statements on racial relations was also presented to viewers for consideration, with declarations such as *Given a fair chance, the Black man can become equal the White man in all things, the only real difference is the colour of his skin*, and *I would be quite willing to have a Black man visit me in my home as long as he was educated or civilised.* Each received responses representing very strong agreements, as did statements about equal pay for similar job performance, equal treatment under the law, equal voting powers, and *As the Black people of Africa become more educated and civilised they should be treated more as the equals of White men.* However, under the notion that interracial marriage would help race problems in Africa, there was a very strong disagreement, yet a strong agreement that *In the British colonies of Africa, the treatment of Black people is generally good.* The eighteen-page survey goes on to ask a series of questions about Africa to test the knowledge of the participant on multiple issues including populations, geographic references, and the effects of race relations upon the influence of Communism.[11] As suggested by Belson, viewers' attitudes to the problems of Africa tend to be liberal, yet their knowledge of the essential facts behind these problems are scanty.[12]

Post-war television and race

As suggested, BBC radio had broadcast programmes on the colour bar in Africa since before the war, but on two occasions during 1952 issues related to immigration and subsequent racism in post-war Britain were explored as an important and potentially explosive topic. Programming for 17 June 1952 over the Light Programme offered Welsh journalist and BBC broadcaster Wynford Vaughn-Thomas reporting on the *Colour Bar in Britain* (feature) with commentary from Vaughn-Thomas. Producer R.D. Smith on 20 October 1952, on the Talks Programme, offered *Race and Recognition: Growing Colour Problem in Britain*, in which racialism was contrasted with the USA, including commentary from American Anthropologist Ruth Landes.[13] As the country continued to adjust to the shock of the *Windrush*'s arrival and subsequent issues, the BBC was beginning to formulate plans to televise programming that addressed misconceptions about race. In a memo sent on 5 January, the Head of Television Talks Mary Adams addressed the first in a series of planned *Race Programmes* filmed by the television newsreel unit, transmitted on BBC television, and hosted by MP Christopher Mayhew. The programme would attempt to address racial differences concerning African versus European ancestry, and was one of the earliest television programmes to broach the sensitive issue of racial conflict, though set in Africa, as immigrants continued to seek employment and housing. Producer James Bredin listed the show as the *Scientific Programme on Race* on 10 November, followed by examinations of South Africa, Kenya, the Gold Coast, Central Africa, and the Sudan in the following weeks. A sum-up show would transmit on 29 January of the following year.[14] A producer for the service, G.H. Noordhorf, felt the subject of race, which Adams considered very important, could be made suitable for television with very little difficulty. Further, Adams noted:

> Grace [Wyndham Goldie] is putting together a series of programmes on the racial question and she wishes to start with a programme dealing entirely with the scientific aspect of the problem. In this programme, for which I should be responsible, the scientific points made would be brought into direct relation with the type of argument, which would be followed in Christopher Mayhew's thesis during the remainder of the series.[15]

In turn, Goldie, serving as Assistant Head of Talks, received a memo later that year from James Bredin (with a copy to Controller Michael Peacock) addressing the planned series, tentatively entitled *Race Relations in Africa*.

The first programme of the series would centre on research conducted by an esteemed scientist who subsequently made anthropological comparisons between races. Three of the principal questions suggested for the programme's guests would be:

1) What is race?
2) What is the effect of a mixed marriage? and
3) Are there such things as superior races?[16]

The presenter of the programme would be Science Editor of the *News Chronicle* Ritchie Calder, who would then interview, among others, MP Christopher Mayhew. Adams and Goldie decided that Mayhew would also appear in a series of six programmes beginning in November of that year, provided a Conservative MP (possibly Julian Amery) hosted a similar series for three to four episodes after Mayhew's show. In response, Adams, in a handwritten note, suggests that Mayhew lead the talks on 5 and 6 November, but only with the understanding that a 'Tory MP [lead the talks] for three [episodes] after Mayhew'.[17] In another memo expressing similar concerns, George Barnes advises Goldie to search for a Conservative MP or ex-MP to speak on foreign affairs. Barnes was worried that Mayhew's views might get television into the same position as sound found itself over the comments of Vernon Bartlett during the 1933 disarmament talks in Geneva. After Germany left the Disarmament Conference, Bartlett commented during the *News at Six* that he believed the British would have acted in similar fashion, if they had been in the same position. The *Evening Standard* noted that if 'contentious views were to be broadcast in an hour of crisis unmatched since 1914, they should be expressed by responsible members of the Government and not by talented attachés of the BBC'.[18]

However, Mayhew had established himself as an authority on racial relations as host of the filmed programme *International Commentary*. The programme, shown fortnightly, investigated issues related to race and its impact on world affairs. Mayhew spent months with camera crews examining racial relations in colonial and postcolonial Africa between Europeans and indigenous citizens. According to an essay written by Mayhew in the *Radio Times*, the show's original intent was to ask what race relations were like in the 'host country', and what makes them what they are, allowing for an ideally open-ended approach to these issues.[19] Goldie proposed that, with assistance from the Television Talks Organiser C. Jackson and the Secretariat's Office, Mayhew and programme researchers would eventually query audiences on what subjects they would like to see examined, an indication of the importance given to audience reaction.[20] Goldie also expressed concerns about the cost of sending Mayhew and a camera operator travelling throughout Africa, and chose to cancel the series despite Mayhew's request to have camera training and do his own filming as a cost-saving measure. She later approved the project but only if a camera operator was used (Goldie felt that Mayhew was not professional enough and lowered BBC standards) and if the budget for the programme was cut to the bare minimum, including Mayhew's fees and expenses.[21] Since scientists had already conducted much of the research for the pending show on race, the programme required very little financial commitment. Goldie's commitment to racial understanding was apparent via her initiatives, but she also suggested in a memo to Littman in Audience Research that concerns existed over reactions to the subject of race relations from White viewers, and

> If there is such hostility, what is its cause and should we expect it in any particular groups or areas? Is there alternatively any sort of predilection towards hearing about Race Relations? Is there a prejudice for or against seeing coloured people in television expressing their own point of view?[22]

The first programme, transmitted on 10 November 1952, was tentatively entitled *The Scientists Look at Race*. Included within the notes and script for the programme were discussions on the ideas about Jews, Negroes, Latins, Aryans, the Island race (British), and 'European'.[23] The scientific theories expressed also implicated postcolonialised and/or neo-colonialised subjects with an African heritage. The layout of the programme would introduce Dr J.C. Trevor, MA, and Lecturer in Physical Anthropology at Cambridge University, who would discuss the way in which the ordinary man sees race: i.e. in terms of posture, gesture, talk, clothes, and walk.[24] Ritchie Calder would then ask how to define race scientifically. Trevor would define physical and cultural aspects of race used by as the scientist as they discussed physical differences between groups using diagrams, racial types who would be present in the studio, and skulls. This would include brain size and measurements, an issue forming a link to the second part of the programme concerned with intelligence. According to the memo, statements and topics for discussion included:

1) He's got Negro blood in him.
2) Are Negroes black because they are so near the sun?
3) Miscegenation – is race crossing a bad thing?
4) Blood groups[25]

The scientists would then jot down specific points they want to make as agreed at a previous meeting. In an insidious reference, the memo then reads that a further meeting of all parties will be held with the intention of persuading the scientists to 'fit what they want to say to the conclusions, which we want them to reach'.[26] The BBC then transmitted the programme, eventually entitled *Race and Colour*, on 10 November 1952. Among those rounding out the panel were doctors and professors specialising in blood research and referencing, along with experts on economics and political science, and a host of well-known newspaper journalists from the London market. Well-known television presenters and BBC management were also included.[27]

Trevor began by reminding the host and audience that race was defined by an 'eminent anthropologist' as a group of people usually occupying the same territory, 'whose ancestors have intermarried over many generations'.[28] Furthermore, he stated,

> When we say that social behaviour is culturally determined, we mean that human beings behave as they do – walk, speak, work, sleep, eat, play, pray, and make love – because they are brought up as members of a group that practises a certain culture. Human beings do not inherit their social behaviour physically as they inherit the shape of their heads; they inherit it as members of a group and we may say therefore, that they inherit it culturally.[29]

Trevor then stated that Britons do not often notice any important differences other than colour, while American films are far more likely to give the impression that Negroes are a class of servile semi-imbeciles. A few moments later, a panel member asked Trevor if he would allow his daughter to marry a Black man. He made it clear that he would have to answer no. He felt that in England White people were somewhat more liberal in their attitudes toward Coloured people than in other countries, but warned that it was still difficult for a Coloured man and his wife, White or Coloured, to gain acceptance. He ended his discussion and concluded the programme by saying that if he had answered yes to that question, it would have meant the coloured problem had been solved.[30]

Despite the controversial issues and subsequent discussions surrounding the talk, many Britons were not impressed. The Viewer Research Report for 10 November 1952 based on 218 questionnaires completed after the programme reflected an overwhelming disappointment many viewers expressed about the programme's focus. According to the Viewer Research Report for *Race and Colour: A Scientific Introduction to the Problem of Race Relations*, the show, which ran at a peak viewing time of 7.45–8.25 p.m., had a disappointing Reaction Index of 54, below the current average (62) for television discussion programmes and talks.[31] When compared to the Viewer Research Weekly Summary, the show had an audience of only 35 per cent of the adult TV public, below an average of 46 per cent for recent scientific talks and demonstrations. More importantly, the programme fell far below the 68 per cent to 81 per cent of viewers for twelve *International*

Commentary programmes that were transmitted between autumn 1950 and spring 1951.[32]

According to the report, the most common criticism of the show was that guest experts had not discussed the real issues of the racial problem or any viable solutions. Some were pleased that a programme would attempt to enlighten them on a subject of major national importance, but felt the scientific discussions were far too technical. Audience members wanted to hear what measures could keep problems at a minimum. Some viewers were inclined to regard their treatment of race and colour as tedious or unpleasant and therefore unsuited to television. Many polled understood that the project was the beginning of a forthcoming series on race relations in Africa, but respondents were not ready for what some regarded as an advanced lecture on anthropology, and there was difficulty in assimilating technical jargon like phrase codes and blood categories. One viewer criticised the panellists for sounding like many doctors at a medical 'confab', and saw no point in worrying whether man 3,000 or 4,000 years ago had a square head, a round head, or no head at all.[33] Soon after management examined these survey results, BBC producers began to consider televised documentaries that specifically examined the *social* impact of West Indian immigration with emphasis upon how these hopeful citizens could be assimilated to English customs. In contrast, J. Grenfell Williams, then Head of Colonial Service expressed pleasure at the programme's content, noting positive perspectives from associates:

> May I say how excellent I thought this programme was? I had several talks with Mrs Wyndham Goldie and with Mayhem before the programme and, of course, I know something of the difficulties, which face any producer who tries to tackle this particular subject … It is interesting that two groups of people, one white South African and one African, have told me that they thought the programme the fairest possible presentation of the case on both sides.[34]

Social realities and a *Question of Colour*

In an effort to examine issues of concern for audiences not addressed by programmes such as *Race and Colour*, BBC producer Anthony de Lotbinière began researching an episode for the *Special Enquiry* newsmagazine on racial relations (BBC, 1953–65). In the episode *Has Britain a Colour Bar?* (31 January 1955) the programme would examine the impact of West Indians and other non-White immigrants upon Birmingham residents, an area in which many had settled. De Lotbinière also requested advice on finding people of colour in Birmingham to talk with, and contacted Dr Kenneth Little, of Edinburgh University. Little already had done research on why Coloured people came to England, relying again upon opinion to construct notions of race. He too had been eager to find out what he could, and used Birmingham because of the large immigrant population from the West Indies.[35]

In the first of two background reports for the programme, researcher Peter Stone was to talk with a host of individuals living in the Birmingham area. The mixture of both White and Coloured participants potentially offered a range of ideas about the racial issues within the city. One of the first, Mr Bradnock, of the city council, was concerned that a special television report might give the council too much publicity. However, his personal view was that 20 per cent of the people in Birmingham would like a colour bar. Certain civic leaders believed that the process of immigration should slow down so that there could be better integration of the Coloured people into the normal population. Discussed were considerations for a social centre where Coloured people could congregate, which were abandoned for fears of stirring up ill feelings among locals. In addition, it was felt that the vast mix of Pakistanis, Indians, Sikhs, West Indians, Arabs, and West Africans could create an interracial rivalry, making a club for Coloured people difficult.[36]

Jamaicans, according to Stone, were unable to immigrate to Panama, Cuba, or America due to the McCarran Act. The General Purposes Committee of the Birmingham City Council estimated that, as of 1952, there were about 4,600 coloured people in the city, which included nearly 2,500 Pakistanis, 1,000 Africans/West Indians, 500 Sikhs and Indians, and around 400 Arabs and kindred races. Another 200 were unidentified. Stone maintained that the numbers of West Indians living in Birmingham could total 8,000 but that 'nobody really knew' the true figure. In the House of Commons on 5 November that year, as noted by Stone, the Minister of Colonial Affairs, Mr Henry Hopkinson, suggested that there must be an imposition of immigration controls.[37] A Mr Keith of the CO stated that over a million pounds was spent in passage money, yet the office provided evidence that there was 'no poverty in Jamaica'. Despite these concerns, supposedly, no difficulty existed in finding full employment in the UK.

Mr Davies, a liaison officer with the local council, had the primary responsibility of dealing with enquiries from Coloured immigrants. Davies reportedly received several invitations each holiday season to have Coloured people attend Christmas parties with local residents, giving him an opportunity to integrate new citizens with local residents. However, when considering assimilation within the job market, Davies complained of West Indians being individualists and therefore not accepting of trade unionism. In addition, when considering the placement of immigrants within Birmingham City Hostel, Davies explained that many West Indians were placed (a fact he did not want widely known), a main reason for colour prejudice among 58,000 Birmingham people still waiting for their own homes. Davies felt that far too many West Indians did not understand the importance of joining a union, a point later disputed by a Black Birmingham doctor, who felt that all Coloured bus conductors were members of their union. Davies' organisation was doing good work for coloured workers, but he 'did not want it to be widely known'.

At the local ministry of labour, an assistant to the Manager of Central Employment explained that many Indians, Pakistanis, West Africans, and Arabs had lived in Birmingham for many years before the West Indians came. Mr A.C. Hutt, manager of the Central Employment Exchange, explained that many, including refugees after the war such as Poles and Lithuanians, had been absorbed into the local population, but Coloured people could never really be absorbed because of their colour. Beyond these concerns were those of sexual miscegenation, and, as Hutt explained, White women would take 'badinage from white men, but not from black'.[38] Stone heard of one factory that banned Black man from working with White women because White women refused contact with them.

A day later, Stone interviewed another West Indian, Mr Jacobs, who was a mechanical engineer with Birmingham City Transport, and who told Stone personally of two instances of a colour bar operating against him. Passed over for promotion several times, Jacobs explained that, on one occasion, there was a supervisory position available, and both he and a White man applied for it. The White man later got the job, but then turned it down. Jacobs applied again, but heard the post would be eliminated. He took the matter up with his union and they decided to take no action. When Jacobs complained to the Union Secretary that he should have attended to it, since it was his future that they were discussing, the Secretary said, 'You blacks are always causing trouble. If I had my way I'd have a colour bar.'

Jacobs had also experienced difficulties with racialism when trying to purchase a house. The firm named Everton's, at Queens Chambers, advertised houses for sale. After applying for one, Jacobs was told the Mortgage Society would not give mortgages to Coloured people. Stone suggested that Jacobs was perfectly willing to say all this in the programme. Stone notes further,

> He told me en passant, of how he had heard on one occasion that there was overtime going, and so he had got there an hour early. Most desirable, of course, but not likely to make him popular with some of his fellow workers. There is in my experience a very similar Jewish type that is completely right in its actions but never achieves popularity – in fact, creates emotional Anti-Semitism.[39]

Stone noted that he mentioned such a case to several people, and the general reaction he got was: 'Quite right too. If they had the niggers in, they wouldn't be able to sell the other houses to the white folk'. Further, an estate agent told Reid, 'These niggers are coming in their thousands every week. We shall soon have the Burma Road all over Birmingham. What I say is keep 'em in the Burma Road.' Stone reported in his notes that Coloured people could always get houses because they provided a payoff for the estate agent, and paid above the listing price, noting, 'it is their only chance to get a house'. Reid noted that estate agents were increasingly selling by private treaty rather than by auction because by auction they had to accept the highest bid even if it came from 'a damned nigger', whereas by private treaty they could keep the district White.

Stone also noted the importance of Dr C.J.K. Piliso, considered the most talked about coloured man in Birmingham, due in part to his outspoken concerns regarding racialism and intolerance. Stone noted that he was the President of the Afro-Caribbean Organisation, a group thought to have Communist ties. As Piliso proceeded to address local colour prejudice, Stone was impressed with his 'fairness when it came to statements of fact'. Piliso noted that Coloured workers often leave their jobs after training, because they fear the colour bar will cancel promotions. He intimated that he felt a sense of security for Coloured workers now that the National Health Service was in place. Similarly, Coloured employees of British Railways needed to have no worries, Piliso also explained, yet local manufacturers like ReVere Motorcars would not employ Coloured labour, nor would they admit it. Piliso considered BSA carmakers liberal in their policy. Piliso noted that many commercial hotels had a colour bar so not to offend their regular customers. The excuse given was that White gentlemen would probably not use a bathroom after the Black gentlemen had. As regards students, although many landladies refused to take any Coloured people, a White landlady who had such a good experience of Coloured students now refused to take any White students. Piliso felt that, in general, Coloured and White workers got on well together at their work and he knew of many instances where the White man had taken his Coloured colleague home for the evening or invited him on Sunday. However, their White wives were not nearly as friendly, due to inexperience with Coloured men.

The doctor confirmed to Stone there was a good deal of concubinage with Coloured men and Irish or country girls who had come to Birmingham to work in industry and had no friends or relatives there. There were reportedly dance balls that would not take Coloured men, and Stone had learned that many would take a Coloured man if he were with a Coloured woman, but not if they thought he was out to get a White girl. Many social clubs did not bar Coloured people but did limit their number. In Piliso's opinion, the importance rested in more encouragement for social assimilation and an interracial centre, not a Coloured club.[40] Also interviewed were Arabs and Pakistani leaders at a local mosque and at the home of a Muslim butcher, respectively. Both men reported 'no real problems' with White people in the area, other than the experience of being the first terminated when cutbacks occurred. Stone also reported that, like the Arabs, Pakistanis kept to themselves, mainly because of their language and religion.

The Coloured worker

Stone indicated that one of the most sensitive areas of concern was that of the Transport Committee which represented bus drivers. He asked about the West Indian conductors trained by the company because, in the four days spent in the city doing advance research, he had not seen any. Mr Smith, Chair of the Transport Committee, advised him that there were in fact 281 Coloured conductors out of a total of 4,700: 213 male and 68 female. There were also 96 drivers in training and six actually driving at that time. Despite a policy that supposedly showed no special arrangements for West Indian workers, a conductor was counting his money at the end of a shift when an Irish conductor came in and slapped him in the back, saying 'Hullo Sambo'. The West Indian did the same in return and said 'Hullo Paddy'. The Irishman hit him back and a fight began. Smith fired both men. A day later, drivers demanded that Irishman get his job back, or they would strike. No such support came forward for the West Indian. Stone reported that the men then asked for a limitation on the amount of West Indians hired.

In a report filed with the Transport and General Workers Union (TGWU) in Birmingham, James Leask OBE suggested that a large problem was fast developing, a problem that could largely be solved by Coloured workers themselves. He noted that since they had come to live in a strange country with people who had very different industrial and social standards, they were obligated to discard any habits that might prove objectionable to the British public with whom they worked. He felt that since Coloured workers were less efficient than the British, they had to develop a skill and proficiency which would ensure that the effort they made was not less than that of the average British worker.[41] It was noted that many foreigners experience language difficulties but West Indians did not, and as conductors they worked more overtime then their White colleagues. The Ministry in London told Stone that more and more employers were asking for West Indians because they were such good workers (better than West Africans). Some even went to the ports to meet them. The only complaint was that they sometimes left to better themselves after they had been trained, but with full employment they were not the only ones to do this.

Stone also had the opportunity to read a resolution that was introduced at a trade union meeting following an inquiry into Coloured immigration. The speech itself, written by Leask, appeared in an article published in the *Birmingham Gazette* of 22 November. Among various points being made about Jamaican workers, it was clear that Indians, Pakistanis, and other Coloured workers were prepared to remain in their own communities, but Jamaicans sought to integrate themselves more fully into the British social life. Leask noted that the majority dictated union policy, and that a fear among members was that if Blacks got the majority vote, they might dictate policy not in the best interests of British trade unionism. Leask explained to Stone that he was willing to speak as a trade union official on the programme, but not on behalf of the TGWU. Further, Leask noted that there was a colour bar among the workers because they were afraid of lowering their working conditions and because they did not want trouble. Stone considered Leask to be an 'honest man who had the guts to say these issues plainly', and thought narrator Rene Cutforth 'could use him in the programme very usefully'. Mr Baker, the Secretary of the Birmingham Trades Council, interviewed by Stone, opposed Leask's attitude about the union and race. He stated that there were indeed Coloured supervisors over White men on the railways. As regards to whether any conductors left the bus service or refused to join it because of Coloured conductors, he felt it was impossible to say because of a big turnover of labour on the buses.

Later, Chief Inspector Lowe drove Stone about; he met a West African who was married to an Irish girl, and was the new father of a sixteen-day-old baby. This man had no complaints about his employer or fellow workers, but was frequently insulted in public. Shortly before, when he was getting on a bus, an Irish had passenger put out his arm and said, 'Not on this bus, you black bastard'. Previously, he had been in a cafe brawl, and did not get a fair deal from the police. In view of his experiences, he did not go out in the evenings more than he could possibly help. He told Stone he would be willing to say all this in the programme. At a different address, a West Indian man married to a White Sunderland girl had encountered racialism. The woman spoke out about the extremely strong anti-colour feeling, especially from the Irish. Whenever they went out, she found them criticised by middle-class people as well as working-class. She described her husband as a hero when he had been in the Merchant Navy, but stated that it was very different now. Stone explained that they had given up going to dance halls because it was too uncomfortable. Stone noted that the majority of the wives of Coloured men in Britain were White, but due to mounting prejudice against mixed marriage there was a tendency for associations with women of a somewhat lower social stature than themselves to occur. As an example, he noted that the Coloured professional and student often married a clerk or typist; the skilled tradesman, the labourer's daughter or factory hand; and the labourer often, though not always, found that only the near-prostitute could afford to face the stigma attached to living with or marrying a Coloured man. More than 3,500 Coloured students had come to England during 1955, and Stone noted how these future leaders and intellectuals of the Commonwealth came in under the Colombo Plan. In general, they were not a problem, but the West Indian influx of workers upset them by taking accommodation and affecting public relations.

When leaving an interview with Mr Bradnock, of Birmingham City Council, Stone also found leaflets distributed around Birmingham that read:

BAN THE COLOUR BAR!
As more coloured friends come across the seas to settle down amongst us, let
us treat them with the respect, which is their due, and make them
feel welcome.
Open your homes to Darkies
More houses for Coloured Folk
Why not Coloured police?
Increase their national assistance
Coloured gents for Councillors
Give them your seat on the bus
Printed by H.W. Owen (the Avon Press) 150 Stratford Road, Birmingham 11
and published by the B.N.C.[42]

Stone considered the matter to be a joke that already received publicity, and he recommended that the programme should not give it more.

He wrote in his report, filed 14 December 1954, that the racism was often due to ignorance and fear, that it increased as the level of education decreased, and that the remedy seemed to be more social welfare to encourage assimilation and reduce ignorance on both sides.[43] The second background report, filed two days later, summarised that no machinery was in place to track immigrants from the Caribbean, but the CO reported that, in the first ten months of 1952, between 7,000 to 11,000 may have come to England, with 8,000 living in Birmingham. Generally racism was apparent, employment was hard to find for Black people, young children were beginning to taunt children of colour born in England ('go back to Mau-Mau land'), and that ignorance and irrational thinking were the primary causes. Stone suggested that journalist Keith Waterhouse of the *Daily Mirror* summed it up best when writing in a series of articles that White Britons took it for granted that 'all coloured people here were pimps, brothel-keepers, and dope traders, proprietors of gambling dens or unemployed stowaways'.[44] As a further example of the mixed opinions evident within the dominant press and popular culture, Stone and other BBC researchers gathered a series of headlines for vignettes during the programme. A headline from the *News of the World* (14 November 1954) read 'Lets Welcome the Jamaicans – They Belong in the Family', whereas the *News Chronicle* (23 October 1954) had urged politicians and citizens to 'Stop Jamaican Invasion'. *The Times* did a special on the 'West Indian Settlers' (8 November 1954), but the *Daily Herald* shouted 'Stay Home Warning for West Indians'.[45] Further, Stone wrote that, after several interviews, he had concluded that at the national level, on an official basis, there was no colour bar; 'yet at the local, personal tacit level there is a hell of a lot'.[46]

Later that month, de Lotbinière forwarded a copy of the first very rough outline sketch for the *Colour Bar* programme to newsreader Rene Cutworth followed by a treatment for the show.[47] According to the rough draft outline for *Special Enquiry No. 3, The Colour Bar*, BBC correspondent Robert Reid was to open the programme by outlining the history of British colonial policies, followed by a discussion of colonials fighting in the services. Their employment in British factories would help to provide reasons for ultimate return to England, after finding their own countries in such poor post-war economic conditions. Excerpts from *Hello West Indies*, developed by the MOI in 1944, were within the script, as were clips of the *Empire Windrush* disembarkation. The script then calls for Reid to address the following points, driving the investigative narrative, 'are they being absorbed? Is a Colour Bar emerging – or not? Housing? Redundancy? What about control-ling immigration? If they're British can we control them?' Scenes follow depicting the arrival of West Indians into New Street Station, Birmingham. As the camera follows one man leaving the station, Reid introduces Cutforth, whose utopic voiceover heralds the tremendous possibilities for new arrivals:

> That man moving into Birmingham to try his luck in a new country will have no difficulty in finding a job. Birmingham's industry has been able to absorb practically every one of them. On the official level, among responsible people in the city's government, among leaders of industry and in the unions, Birmingham's attitude to this invasion has followed the highest traditions of British fair-mindedness and democracy.[48]

Specific issues for discussion then appeared within the rough outline treatment for the new *Colour Bar* episode. As development of the show continued, it was determined that a principal focus of the show would be how West Indians were settling in since their arrival in Birmingham. A rough draft treatment of the programme, written 28 January 1955 by de Lotbinière, suggested that host Robert Reid would open the programme by introducing the subject. He would then outline a brief history of this new, large-scale immigration from the West Indies via the following points from the outline script:

1) British Colonial policy has fostered belief in Britain as the Mother Country.
2) During war, we were happy to have colonials fighting in the Services and working in British factories. FILM TO ILLUSTRATE THIS (from Hello West Indies)
3) After [the] war, a few stayed in Britain. Others on return to their own countries found poor economic conditions and they later came back to this country. FILM: Immigrants landing from Empire Windrush in 1949 with sound piece by Jamaican. Since then – with jobs going in this country – many thousands more have come over.
   Many immigrants are assisted to get here by societies making loans at 10% interest. HEADLINES OF CURRENT SITUATION[49]

Film would include shots of two Coloured men coming out of the Labour Exchange with narration stating that it may not be the job he wants, but 'most coloured men find jobs worth seven or eight pounds a week within a few days of landing. Places *have* been found for coloured workers in all types of jobs'. Several factory exteriors feature images of Indians, Pakistanis, and West Indians, signalling an obvious contribution to the local workforce. As a newspaper headline screams, 'No more blacks on buses!' Cutforth provides a history of Coloured people working as conductors, engaging with White citizens and punching tickets. Within the programme notes, an interview planned with a 'Mr Olban', lists him as either a 'conductor or driver', and plans to give an account of his relationship with White co-workers, which Lotbinière notes should be 'fairly reasonable, I think – I hope!'[50]

However, the narration also features an interview with the head of the local busmen's union, Harry Green, who states that as the population of Blacks working in garages and on the buses grew, Whites did not like it because they said that having Blacks on the job lowered their position (Figure 3). Ultimately, comparisons made between Blacks and the Whites they worked alongside in bus garages yielded predictable results. Complaints included how Coloured workers often had nowhere to go after their shift ended, sat around the canteen all day, and 'grabbed' the overtime jobs. Cutforth then begins to address the problems of accommodation for West Indian immigrants. Sequences planned show a Black man, presumably an African or West Indian, walking up to a couple of doors, greeted by a landlady who shakes her head no. The soundtrack to be dubbed in would feature the voices of landladies saying 'sorry the room just been taken' or 'I don't have niggers here'. The narrative then addresses the Burma Road area of Birmingham, a neighbourhood once considered prosperous. Cutforth explains that Black men hold short leases and rent rooms to immigrants.[51]

One unidentified householder explains that he accepts Africans and Indians, but would be deeply concerned if they tried to buy the other half of his house. His biggest concern is that the value of the house would go down

Figure 3 Birmingham Union leader Harry Green offers matter of fact reasons for racialism to Rene Cutforth (3a), noting that white busmen believed that having blacks on the job lowered their position (3b).

'in no time'. James Walker, a Jamaican who lives in the same house, explains to Cutforth that all the fuss in England about colour is surprising, particularly considering how easily Blacks and Whites mix in Jamaica. Walker explains, 'we've got the same queen – we fought in the same war – now on coming to England we find we're different!'

As the narrative continues, Cutforth reminds audiences that the impact of Coloured people takes time to get over, followed by, 'let's face it – these people *are* different'. During this voiceover, audiences also see the interior of a mosque within a slum house. The sounds of the Arabs chanting lead Cutworth to say that not only did immigrants bring different religions, but different manners, customs and a way of life that 'varies as much between their own race as it does to others'. As his voiceover makes this pronouncement of a discomforting diversity, Sikhs are shown buying and cooking rice, and Jamaicans play dice and hang out on street corners, dressed in what the script describes as clothing that is 'gaudy with a large hat[s] and colourful tie[s]'. A local White man, identified as 'Tony', explains to Cutworth that some of the West Indians are pretty rough characters, and others are as 'quiet as the day'. However, he then states that if given any of them 'receive an inch, they'll take a mile', further explaining that he would not have any of them in his house or 'around the missus'.

As the programme moves toward a conclusion, Cutforth makes an appraisal of the situation in Birmingham by stating that, even if coloured people are settling in reasonably well, there are still strong reasons for anxiety about the future. Coloured people need restrictions, two White bus workers explain, and, if they did become permanent staff, unemployed White workers would be angry if they had to get tickets on buses from Coloured men. As a film concludes, a third worker for the bus company explains that the problems in Birmingham will become worse if the colour bar continues.[52] Reid then planned to interview Councillor Major H.N. White, Mayor of Lambeth, back in the studio. White's office had sponsored a 'No Colour Bar' dance months before the planned interview, in an attempt to foster racial harmony (Figure 4). He invited an equal number of Whites and West Indians, and encouraged interracial coupling on the dance floor, as 'the rhythm of the Mambo was doing its bit towards racial harmony'.[53] After conferring with staff, De Lotbinière listed suggested questions to ask Councillor White in the studio:

> 1) How do the Jamaicans come to be in Lambeth in such great numbers? 2) What is the most serious aspect of this problem so far as Lambeth is concerned? 3) With your experience what do your think can be done to enable black people and white people to get along together in a community such as Lambeth? In addition 5), there is nothing at the moment to keep a coloured British subject from coming here. Do you think the British government should pose some restrictions?[54]

Figure 4 While Major H.N. White, Mayor of Lambeth, helped to organise the No Colour Bar to promote racial harmony (4a), he also called for a revitalisation of the West Indian economy to stop immigration and subsequent overcrowding (4b).

In the following scene, newspaper headlines depict what the script calls 'the most frightful crimes committed by black men', leading Cutworth to exclaim that popular belief would have it that all 'Coloured men are dope peddlers, sex maniacs, and pimps'. General scenes planned for the Jungle room of the Eagle Pub would film West Indians at a popular gathering place. Stone found the location to be crammed to the door with Coloured men and White prostitutes. The place was considered a rough quarter, and the landlord, named Tony, said that many pubs and neighbourhood houses refuse to serve Coloured men, particularly the Bingley Hotel, where pseudo-socialite Lady Docker was once a barmaid. For the sake of the programme, Tony was willing to send Coloured men to the Bingley so the cameras could film them being refused service. Stone considered this impossible due to likely restrictions on the part of managers of the pub, but Cutforth could be there, and say that he saw the refusal of service. Two more pubs in the area visited were considered rather rough, not because of the Blacks, but the Irish. Two days later, Stone visited the Hope and Anchor, and the owner told him that though he did not refuse drinks to Coloured people, he did treat them quite coolly. He explained that the difference was 'when you [as a white patron] come in, I say, "Good Morning, Sir, what will you have?" When they come in, I stand dumb, and if they order a drink, I serve it to them. I don't want 'em here'.

The narrator states that popular belief would have it that all Coloured men are dope peddlers, sex maniacs, and pimps, as images show a Black man sitting with a White girl as White men sitting nearby glare. The script goes on to discuss while there is 'no friction now, there are two strong reasons for anxiety in the future, given that there is still a certain amount of prejudice against working alongside coloured people … what about the restricting of promotions?' In the rough treatment, bus union President Green says, 'we will keep them because after two years, they join the permanent staff, but they'll be trouble from unemployed white workers if they have to get tickets on the buses from coloured men'.

As part of this examination, de Lotbinière and his crew planned to interview West Indian bus drivers that had begun working for the local transport companies. This effort was particularly important in contextualising the immigrant experience from those who had experienced this transition first-hand. However, according to a rough outline treatment of the programme *Special Enquiry Number 3: The Color Bar*, White drivers at the Hockley bus garage in Birmingham reacted in a most unfavourable way to the attention these men might receive.[55] Background information notes complied by de Lotbinière's assistant Peter Stone indicated that a great deal of resistance to the interviews existed among White people working with West Indians. Trade unionists had already rebelled when the city had announced plans to hire close to 300 Black bus drivers and/or conductors, but cancelled the action after a nationwide protest of service disruption and unfair labour practices. In some cases White drivers felt that an unfair amount of attention and praise would be given to these men on the programme. Within days, headlines of the *Birmingham Gazette* read 'Bus Strike Threat Stops TV Film: Undue Publicity for Coloured Men: So BBC Won't take Cameras to Hockley'.[56] Despite best intentions, the BBC initially cancelled the show after weeks of research and filming. A primary reason was that the matter seemed too difficult to broach, and a city beginning to experience some post-war growth could not afford a bus strike. Later that year, de Lotbinière began to research the idea of returning to Birmingham to continue the project. The producer also followed up with an apologetic letter to the head of the local busmen's union, Harry Green, indicating how sorry he and his staff were to cause ill-feeling down at the garages. He followed with a reassurance that:

> We went down to Hockley yesterday – and we were invited into the canteen for a cup of tea – on the strict understanding that we did not talk a word about the buses or coloured men. It was a very good arrangement and we talked hard about the Eighth Army and coal mining! Our camera, by the way, was left locked up in the car outside![57]

After writing a letter to owner H.W.G. Evans of Mitchells and Butlers Ltd requesting permission to film at the Eagle pub during business hours on 10 January 1955,[58] Anthony de Lotbinière and a BBC camera crew crafted a narrative of proper behaviour for immigrants in an English social setting. A scene-by-scene analysis of a rough outline treatment for the programme reveals a mixture of highly cautious optimism with a general sense of malaise toward the West Indian worker.

One segment transmitted features two young West Indian men coming into the pub, dressed in overcoats. The scene (staged for dramatic effect as the show's treatment indicates) shows us many White male patrons of varied ages talking and drinking. One of the Black men pounds his fist on the bar to get the bartender's attention. The voice of the narrator – which sounds White, middle-aged, and British – says 'Manners are different, too. In Jamaica, this is the normal way to attract the attention of the man behind the bar' (Figure 5). The camera then shows patrons grow immediately silent and gaze at the duo. The narrator's voice from the *Special Enquiry* featured series states 'In English pubs, they don't approve of it. Innocent actions and gestures are misunderstood and suspicion hardens on both sides'.[59]

Of the fifty-one scenes in the treatment for the programme, thirty highlight issues of unemployment, racism, fears of miscegenation, housing issues, and labour disputes. Sequences feature West Indian citizens as

Figure 5 In *Has Britain a Colour Bar?*, the narrator addresses the cultural differences between West Indian men ordering a drink (5a), and the barman's displeasure at his unintentional rudeness (5b). The sequence highlights the intercultural differences between them, reinscribing the difficulties for immigrants.

misunderstood or forlorn over their choice to immigrate. Dramatised and actual interviews with property owners and 'average' (White) citizens provide dystopic responses to questions such as 'Is there an active colour prejudice in Birmingham?', further codifying concerns over the Black and Asian presence in the city. Reminders of racism, housing problems, and the difficulty in transition abound, but primarily from a White perspective. The rough draft outline suggests multiple scenes showing West Indians, Arabs, and an African, but the programme provides only one actual interview with a Jamaican man (James Walker) on his perceptions of life in the city. In other scenes meant to highlight lifestyle choices, West Indians shoot dice, hang out on street corners, and sit with White women in pubs as White men scowl.[60]

The Television Press Officer gathered selected articles from 31 January 1955 about the programme. Overall, those papers selected offered high praise (as written by R. Cannell of the *Daily Express*); favourable comments came from Clifford Davies and James Thomas of the *Daily Mirror* and *News Chronicle* respectively; and Mark Johns of the *Daily Sketch* found the episode responsible, courageous, and well done. In a letter addressing concerns over a violation of House regulations, Robin Whitworth, Documentary Organiser for Television, contacted John Eden, the Conservative Member of Parliament for Bournemouth West.[61] The matter had been raised by Geoffrey Finsberg – who was serving as National Chairman of the Young Conservatives that year, and who took senior rules in the National Union of Conservative and Unionist Associations – as he served as Borough Councillor in Hampstead. Whitworth had already responded to Finsberg's concerns on 8 February, explaining that the BBC did not broadcast programmes on subjects discussed in either House, and, in the case of the *Colour Bar* programme, there was no departure from usual practice. In the letter, Whitworth noted that the programme did not breach rules related to subjects discussed in either House within a fortnight after transmission, as the rule only applied to full-dress or important debates.[62]

In another letter of concern about the programme, Eric Wilson, the general secretary of the Birmingham and district property owners association, expressed concern to the editor of the *Radio Times*, who passed the letter on to Lotbinière's office. Within the show's narration, Cutforth described the concerns of an inhumane landlord when renting to West Indians. Wilson urged that a clearer distinction was necessary between the proprietor and the actual property owner, who may be more liberal in his or her renting practices.[63] Other concerns were expressed to Swallow's office about the usage of the TGWU in the piece, but not other organisations. The protest came from a Mr Bolas, a representative of the TGWU, who felt that the programme did not offer enough images of Black people doing well in areas other than transport. According to Swallow's response it drew attention to an industrial sequence showing 'many shots of coloured men in engineering', which he claimed was designed to show that, at that point in time in Birmingham's industry, Coloured and White workers were getting on well together with no evidence of colour prejudice. He noted the fact that the programme indicated that all White workers in Birmingham got on well with their Coloured industrial colleagues. Swallow further expressed concerns over criticism from the office of the Controller, Midland Region, over a lack of consultation. Swallow noted 'we cannot consult *every* [transport union] organisation, every time'.[64]

Audiences did watch the programme, according to research reports for week five of 1955. Documentary programmes transmitted for the first nine months of 1955 recorded an Audience Reaction Index of 75 as an average; the programme generated an Index of 77. The choice of only one West Indian interviewee to address racism reinforced the strategy of White British discursive authority to frame these issues strategically, in this case for docu-dramatic impact. However, the reaction of the BBC to the White Hockley drivers in Birmingham immediately altered the organisation's creative ability to frame citizens' reactions and the stories of the West Indian experience in England. In this instance, management desire to take a safer approach to the issue of racial integration shunted its cultural authority and practice (as the evidence provided above has shown).

The men from the sun

BBC newsreels and special reports discussed the influx of West Indians into a country that had now changed forever, as many citizens and audiences perceived these immigrants as competitors for jobs and housing. In Brixton, slogans had already appeared on walls screaming 'Keep Britain White', often initiated by followers of fascist Oswald Mosley. Many refused admittance to Blacks, fearful of retaliation in the form of vandalism by Whites after hours. The worry over the reactions of other White people often reinforced some of these practices. One woman who allowed Coloured students to room in her home reported that her neighbours stopped talking to her. On the phone, West Indians were routinely told that rooms were available, only to find the landlady refusing to answer the door after seeing in person who had called.

As another means of reaching audiences educationally and ideologically where these issues were concerned, the Television Service began to consider the use of dramatic teleplays. When survey responses for *Race and Colour* were considered, it was believed that certain viewers were more likely to glean information on social issues from light programming than from talks or newsmagazines. Another precedent for a hardhitting teleplay was *The End*

Begins (BBC, 17 May 1956), a science fiction scenario featuring Earl Cameron. The post-apocalyptic story, written by Ray Rigby and directed by Hal Burton, features a group of survivors building a new life on a remote island, and was considered 'gripping' by the most viewers surveyed in an audience research report for week 20 of 1956. According to the audience research report for week 20, the programme had an estimated audience of 20 per cent of the adult population of the UK, equivalent to 46 per cent of the adult TV-watching public. The majority of those surveyed praised the excellent performance of Earl Cameron as Hank Christians. Yet there was a certain amount of controversy about the introduction of the colour problem into the picture, with some viewers expressing disapproval of the fact that the one marriageable woman on the island chose the Black man for her partner, or feeling that too much emphasis was placed on the colour question. Others expressed appreciation of the sympathetic treatment of the case for the Coloured man.[65]

The now famous *A Man from the Sun* (BBC, 8 November 1956) was one of the first teleplays to present West Indian immigrants and their lives. It was also one of the first docudramas that dealt with the harsh realities of the immigrant experience, this time from the perspective of the West Indian immigrant, not British nationalists reacting to immigration. British producer and writer John Elliot had written this docudrama with the intention of highlighting the contrast between what he described as the mythical image of a cosy Britain which people were receiving as part of their colonial education, and the grotty Britain which the West Indian immigrants encountered when they first arrived in the country.[66]

Elliot developed a reputation as an expert documentary filmmaker in the army, and later joined the BBC in 1949. Ultimately, he became a respected television writer and producer who, after scouting locations in London's Black community of Brixton, approached the BBC in 1956 about producing the teleplay. He first discussed the idea with the documentary section of the Drama Department, whose dramatised documentaries addressed subjects considered too sensitive for actual portrayals. After receiving a green light for the project, Elliot wrote the script and began reviewing stock footage of Black people living in and around the Brixton area. By November, the actors were in the studio at Alexandra Palace ready to begin the live performance. There was continued concern at the BBC over how White viewers, particularly those not comfortable with the BBC's previous attempts to address race, would perceive the drama. The play proved to be controversial, yet the service stood behind Elliot's creative standards and storyline.

The cast featured, among others, West Indian actors Errol John as the immigrant settler Cleve, Cy Grant as cultural guide Alvin, and Earl Cameron as a West Indian community leader (Figure 6). In one scene that addresses some of the confusion evident as West Indian settlers are arriving at a dock,

Cy Grant's character plays an ombudsman or guide placed to assist settlers in finding their way. Each West Indian (including John's Cleve) is speaking in heavy Jamaican patois and is dark in complexion. They seem frightened, angry, or confused. Grant's Alvin is light-skinned and speaks perfect English. He answers each question accurately yet succinctly without emotion or empathy. He eventually gives a booklet to one of the arriving men and states that it contains useful information about England. The text represents a cultural guide for these citizens that assists them in learning how to get along in England, eerily reminiscent of the *Going to Britain* later published by the BBC for potential immigrants, as discussed later in this chapter. This scene gives a sense of disillusionment easily overcome by reading a prepared text on life in England.

In another scene, Cleve has carefully arranged temporary employment as a construction worker. As a scene opens with the image of a pounding hammer, the Banana Boat song plays within the soundtrack. As the chorus sings, 'Daylight come an me *wont* [sic] go home', Cleve is shown drawing his coat tightly to his chest, reluctantly braving the cold. The scene and its narrative context highlight his disillusionment, and his dissatisfaction is obvious. Moments later within the following scene, a White British working speaking with a cockney accent (an allusion to a lower class of British citizen) teases him about the smell of his hair, and refers to him as 'Sambo' and 'a nig' (Figure 7). The disagreement erupts into a near fight as the White worker shoves Cleve. As Cleve grabs a hammer, the supervisor stops him (Figure 8). The cockney worker screams to his co-workers that hold him, 'let me go and I'll murder the black bastard'.[67]

The Research Department reported that the general effect of the show was to make viewers feel that they would have to revise their ideas about the Coloured worker in the UK. The majority of viewers in the sample felt the programme did a good job and provided a valuable public service by spotlighting the hardships of the immigrants already settled in Britain. According to the audience research report for week 45, the programme had an estimated audience of 18 per cent of the adult population of the UK, equivalent to 39 per cent of the adult TV-watching public. Although any factual information presented was in a fictional setting, general comments suggested that the narrative presented challenges just as clearly as any discussion or talk. Moreover, the programme made its mark as a piece of television with strong human appeal. The report indicated that viewers enjoyed following the trials and tribulations of Cleve and Ethlyn (Gloria Ann Simpson), and felt compassion for their efforts to find housing and employment, causing a majority of those surveyed to revise their ideas about the Coloured worker in the UK, as deserving more sympathy and understanding than before.

Figure 6 Errol John as the immigrant settler Cleve breaks the fourth wall, while dictating a letter to his cousin about a planned trip to London (6a). As West Indian settlers arrive, each seems frightened, angry, or confused – again framing the process of immigration as initially difficult and daunting (with Earl Cameron) (6b).

Figure 7 As a scene opens, immigrant Cleve draws his coat tightly to his chest. The narrative context that highlights his disillusionment and dissatisfaction is obvious (7a). Moments later, a white worker refers to him as 'Sambo' and a 'nig' (7b).

Figure 8 The disagreement erupts into a near fight (8a) as the supervisor (John Hawkins) stops them (8b). The notion that racialism on the job is expected creates a dystopic notion of life in Britain.

On the debit side, complaints indicated that the programme did not go deep enough and was inclined to show the best side of Coloured people's behaviour. For example, a housewife who frankly admitted that she was the kind of person who looked for a seat away from Coloured people said the 'knowledge of what's happening right now in Brixton in regard to housing and jobs is enough to make me wonder if this was a realistic picture'. A retired school superintendent added that he regretted to say that his personal experience was vastly different from what was depicted in the story. A dance hall Master of Ceremonies said he found 'Negroes' very difficult and arrogant as compared to the characters in the show. One household felt that overall, with the state of ignorance and prejudice in Britain as it was, things were not likely to carry any easier. The actors, thought to have given a well-rounded portrait of the people they were supposed to represent, were trained English actors. Yet their portrayals with West Indian accents caused a poultry farmer to report that they really brought a touch of their native sunshine with them.[68]

Those West Indians who had actually arrived on the *Empire Windrush* felt a great degree of disappointment and anger at the treatment received from White people because of mass xenophobia, an issue generally left unexplored by this programme.[69] Various reactions to the show indicated that West Indian immigration was no blue-sky tale, and almost every kind of difficulty from the racial discrimination practised by landladies and employers to the temptations of easy money and vice rings, was covered within the programme's script. The programme attempted to explore difficulties faced by these immigrants, yet, as a documentary drama, many considered it an effete representation of a highly difficult time. Elliott's intentions were to examine the difficulties Caribbean settlers had to endure, yet the programme lacked the harsh reality many had to face when confronting racism at hotels or rooming houses where landladies refused to rent to Blacks. There was also too little discussion of violence encountered from Teddy Boys or other working-class Britons.

A comparison can be made between the protagonists of the drama and actual passengers who arrived aboard the *Windrush* – as presented in a *Daily Mail* article entitled 'Verdict on the Promised Land' from 1988, which gave the experiences of four West Indians people who had been on the vessel. Featured was Nick Collins, who had nearly finished technical school in Kingston when he left the islands for England seeking a chance to go to college. When he first arrived, he worked in a factory making sweets, then eventually as a welder. At the time of the interview, he was married to an English woman and lived in Hounslow, West London. When contrasting his perspective with that of the fictitious Cleve, there is an understanding of the far more gentle nature of the programme. Under the subheading of 'Bitter', Collins explained:

When we docked, I remember feeling excitement and apprehension, thinking: What have I done? In the early years, I had doors slammed in my face. For a few years, it made me bitter ... You never become immune to that sort of thing, but you must have pride in yourself ... The young black people [today] are neither West Indian nor British. It will take another generation before they are fully accepted as British ... Now a third of the people are neo-fascists, a third are really responsible, nice people and a third don't care about anything as long as there's beer in the pubs.[70]

The BBC and Elliot had accomplished a somewhat noble effort, but in the service's attempt to produce empathy for these immigrants they had weakened the true impact this transition had upon many West Indians. During the 1950s, as immigration increased, BBC television programming continued to construct West Indian behaviour as often alien to White Britons. Documentaries such as *Colour Bar* continued to make suggestions of proper behaviour for new immigrants and address racial tension, programmes such as *Man from the Sun* reinforced the difficulty West Indians experienced coming to the UK. Two years later, the BBC planned a follow up to issues of racial prejudice in Birmingham with *Special Enquiry: A Question of Colour*. However, a major civil disturbance created even more attention over the race issue.

Nottingham, Notting Hill and the BBC

During late August and early September of 1958, riots began in the Midlands city of Nottingham and in the Notting Hill area of London between White, working-class Teddy Boys and West Indians who had settled there. Caribbeans competed with working-class White families for decent housing, a situation exploited by unscrupulous property owners who provided less than desirable rooms for high prices. Fascists like Oswald Mosley also exacerbated these tensions, drawing upon White fears of a lack of control over the flow of colonials from India and, in particular, the West Indies. Cyril Osborne, Conservative MP for Louth, launched a campaign amongst Conservative party members and a cautious public to end immigration. While net migration to the UK was only 12,000 between 1951 and 1961, and decreased thereafter, the presence of these settlers and the backlash created among some Whites seemed to amplify the potential for further conflicts, which most likely culminated in the murder of West Indian carpenter Kelso Cochrane in 1959, an event that also galvanised white and black to move toward racial harmony (Figure 9a). Meanwhile, as Mosley planned to speak in Notting Hill (Figure 9b), 'Teddy Boys' became increasingly hostile toward Black families in Nottingham and in Notting Hill, leading to significant racial violence.

Figure 9 Crowds of all ethnicities join the funeral procession for Kelso Cochrane, as detailed by British Pathé (9a). Tensions were apparent, particularly since Oswald Mosely had arranged to speak in the same area later that week (9b).

Between 24 August and 17 September, 51 Coloured people were arrested in the Metropolitan Police District in London, including 34 in Notting Hill, while 126 White people were arrested, including 73 in the Notting Hill area. In Nottingham, the disturbances on 23 and 30 August resulted in 23 White arrests and two Coloured.[71] Attacks in Birmingham, Liverpool, Deptford, and Camden Town had also occurred in 1958, as right-wing groups such as the White Defence League and the Union Movement (UM) set up branches in Brixton and Notting Hill. Sir Oswald Mosley, founder of the pre-war British Union of Fascists, returned to active politics following the war, and held meetings and street-corner rallies calling for an end to immigration, as wall slogans and leaflets urged 'Keep Africa Black – Keep Britain White'. Anti-immigration sentiments in this same year encouraged Mosley to run for election in North Kensington during the 1959 General Elections.

In 1958, Nottingham was suffering from a major recession, and the post-war economic boom was beginning to wane. Factories shut down and many workers were made redundant. By this time, many of the more depressed neighbourhoods had also become home for scores of West Indian immigrants, many of whom could not find employment. The fighting that erupted on 23 August 1958 was thought to have been started by Teddy Boys after a white woman was seen arguing with a black man at closing time.[72] Windows were smashed at Caribbean-themed cafés and shops, as White teens assaulted several Black residents near St Ann's Well Road. This followed reports of bricks being thrown through windows in Black neighbourhoods. West Indians also retaliated by reportedly stabbing some White people with flick knives.

In a similar fashion, the Notting Hill riots began in August of 1958 when White men attacked a White woman married to a West Indian as she was walking home. She had allegedly been seen the previous night with her Jamaican husband near the Latimer Road tube station. The attackers had shouted racial insults at him for being with a White woman, but were shocked when she cursed at them. The next night, violence erupted in her building, leading her to be beaten with an iron bar. Majbritt Morrison, in the tawdry autobiography *Jungle West 11*, described how sexual miscegenation might have been the true reasons behind the Notting Hill disturbance:

> As I came out on Bramley Road there was a crowd of people – maybe a hundred or two-hundred. I went through the crowd and one of Teddy boys recognised me and shouted loud, 'There is another black man's trollop. Get her, kill her,' I heard him shout ... police came over to me and led me to the police van and toke [sic] me to Notting Hill Gate police station. I wundered [sic] what made them pick our house to start a race riot. The reason I learned a year later. The Teds were after a coloured man named Sporty who had two young [white] girl friends. This jealousy started the Notting Hill race riots – Sporty actually lived next door.[73]

Soon White mobs roamed the streets, as rioting spread throughout west London, with the sections Notting Hill and Notting Dale experiencing the worst.[74] Later that night, mobs of over 400 White people, many but not all of them Teddy Boys, were seen on Bramley Road attacking the homes and apartments of West Indian residents. Rioting and attacks continued every night until 5 September. A report to the Metropolitan Police Commissioner stated that 108 people were charged with grievous bodily harm, rioting, and possessing offensive weapons. Most were White. Eric R. Guest, the magistrate for West London, intervened to ask Notting Hill residents to stay indoors as a voluntary curfew began. While many West Indians stayed away from the area, many others fought back, threatening Whites with knives and bricks. They too were arrested along with Whites.[75]

By September of 1958 following the BBC's reports of the disturbances at Notting Hill and in Nottingham, the matter of racial violence was impossible to ignore, despite attempts by the Conservative government to downplay racialism, and frame the conflicts as 'Black vs. white hooliganism'. Between the dates of 25 August and 7 September, BBC television news featured no fewer than 32 separate reports on the Nottingham and Notting Hill riots.[76] On 1 September, the BBC reported that for the 'second night running' there were more disturbances between White and Coloured people in the Notting Hill area of London. Three men were reported 'injured and in the hospital with cuts and bruises, while 17 people were arrested some charged with using insulting behaviour, others with obstructing the police'.[77] One day before, the BBC Home Service had reported incidents in Nottingham, as 'the scene of clashes last weekend between white and Coloured men'.[78] However, it was reported, with regard to the skirmishes at Notting Hill, 'this time no Coloured people were involved'. The police had to use loudspeakers to control the crowd after some fighting broke out and fireworks had been set off. The Chief Constable noted that 24 people had been arrested and charged with various offences under the Public Order Act.[79] A number of young people were also arrested with possession of 'flick knives'. The police said Teddy Boys who had simply drunk too much, while 'Coloured people had behaved in an exemplary manner by keeping clear of the area', had caused the trouble.[80] Fire brigade-unions protested to the Home Secretary about Nottingham fire-fighters having to use fire hoses to restore order, perhaps due to reports of firemen doing the same to Negro protestors in Little Rock in the USA.[81] Ultimately, disturbances involving more than 200 people were reported, as were multiple incidents of violence involving more 'flick knives'. The Deputy Town Clerk of London blamed the trouble on 'sensational' publicity, citing how one freelance camera operator lit a flare in order to film a 'mock scuffle'.[82]

According to Ian Burrell of *The Independent*, the Home Office and

Scotland Yard tried to cover up the Notting Hill race riots of the 1950s by portraying them as a simple clash between Coloured and White 'ruffians'. Senior officials and police chiefs tried to present the riots as a 'law and order' issue to protect the Government from political embarrassment internationally. Documents released by the Public Record Office at the Kew Archives in 2003 show that police officers warned superiors that racial prejudices in the area would soon lead to 'serious disturbances', but were ignored. The documents also disclose that the CO wanted to address racial prejudice in Notting Hill because of concerns voiced by Commonwealth governments, but was rebuffed by the Home Office. Police Constable Michael Leach, based in Notting Hill, noted that crowds of several hundred people, all White, would gather to 'shout obscene remarks like, 'We will get the black bastards.' However, according to an internal police memo in September 1958, the divisional commander of the Metropolitan Police rejected the notion of a race riot, noting, 'Much of the trouble was caused by ruffians, both coloured and white, who seized the opportunity to engage in hooliganism'. While the presence of West Indians was allegedly underscoring racial tensions, Sir Oswald Mosley became the MP for Kensington North; Chief Minister to Jamaica, Mr Norman Manley, urged for more tolerance and resistance to colour prejudice; and R.A. Butler, the Conservative Home Secretary, questioned whether White Britons could continue to allow the immigration of 'generally unskilled' labour.[83] In addition, Butler called for 'no exaggeration' of these events in the news media, especially overseas. Meanwhile, he emphasised that the government was carefully reviewing the free admission of immigrants into Britain.[84] Despite this upheaval, in November of 1958 the House of Commons addressed colour violence and prejudice, and warned that the events of Notting Hill and Nottingham should not allow the country to discriminate against colonial immigration.[85]

More reports were transmitted on the Sunday news bulletins at 6.00 p.m., 7.23 p.m., 10.00 p.m. and 11.00 p.m. of smashed windows and arrests among White teens. As the days progressed, a London magistrate urged youngsters to stay indoors, while a Coloured man was sentenced to two months in prison for possession of an open razor, four others were fined, and thirty-seven were remanded in custody. The BBC also reported that while an 'air of tension and expectancy existed as white people gathered in the streets, hardly any Coloured people were to be seen'. On the *News Summary for Sunday*, Scotland Yard insisted that the Metropolitan Police would carry out their duty of preserving the Queen's peace without fear, favour, or discrimination.[86] During that afternoon, papers had reported that a West African student was nearly lynched by White mobs in Notting Hill, as a young assailant told the reporter, 'just tell your readers that Little Rock learned [sic] us a lesson' (Figure 10).[87] By 3 September, the Home Secretary called for a

Figure 10 As the events in Notting Hill worsened, a West African student was chased into a greengrocer's, and nearly lynched by white mobs. A young Ted told the reporter of the lessons they learned from Little Rock and the racialism displayed there.

detailed report on the disturbances in Nottingham and West London from the new Metropolitan Police commissioner, Joseph Simpson. George Rogers, Labour MP for Kensington North, told BBC News that 'hooligans' did not start the racial troubles. Instead, it was the reaction of people 'very sorely tried by the behaviour of the West Indians' (the news script had been altered to read 'some West Indians').[88] A segment on 10 Downing Street, and reactions to the racial disturbances, found Home Secretary Mr Butler reporting to the Prime Minister about the incidents. The government made it clear that an impartial, strict enforcement of the law would take place, as would the confiscation of offensive weapons. Another visitor to the Home Office was Rogers, who told Leonard Parkin,

> Oh, primarily it's two things – the very bad housing in the constituency, and crime by certain section of the immigrants … people are very annoyed when they see houses which they think they ought to have because they have been there all their lives given to people who have only just come to the country. Also that it is this question of Coloured landlordism, which is that both in exploiting their own people and white tenants and also in making the lives of white families very miserable because they want to get out.

He added that he was going to insist the government take action, now that 'the riots have woken them up to the seriousness of the problem'.[89]

Subsequent days found more reports from the BBC of disturbances, hooliganism, and arrests. Blamed were fascist organisations, as were some West Indian males retaliating against the actions of Teddy Boys. Number 10 Downing Street reported that the government was closely examining the 'result of allowing the free entry of immigrants into Britain from commonwealth and colonial countries'. The BBC also reported that the Colonial Secretary, Mr Lennox Boyd, was returning to London from Bermuda on 5 September – in other words the next day – and arriving at about the same time would be Chief Minister Manley, along with the Deputy Prime Minister of the West Indies Federation, Dr La Corbiniere. The men were reportedly coming to 'investigate the racial situation at first hand'. The Ghanaian Finance Minister, Mr Gbedemah, stopped over in London on his way to a series of meetings in Canada, and explained that 'his people were distressed that these things should be happening in Britain, of all places. They hoped they were only superficial and would come to an abrupt end'.[90] When interviewed by David Holmes, Manley explained that everyone in the West Indies was deeply disturbed, particularly because 'The West Indies are making a magnificent job of building up a multiracial society, and always looked to England to give a leave in that direction', particularly when considering what Manley called 'an issue of world importance'. He also explained that he was there to assist and was at the 'disposal of the British government', and to 'see my own people', and to let them know that 'we give help'. When asked about the way people were behaving against West Indian immigrants generally, Manley was convinced that the vast majority of people in England treated strangers in accordance with traditions of decency and tolerance. Later that day Manley walked through Brixton, where crowds of West Indians welcomed him.

Accompanied by an officer of the British Caribbean Welfare Service, he visited some West Indian immigrants in their homes, and others in markets and on the street. During the three-hour tour, Manley visited the Racial Brotherhood Association, an organisation hoping to keep Brixton free of racial classes.[91] The General Secretary of the Trades Union Congress (TUC), Sir Vincent Tewson, from a meeting in Bournemouth, explained that the TUC was shocked by what was happening, and that this is the 'sort of thing that does a great deal of harm to a movement which has contacts with Coloured people in more than 35 British territories overseas'.[92] Tom Driberg, Chair of the Labour Party, called the riots 'a blot on the consciousness of Britain'.[93] A declaration from the organisation stated that all delegates were deeply disturbed at the recent isolated outbreaks. The group told the BBC that evidence was accumulating that elements which stirred racial hatred before the war were 'once more fanning the flames of violence'. Meanwhile, trade unionists felt that it was their duty as responsible citizens to aid the authorities in preventing further occurrences, while respecting the laws and obligations of citizenship.[94] A formal statement denouncing the racial violence was approved during the TUC's final session that week; as Tewson noted, 'we want our people to work to ensure that here in this land, we have no Little Rock'.[95] On that same day the BBC reported that pamphlets were being handed out in North Kensington blaming both the Tory and Labour parties for the conditions of the area, and explained that the 'real culprits' were the 'old party politicians'. The pamphlet ended with a statement, 'Back Mosley in the Fight'.[96]

On 5 September, the Home Service ran a special report on Notting Hill, which provided an opportunity for members of the community to express their concerns, including West Indians and West Africans. Reporters John Tidmarsh and Leonard Parkin provided on-the-spot recordings and a background report on the area itself. In addition to the progressive beauty of a 'new underground station being built at Notting Hill Gate', the line of 'greengrocers and antique shops' were described in detail. However, Parkin added that soon after passing through this area one could find oneself having driven 'into a pretty seedy area … the district of north Kensington, which is literally poles apart from the more sedate south Kensington; a very long way away on what the snobs used to call the right side of the park'. Parkin continued to describe the rough undesirability of the area, a place in which 'young people played long after dark, and some hung around pub doorways waiting for their parents'. Considered a 'rough, hardworking part of London', the area was one where 'a sizable black population' lived side by side – and often in the same partitioned houses – as Whites. Both groups 'stand on street corners, or hang out of the flat windows', giving the impression that 'there's not a lot privacy and that the rooms in the basements and behind the curtains windows are not homes so much as places to live; places to sleep'. Parkin described this mosaic as having recently become a 'tough vicious area with a tension and a feeling of distrust that you can almost touch'. Tidmarsh then followed by conducting a series of interviews with people in the area.

In the first of these, listeners heard a male voice describe the Notting Hill mêlée as 'not a race riot at all. It's a riot against a certain type of people. It's a revolt against the vice that's come into the vicinity'. Another male voice states that the Government 'allowed these people: they come over from the West Indies and Jamaica and they've got these young girls, white girls, they've got them out on the beat as prostitutes and they're living on the immoral earnings of them, and that is the root of all the matter, that is definitely a fact. One of [the West Indians] has got a club – one of them has got a club now in the West End, he's got quite a big club and he's got, at least to my knowledge, half a dozen girls out on the game and that is why the white people are angry towards them'. When Mr Pilgrim of the British Caribbean welfare service was asked to discuss the criminality of these men, he explained that those working in vice were clearly within the minority. Many more worked on the Underground, as well as in factories, post offices, and some commercial concerns. This included West Indians and West African students in the Notting Hill area. Pilgrim also reminded the reporter that Notting Hill had 'never had a great reputation for respectability'. He felt that the reason some had got involved in a bad situation or illegal trade was that it 'existed already, and it wasn't a West Indian who introduced this to the area'.

Accommodations were again a factor, as another male voice reported that the 'trouble with blacks is not caused by the Teddy Boys', but was actually caused by 'blacks buying property and leading old people to live a dog's life'. The man also complained about 'radiograms blaring away 'ere until three and four in the morning when people have to get up and go to work, and they're sitting on windowsills with hardly anything on, whistling at the girls and women as they pass by'. In a telephone interview with Mr Chesworth, representing North Kensington on the London County council, the problem of Black property owners and slum housing came up. Chesworth explained that, though a housing shortage existed, trouble came from the fact that 'landlords from every part of England, Scotland, Wales and from overseas have brought up the houses which a contain people paying small rents in rent control rooms or apartments'. As for overcrowding, Chesworth believed that the population of the North Kensington area was the same as it was 'two or three years ago' because it was a 'very mobile population'. There was a 'constant coming and going'. He agreed that there were more West Indians now, but that the actual population remained 'pretty static'.

Also interviewed was a Jamaican woman who worked in a local welfare office, addressing the challenges of Coloured people finding accommodation. She stated that in Jamaica there were 'hundreds of white people', and she had 'never heard a single Jamaican during the thirty years [she] lived there, bear any resentment [to] the British or Europeans having a house in Jamaica. I think it's very shocking and very wearing for [whites in Notting Hill] to expect the coloured people should live in trees'.

A local in Anglican minister from the area reviewed what might have started the troubles of the past week. Richard Wallace responded that he had not been aware of any tensions and was very surprised when the 'riots all began'. He also explained that he was in touch with quite a number of West Indians from his church, and 'quite a number of them play an active part in the parish and on the local church council'. However, he had never known of any racial tensions. When asked about the presence of the Teddy Boys, Wallace explained that he felt that many had no idea of the racist implications. He mentioned that, when walking through a crowd the night before, he had asked a Ted what all the fuss was about, and he received the reply that it was a 'racial problem. When I asked him what the racial problem was, he could not answer. He explained that many involved themselves for sport, inviting their friends to "get into it". When asked if he thought some sort of organisation was behind the skirmishes, Wallace felt that 'some [Ted] scraps with West Indians and one thing starts another'.

Parkin interviewed by telephone a member of Mosley's UM, Mr Hamm. When asked what they hope to accomplish by holding meetings in Notting Hill Gate, they explained that the meetings were part of normal political activities with the aim of 'swinging public opinion towards the union movement'. Hamm further stated that, in relation to the riots, the organisation 'deplores violence as much as any other decent person does'. When UM pamphlets called for 'action now', and to 'fight with us', he suggested, this meant political action. He was also pleased that large crowds came to the speeches.

Pilgrim disagreed and felt that there had been a considerable amount of groundwork already laid by stirring the racial hatred in the area. He mentions the evidence of pamphlets being distributed by the UM that encouraged 'white people of Kensington to fight for their country and help to send the blacks back to their country'. A West Indian woman was interviewed who ran a 'coloured club' in the area, and she explained that she received a telephone call the night before the riots from a White friend. This person suggested that they should be as 'cautious as possible and make sure they had plenty of people in the club to protect them', because Teds were out to bomb the club and 'wreck the place'. For protection, she explained that she had a 'few of the boys down sitting around just in case someone tried to charge the place'. When a reporter asked why she did not get police protection, she explained that there was no point in it because some people had called for police protection at ten in the morning, and did not receive it until midnight. She also placed no blame on the police because many of them were on the streets, trying to 'cut down the trouble', and their hands were 'very, very full running around trying to keep people indoors. But, how can you ask a person you go home and sit in a house, when the houses are going to be bombed?' She noted how Teds were 'round right now on motor bikes', marking all the houses where Coloureds lived, so the 'boys know where to bomb, or where not to bomb'. When asked if she thought there was some organisation behind the White violence, she responded that children were not using their own initiative – 'they're doing it because they've been roused up and they're being told to do'.[97]

Further, concerns over racial unrest came from members of Birmingham's West Indian community, due in part to the recent problems at Notting Hill. Pilgrim criticised the BBC for including a fictional news bulletin of race riots continuing in Birmingham during the first instalment of the highly popular *Quatermass and the Pit* (BBC, 22 December 1958–26 January 1959). Pilgrim considered the reference 'particularly unfortunate because it might create an anti-West Indian attitude among English people at a time when the coloured leaders were encouraging sympathy between the races'. Piliso of the Afro Caribbean Association said that, in allowing the dialogue, the BBC had 'misrepresented conditions in Birmingham', leading a BBC official to remind readers that the news bulletin was 'completely imaginary', and took place within a show. The future depicted within the teleplay contained such items as a rocket landing on the moon, and other 'Jules Verne sort of stuff. No slur on Birmingham was implied and no reference to past events nor prophecy of the future was intended'.[98] Once again, the BBC was reminded of their responsibility for education and the examination of racial attitudes; the onus was on them to maintain these aspects of their service as the overall national identity of the country changed with each boatload of immigrants.

In a survey sponsored by the Audience Research Department, the Gallup Poll and the BBC on 3 and 4 September polled a select audience on their perceptions of 'coloured people' following the riots. Nearly everyone had heard of the 'recent disturbances between white and coloured people in

Nottingham and London', and when asked whom was 'chiefly to blame, white or coloured', 21 per cent expressed no opinion, while 27 per cent said 'white', 9 per cent 'coloured' and 35 per cent felt both groups were somewhat responsible for the tensions. General opinions about immigration found that 65 per cent were in favour of 'laws to restrict entry to Britain from the Commonwealth', but most thought such laws should apply to both White and Coloured people, 21 per cent were against such legislation, and 14 were neutral. Where jobs were concerned, 48 per cent were in favour of 'coloured people from the Commonwealth' being 'allowed to compete for jobs in Great Britain' and 37 per cent against. However, 54 per cent were against 'coloured people from the Commonwealth' being placed on council housing lists along with 'people born in Great Britain'. Most polled, at 70 per cent, indicated they would not move 'if coloured people came to live next door', yet 26 per cent would move, if 'great numbers' of coloured people came to live in their district. The answers of men and women differed very little, yet women were more inclined to respond 'didn't know', to many questions, as were 16–21-year-olds, yet both genders expressed a strong opposition to mixed marriages, with 71 per cent disapproval. Half the people claimed to know coloured people personally, citing that they were 'no different from other people', with the 16–21-year-olds indicating *slightly* (report's emphasis) more tolerant attitudes, but giving responses that were generally very similar to those of their elders. There was also little to 'distinguish the replies in the London area from those of the rest of Great Britain'.[99]

Labour minister Lord Pakenham, in putting a motion before the House of Lords, called attention to recent outbursts of 'colour prejudice and violence', and noted that arrest figures and violent behaviour represented 'looking into an abyss from which we must draw back, and draw back at once', for the sake of 'British traditions and the ideals that we most prize and pride ourselves on'.[100] Figures provided by the government estimated the Coloured population in Britain to be about 190,000 out of a population of 50 million, making four out of every 1,000 people Coloured. Of these, 100,000 may have come from the West Indies and 50,000 from India and Pakistan; Pakenham noted that 'most of these coloured people are recent immigrants or the children of recent immigrants, though there have been some coloured families in this country for generations'. Immigration from the West Indies continued, but India and Pakistan had taken some steps to 'discourage and reduce the flow from those countries'. The consensus was that immigrants of colour often performed essential tasks for which labour had not otherwise been available, while restricting the free entry of Commonwealth citizens could create an ideological backlash, denying British emigrants entry into Commonwealth countries. Despite examinations of practices that allowed free entry from Commonwealth and colonial countries, two and a half months had passed since discussions had begun, causing Pakenham to 'ask the Government for a clear, unequivocal statement as to where they stand on at any rate the main issues'. Pakenham compared current measures to the McCarran-Walter Act and reminded others that the 'new quota system' introduced by the United States of America in 1952 'drastically reduced opportunities for West Indians to follow their traditional search for employment in that country'. While most Lords agreed in principle to the detrimental aspects of Butler's labour considerations, Lord Silkin noted that the matter of restricted entry was an option for the future, despite its discriminatory leanings.[101]

The horrific events of Notting Hill and Nottingham demonstrated to the British population the extreme difficulties West Indian immigrants were experiencing, yet the blame for racial tension and related situations often put onto lower-income Whites for their intolerance and the immigrants for their ignorance of housing laws and social practices. While the social problems their presence supposedly caused were paramount in the minds of many, notions of place and presence were being reformed and disrupted with each new wave of immigrants. Kenneth Little noted in the *New Statesman* that 'attacks upon coloured people should not be seen as racial hostility alone, but as the symptom of much deeper social tensions', due to 'rapid change and unevenness in our society's development', and that 'the whole programme of coloured integration may require reconsideration' as the 'general life of the community' becomes 'invigorated'.[102] However, continued concerns over housing and economic issues led in part to the Commonwealth Immigrants Act 1962, which, under Macmillan's Conservative government, restricted citizens of the United Kingdom and colonies (CUKCs) with passports not issued by a colonial Governor of a colony or the Commander of a British protectorate from entering the country. The Act also increased the residence requirement for Commonwealth citizens applying for registration as CUKCs from a one-year to a five-year period, permitted only those with government-issued employment vouchers to settle, and greatly affected immigrants from Asia and Africa.

As the House of Commons began debate on further restrictions of Coloured immigrants to England, the West Indies Commission in London issued a paper noting the benefit of how money sent home to the islands by West Indians in Britain helped the overall economy. West Indies immigration alleviated England's labour scarcity within northern industrial areas, the Midlands, and London via employment with 'British Railways, London Transport, hospitals and the catering trade'. The panel disputed notions of casual immigration, reminding those in favour of restrictions that authorities in the West Indies were aware of 'pressure from Britain to slow down Immigration'. The West Indies Commission also noted how 'frequent articles in the press', along with radio warnings, 'cautioned the migrants', a likely reference to aforementioned BBC programmes aimed at the Caribbean, and noted in the *Going to Britain* handbook.[103] While touring the West Indies in March of 1961, Prime Minister Macmillan, after having an 'emergency meeting with President Kennedy', had separate meetings with Sir Grantley Adams, Governor of Trinidad, and members of his cabinet on a number of subjects, including the question of the migration of West Indians to the United Kingdom. In a notion of liberalism that moved beyond economic matters of trade, Adams, members of the cabinet and various academics emphasised the 'West Indian view that no barriers should be put up by Britain on the entry of West Indians', and more concern over the welfare of those 'now living in Britain'.[104]

Another *A Question of Colour*

In 1958, an additional programme from the *Special Enquiry* series attempted to demonstrate that assimilation could occur, if not generally accepted. As a follow up to the *Colour Bar* episode, the BBC transmitted the instalment *A Question of Colour* on Friday, 14 November 1958. David Martin of the BBC's Midland Film Unit produced the programme in which a crew returned to Birmingham to find out how racial relations had improved in the city. According to Norman Swallow, Assistant Head of Films for Television, the second story in Birmingham was to be 'a cheerful one, at least on the surface. A great deal more cheerful than it was in 1954.' In his memo called *Question of Colour Notes*, he suggests that as host Robert Reid opens the programme, audiences be reminded that

> [The BBC] came to Birmingham for only one reason – because we came here four years ago. We came then because Birmingham had so many coloured immigrants, and it still has (figures here maybe?). However, in Birmingham, as you'll see, the story is better than it was in 1954. No violence here. If you're looking for violence, then this isn't your programme. If you're looking for evidence to support a restriction on coloured immigration, this isn't your programme.[105]

In a critique of the overall programme, Swallow suggests that audiences would expect drama and violence, due to the recent Nottingham and Notting Hill riots, and Martin would give them neither within the programme. He further suggests that Martin should find a means of 'coming clean from the start', by saying this would not be a 'sensational' report, and referring to Birmingham in a manner than would seem to be an example to other places.[106]

Swallow, in a reference to the Hockley Garage problem from the first documentary, wrote

> I still think the exterior (1954) of the Garage would be effective if [the
> presenter] could say this was as near as our cameras could get to the Hockley
> Garage 4 years ago. This year I went inside ... (Interview with busmen to
> follow). [Also] See what you can do with the Personnel Manager, who struck
> me as a bit of a phoney.[107]

The racialism previously encountered by the BBC crew would now be
exposed to audiences in the follow-up programme. Individuals that
expressed racist views would also be re-examined. In a reference to a racist
landlady, probably thought to be within her rights, Swallow suggested:

> Put the splendid landlady later on. Cut her down as discussed. [Then] end,
> after the sequences, with street scenes of Birmingham. Over these [the
> presenter] says that this city and its people are perhaps an example to the rest
> of Britain. Proving that a colour bar is neither necessary nor excusable.
> Proving that men and women of different races can live and work in harmony
> if only they have the will to do so. Proving that Britain, in 1958, is still a place
> that can promise a worthy future for everybody ... whatever his colour ... (Cut
> to shot of coloured child ...) whatever his age. (Or something of the sort!)[108]

Swallow's directive was clearly pro-integration as the service demonstrated
a desire to heal social rifts and expose racist practices.

Reportedly, in Birmingham's schools, there had been at first 'great colour
prejudice' from both students and teachers, which resulted in many
coloured children going home crying. However, things had improved, and
Stone planned to recommend some very happy shots of Coloured and White
children together in the schools in the Balsall Heath, Handsworth, and
Aston areas. However, there was concern by a local organisation that highlighting the adaptation of Black children in a local school could raise issues
of racial and cultural difference. As a means of accentuating positive aspects
of the immigrant experience in Birmingham it was suggested that the show's
title avoided the words 'prejudice' and 'bar'. Writing to Swallow, Martin
stressed that

> The one stumbling block has been the continued refusal of the Education
> Committee to give us facilities to film any of their schools, or even to interview
> the Youth Employment Officer. They give us their reasons for this refusal that
> the integration of coloured children into Birmingham schools is proceeding so
> smoothly and satisfactorily that they feel any publicity given to the subject
> might arouse latent colour prejudice.[109]

Audience reaction, based upon questionnaires completed by a sample of the
audience, provided a Reaction Index of 73; the fifteen other programmes in

the Special Inquiry series averaged 71. By comparison, the *Colour Bar* show had gained an Index of 77. Audiences felt that a return visit to Birmingham to find out how Coloured people were doing seemed like a good idea for the programme's premise, yet some believed that in dealing with one city the programme did not address the national situation fairly. In addition, it was felt that no new or surprising information had been included in the broadcast, and that the subject, perhaps due to the riots, had been publicised more than adequately in preceding weeks. Otherwise, the sample considered it an interesting and a useful programme that looked at a social problem clearly and without bias, providing increased understanding of the problems of both White and Coloured people, which was necessary if a satisfactory solution were to be found. Several viewers also found the overall picture of racial relations encouraging. Otherwise, comments from those interviewed were of a general nature, with most viewers in the sample feeling that the subjects had been well chosen, forming a representative cross-section of immigrants and that they behaved naturally in front of the cameras, and answered the questions put to them frankly and sincerely.[110] However, despite these reactions, there were concerns over an increase in immigration, perhaps due in part to the events of Nottingham and Notting Hill. How the BBC would address these matters of racial and cultural difference remained an on-going challenge.

Notes

1 From Collins to HTel.LE 2 February 1950, T16/175/1, BBC WAC. All references BBC WAC unless otherwise noted.
2 Goldie, *Facing the Nation*, 52.
3 Paulu, *British Broadcasting in Transition*.
4 Goldie, *Facing the Nation*, 56.
5 Television Newsreel, programme 50, 25 June 1948.
6. Luke McKerman, ed., *Yesterday's News: The British Cinema Newsreel Reader*. London: BUFVC, 2002: 76.
7 P.H. Dorte, 'The BBC television newsreel', in McKerman, ed., *Yesterday's News: The British Cinema Newsreel Reader*. London: BUFVC, 2002: 55.
8 British Pathé films, Pathé Reporter News, 25 June 1948.
9 From McGiven, 24 August 1951, T16/175/1.
10 Controller, Television Programmes to McGiven, 29 August 1951, T16/162/1.
11 Viewer Research Report, 10 November 1952, VR/52/458.
12 Belson, *The Impact of Television*.
13 Programme Index on *Colour Bar programmes, 1952, T/4/55*.
14 Brendin to Goldie, 29 September 1952, T/32/209.
15 Adams to Noordhorf, 5 January 1952, T/32/209.
16 *Ibid.*, 2.

17 Adams to Barnes, 3 July 1952, T32/209/1.
18 David Wilby, 'Vernon Bartlett comments 1933', *The BBC Story*, 2006, www.bbc.co.uk/historyofthebbc/resources/bbcandgov/pdf/bartlett.pdf (accessed on 6 December 2009).
19 Christopher Mayhew, 'The problem of race relations', *Radio Times*, 21 November 1952: 45.
20 Goldie to Bredin and Swallow, 15 January 1952, T/32/209.
21 Adams regarding Mayhew, 28 July 1952, T/32/209.
22 Goldie to Littman, 15 September 1952, T/32/209.
23 Bredin to Goldie, 15 October 1952, T/32/209.
24 *Ibid.*
25 Noordhof to Supply Manager, *Race and Colour*, 7 November 1952, T/32/209.
26 *Ibid.*, 2.
27 Viewer Research Report for Race and Colour: A Scientific Introduction to the Problem of Race Relations, BBC WAC.
28 *Ibid.*, 3.
29 *Ibid.*, 4.
30 *Ibid.*
31 *Ibid.*
32 *Ibid.*
33 *Ibid.*
34 Williams to Goldie, HTel.T and CTel.P, 26 November 1952, T/16/175.
35 Lotbinière to Little, 6 December 1954, T/4/55.
36 Production notes for *Special Enquiry*, T/4/55.
37 House of Commons Sitting of 21 June 1955, Vol. 542 cc1152–269. Record of proceedings (Hansard) [serial on the internet] 1955 (accessed on 8 December 2009). Available from: http://hansard.millbanksystems.com/commons/1955 /jun/21/colonial-affairs.
38 Production notes for *Special Enquiry*, 14 December 1954, T/4/55.
39 *Ibid.*
40 Piliso to Stone, 14 December 1954, T/4/55.
41 Kew Archives, CAB/129/40.
42 Production notes for *Special Enquiry*, 16 December 1954, T/4/55BNC.
43 *Ibid.*
44 *Ibid.*
45 Newspaper headlines for the *Colour Bar*, 21 January 1954, T/4/55.
46 Production notes for *Special Enquiry*, 16 December 1954, T/4/55.
47 De Lotbinière to Cutworth, 23 December 1954, T/4/55.
48 Rough draft treatment for *Special Enquiry* – Third Year; Number 3: *The Colour Bar*, Second Background Information, T/4/55.
49 Rough outline treatment, the *Colour Bar*, 14 December 1954, T/4/55.
50 *Ibid.*
51 Rough outline treatment, 16 December 1954, T/4/55.
52 *Ibid.*
53 *Lambeth No Colour Bar Dance*. British Pathé, 17 February 1955.

54 Rough outline treatment, 16 December 1954, T/4/55.
55 Stone to Lotbinière, 11 November 1954, T/4/55.
56 Anonymous, *Birmingham Gazette*, 5 January 1955: 1.
57 Lotbinière to Green, 14 January 1955, T/4/55.
58 Lotbinière to Evans, 30 December 1954, T4/5/1.
59 *Has Britain a Colour Bar?*, BBC, 31 January 1955.
60 Rough outline treatment, 14 December 1954, T/4/55.
61 Whitworth to Eden, 9 February 1955, T4/55.
62 Whitworth to Finsberg, 8 February 1955, T4/55.
63 Lotbinière to Wilson, 2 February 1955, T4/55.
64 Swallow to ACP (Tel.), 1 March 1955, T4/55.
65 Audience Research Report, 5 June 1956, R9 July 1922.
66 *Black and White in Colour*. Dir. Isaac Julien, Prod. Colin MacCabe for BFI TV/BBC Television, 1992.
67 *A Man from the Sun*. Dir. Isaac Julien, Prod. John Elliott, BBC, 1956.
68 Viewer Research Report, 8 November 1955, R9/7/25.
69 Trevor Phillips, personal interview, 21 August 1998.
70 Gil Swain, 'Verdict on the promised land', *Daily Mail*, 21 May 1988: 4.
71 House of Lords sitting of 19 November 1958, vol. 212. Record of proceedings (Hansard), http://hansard.millbanksystems.com/lords/1958/nov/19/colour-prejudice-and-violence (accessed on 2 February 2011); pp. 632–724.
72 D. Lowe, 'Bygones: the race riots, 50 years on', *Nottingham Post*, 4 September 2008. www.thisisnottingham.co.uk/news/Bygones-race-riots-50-years/article-306378-detail/article.html (accessed 25 February 2011).
73 Majbritt Morrison, *Jungle West 11*. London: Tandem, 1964: 36–7.
74 Anonymous, 'Renewed racial disturbances in London' *The Times*, 2 September 1958.
75 Anonymous, 'Magistrate asks for voluntary curfew', *The Times*, 4 September 1958.
76 BBC News Scripts, BBC Home Service, 25 July–7 September 1958.
77 Talks Script – 'At home and abroad' – BBC Home Service, 1 September 1958.
78 BBC News Script – 'Nottingham' – BBC Television, 25 August 1958.
79 Attacks on the Jewish community by Oswald Mosley and the British Union of Fascists (BUF) at public meetings led to violence in Britain. In November 1936, the Cable Street Riot took place when left-wing organisations attempted to stop the BUF from marching through the Jewish areas of London. Parliament reacted by passing the Public Order Act, giving the power to the Home Secretary, and thereby to chief constables by proxy, to ban potentially disruptive marches. The Act also made it an offence to wear political uniforms and to use threatening and abusive words.
80 Talks Script – 'At home and abroad' – BBC Home Service – 1 September 1958.
81 BBC News Script – 'Nottingham' – BBC Television – 25 August 1958.
82 BBC News Script – 'Riots' – BBC Television – 25 August 1958.
83 Ian Burrell, 'The Home Office cover-up of Notting Hill's race riots', *The Independent*, Saturday, 23 August 2003.

84 *The Promised Land?*, BBC2, 22 July 1982.

85 House of Commons Sitting of 19 November 1958, vol. 212. Record of proceedings (Hansard) [serial on the internet] 1958(accessed on 28 December 2009); pp. 632–724.

86 BBC News Script – 'Notting Hill' – BBC Television – 2 September 1958.

87 Anonymous, '"Lynch him," cried as coloured man is chased', *The Guardian*, 2 September 1958: 1.

88 BBC News Script – 'Racial' – BBC Television – 3 September 1958.

89 BBC News Script – 'Rogers' – BBC Television – 3 September 1958.

90 BBC News Script – 'Racial' – BBC Television – 4 September 1958.

91 BBC News Script – 'Butler and Racial' – BBC Television – 5 September 1958.

92 BBC News Script – 'TUC for 6pm' – BBC Television – 3 September 1958.

93 Anonymous, 'Thirty charged at Notting Hill: another evening of racial unrest', *The Guardian*, 2 September 1958: 1.

94 BBC News Script – 'TUC (OB)' – BBC Television – 4 September 1958.

95 BBC News Script – 'TUC for 10 pm' – BBC Television – 5 September 1958.

96 BBC News Script – 'TUC' – BBC Television – 5 September 1958.

97 Talks Script – 'At home and abroad' – BBC Home Service – 5 September 1958.

98 Anonymous, 'Coloured leaders criticize BBC', *The Times*, 24 December 1958: 4.

99 Audience Research Report, 29 February 1958, R/51/781.

100 House of Lords sitting of 19 November 1958, vol. 212. Record of Proceedings (Hansard) 1958, pp. 632–724.

101 *Ibid.*

102 Kenneth Little, 'Integration without tears', *New Statesman*, 20 September 1958.

103 Anonymous, 'West Indian immigration: plea against restriction', *The Times*, 17 February 1961: 11.

104 Anonymous, 'West Indians oppose barriers to British immigration', *The Times*, 27 March 1961: 11.

105 *Ibid.*

106 Swallow to Martin, 18 September 1958, T/32/1569.

107 *Ibid.*

108 *Ibid.*

109 Martin to Swallow, 18 September 1958, T/32/1569.

110 Audience Research Department, *A Question of Colour*, 26 November 1958.

3

Voices of contention and BBC programming

You see, the white man is a very funny creature. He likes his change in scenery. He likes his variety in life … Yet the English man, or the white man for that matter, doesn't want the variety of the human species. He likes to see white only.

Pastor Dunn in *The Colony* (BBC, 1964)

As suggested by Rich's work in *Race and Empire*, the coming of World War Two sparked a new move toward improved race relations, which coincided with the gradual disintegration of the colonial empire. He notes how, as the Colonial Development and Welfare Act passed in 1940, after decades of imperialism being 'least challenged politically by colonial nationalism, the British establishment turned its mind towards colonial development at precisely the point when its rule began to be undermined'.[1] The Crown's need for support among its colonies is apparent in the numerous radio broadcasts, newsreels, and films featuring West Indian troops as part of the war effort. However, as the war ended, concerns continued over an increase of immigration from the West Indies. A report from the Manley adminis-tration on the economic impact of these settlers led to the establishment of the British Caribbean Welfare Service on 5 June 1956, under the control of Ivo de Souza, Welfare Liaison Officer for the British Caribbean Welfare Service and the CO. According to figures compiled by de Souza's office, the total number of West Indians entering the UK in 1955 was around 25,000 with an equal number expected in 1956. The number of West Indians in the country in that year totalled approximately 55,000 to 60,000, as compared to a labour force of 22 million.[2] A meeting held on 28 June 1956 by the British Caribbean Welfare Service to discuss immigration issues drew nearly one hundred White British attendees. The group reminded attendees that no press would attend, in order to give freedom of discussion. In turn, the London Council of Social Service stated that they sought to serve as a consultancy for immigrants and the multitude of agencies they encoun-tered, and the Colonial Office also took part. The meeting indicated a poor understanding by these organisations of both immigration processes and the dynamics of race relations. However, as the nation further considered the problematic issues brought forward by race relations, the government under PM Macmillan was compelled to intervene in the area, particularly in regard to the increase in West Indian immigration: initially from the West Indies, but in the late 1950s increasingly from India and Pakistan. As Commonwealth residents, Asians were also British subjects without citizenship and, under the terms of the 1948 Act, held the right of free entry to Britain.

Kathleen Paul notes that, by 1957, the Working Party on Social and Economic Problems had become highly concerned over the increased immigration of Asians from both countries, considered to be of poor social standards, unskilled, and undesirable. The sheer nature of Britain's relationship with India as compared to the British West Indies had already shaped immigration laws, potential housing, and employment. Paul also notes that support for West Indian migrants stemmed from the fact that they were often skilled or semi-skilled individuals, concerned with economic improvement and a desire to enhance their middle-class status by journeying to the motherland. The 'relative value of West Indian migration during the mid-1950s may have provided a lesser evil when compared to Asian immigration later in the decade, yet there remained overwhelming concerns over social assimilation'.[3] BBC television programming in the 1950s – such as *Has Britain a Colour Bar?*, *A Question of Colour*, and *Man from the Sun* – attempted to provide a studied, though somewhat patronising, perspective on the issues of race and immigrants. Since each programme received mainly positive responses in audience research reports, the structured polysemy offered on these BBC programmes affected the control of public opinion, avoiding the damage to Commonwealth unity yet reinforcing the vigour of some West Indian groups on television. The nobility assigned to others also bore a problematic construct, as Pathé newsreels shown on the BBC addressed this continued influx as 'Our Jamaican Problem'. One such script, as broadcast, reminds viewers that, despite the concerns expressed, 'we cannot deny them entry', because, as British citizens, each was entitled to the identical rights of anyone else in the Empire. Discussed are employment problems in the West Indies, and further outcries over West Indians, despite little criticism over 'thousands of white foreigners (including 15,000 former enemies) that have made their homes' in England.[4]

As ministers in the government considered more inter-departmental enquiries into the social consequences of increased immigration, they wanted not to simply monitor expressions of public concern, but also 'control its expression'. Thus they rejected the idea of ascertaining the public mind on the subject by stimulating discussion in the press for fear that the result might be an explosion of opinion in favour of 'immediate action', which they could not undertake, having not yet decided on its form.[5] It would seem apparent that the BBC could, and ultimately would, assist the assimilation of both Blacks and Asians greatly, through programming that fostered public education about life in England, and social customs.

A reassessment of racial imagery

As the BBC began to incorporate more issues about the racial question into its news and documentary programming, there was an attempt to calculate the amount of Black and other Coloured people that had appeared on the BBC throughout the 1950s. There had been discussions at a meeting of the Northern Ireland Advisory Council, led by Controller Robert McCall, that the service had only used Coloured people for popular programmes that addressed music, controversial race issues, and special series. In an effort to address this concern, an urgent memo by Controller, Northern Ireland (CNI), Robert McCall sent to Norman Swallow, on the 'Racial Problem', addressed information regarding certain programmes. The memo enquired about the number and nature of the programmes people of colour had appeared on. McCall stated:

> At the last meeting of the NI Advisory Council, there was some discussion of the incidence of programmes that provide opportunities for coloured people to be heard as artists or to express their views. One of the members had the impression that the BBC only used coloured people for popular programmes such as Jazz Sessions, The Six-Five Special, and so on. I suggested that this was not entirely true and that in fact coloured people were frequently employed in programmes of high quality ... I was asked, however, to provide the Council with a sample list of the programmes to which I referred. I therefore would like urgently to have your cooperation and that of your Heads of Programme Departments. What I really want from each Departmental Head is half a dozen examples of programmes, in which, during the past year, coloured people – Indian, African, West Indian, etc. – have been heard as serious artists or have taken part in serious programmes such as discussions or talks.[6]

In response, Lionel Salter, Head of Music Productions, Television responded with a roster of coloured artists in serious programmes. Salter noted his department's output with broadcast dates for that year, apart from Elizabeth Welch. Noted were a film of the National Orchestra of All India Radio (17 April), a performance by the National Dancers of Ceylon (3 August), and two other performances of Indian actors and dances: in a production of *Salome* (11 September) and within a segment of *Music for You* (17 April). Performances by African-Americans included famed soprano Gloria Davy by Eurovision from Brussels in an operatic recital (28 April), and on two episodes of *Music for You* (10 August and 2 November). The soprano Leonora Lafayette singing in *Aida* also appeared on the programme. Only one West Indian was noted, Boscoe Holder doing songs and dances of the West Indies (24 July).[7]

In a follow-up memo that addressed Coloured speakers in religious television programmes during 1958, Oliver Hunkin, Assistant Head of Religious Broadcasting, Television, wrote to Swallow to note guests on specific shows. On an episode of *Meeting Point* (16 February), Mrs Ta Upu Pere and Mrs Edrisinha discussed Christianity, and Sri Lankan evangelist and ecumenical leader Dr D.T. Niles appeared on *Epilogue* (13 April). The organisation the Quest of Nations appeared with overseas students, including those from West Africa, to discuss their lives in England on *Meeting Point* (11 May); on another episode of the series (1 June), African musicologist Tom Nabeta interviewed the Bishop of Uganda. Author Angela Christian from Ghana spoke on colour prejudice during a *Meeting Point* of 12 October, and Rev. Vedaneyagon Gnanamuthu spoke on the Church in India (28 December).[8]

The School Broadcasting Organiser for Television, Cyril Jackson, provided a list of Coloured people used from September 1957 until July of 1958, specifically on the *Living in the Commonwealth* series. These segments allowed speakers of colour from various countries to provide a demonstration of their cultures to pupils and other audiences. Groups recognised by the BBC as cultural societies assisted the organisation in finding guests for most programmes: a list of such societies included the West Indian Students Union, the Stepney League of Coloured Peoples, the All Nations Social Club, the African West Indian Services, and the Anglo Caribbean Clubs.[9] Of the nineteen shows listed, many featured spokespeople from Ceylon, Pakistan, India, New Zealand, China, and Malaya. Three Africans featured in specific programmes that addressed culture from western regions of the continent. From the West Indies, authors Errol John (22 April 1958), George Lamming (29 May 1958), and Andrew Salkey (5 June 1958) read excerpts and spoke about their personal histories. Also featured were dubbed commentaries on film by Errol John about West Indian immigration (11 July 1957), and a West Indian immigrant film with an unknown interviewee from the United Nations Declaration of Human Rights Committee (12 May 1957). Cyril Jackson added a handwritten note, 'I think it is a fair point to make that the *Living in the Commonwealth* series was 1/4 our weekly output!'[10]

Head of Drama, Television, Michael Barry, noted that Coloured actors appeared in dramatic fare, but only when the programme offered 'suitable roles'. In a direct comparison and challenge to American constructs of race, Barry notes that the post-war drama had tended to provide more serious occasions than the Negro butler in some American plays, which had become a cliché. Noted was African-American actor Gordon Heath, who came to

England to appear in the television version of *The Concert* (5 July 1959) (though Earl Cameron appeared in the programme, he is not mentioned) and afterwards in the BBC television production of *Othello* (15 December 1955). Barry also suggested that BBC television had, during 1958, provided the young West Indian playwright Evan Jones with productions of his two first plays, *The Widows of Jaffa* and *In a Backward Country*, though no transmission date for either play is on record. Barry also notes his pleasure at the first prize awarded to the West Indian actor Errol John for his play *Moon on a Rainbow Shawl* in the *Observer* play competition. John had received from Barry a bursary that allowed him to study theatre in the USA for twelve months; Barry notes that he did this in his position as Head of Drama,[11] yet his writing that he did so 'on behalf of the BBC', is stricken out in the memo.

A report filed on Coloured speakers from the *Tonight* programmes of 1958 included the PM of Western Nigeria, Tom Mboya of Kenya's Legislative Council, a university lecturer from Rhodesia about that country's colour bar, singer Harry Belafonte, and a Malayan student who had hitchhiked around the world to come to a university in England. The Premier Chieftainess of Sierra Leone discussed the position of women in Sierra Leone, and three other Asian women discussed forthcoming books. However, on 10 September 1959, Dr La Corbiniere, Deputy PM of the West Indian Federation, discussed the race riots in Notting Hill and Nottingham, as did Nigerians and West Indians in London on 1 September in a filmed report.[12] Also noted was the Midland Region's *Question of Colour*. Also weighing in was Goldie, whose office provided a roster of Coloured people appearing on *Panorama* during 1958. Under the subject line of programmes dealing with the colour problem, eleven guests were listed, with several guests from Africa, India, Ceylon, the United Arab Republic, and China. The Ministers of Trade and Industry discussed agreements between the UK and British Guiana on 30 June, and the Ministers of Labour and Home Affairs appeared on 22 September to discuss emigration and unemployment in Jamaica. *Press Conference* had four guests of colour, none from the West Indies.[13]

Miss A.J. Wright, the secretary to Kenneth Adam, C.P. (Tel), forwarded an acknowledgement that indicated which contributors would be forwarded to McCall. Besides religion, drama, music, and schools, the editors of Women's Programmes explained in the memo that the department had recently provided a thirteen-minute programme on mixed marriages. They also suggested that they quite often had Coloured people in their programmes – a Nigerian midwife, for example. Also mentioned was the recent production of *A Question of Colour* as part of the *Second Enquiry* series.[14] Ultimately, a final report to the CNI states that the general picture of Coloured guests in BBC television programming was very different from the council's impression. In addition to the aforementioned programmes, the *BBC Sunday Night Theatre* featured a production of *The Green Pastures* (14 September 1958), with West Indians Robert Adams, Earl Cameron, Nadia Catouse, and the all-coloured cast of the 1936 film. McCall's response to Adams, sent under the ominous subject line of 'the racial problem', was an expression of thanks.[15]

As another reaction to the irritation of racial problems, the Controller of Program Planning for Sound, H. Rooney Pelletier, confirmed the development of a new post-Notting Hill programme on how the West Indian lives. The programme, placed early in the first quarter of the corporation's broadcast schedule for 1959, was envisaged as a story told by the West Indians themselves and by those people whose decisions affected the lives of West Indians in the UK. Suggested interviewees included officials from London Transport, and from various hospitals where West Indians traditionally worked, and the proposed programme would not confine itself to Notting Hill, nor seek to discuss solutions to the queries and problems that it would stimulate in people's minds; such discussion was the function of other programmes, it was suggested.[16] In a memo dated 18 November 1958, the Assistant Head of the African, Caribbean and Colonial Services, D.P. Wolferstan, wrote to the Controller of Overseas Services to address the possibility of special broadcasts for Caribbean immigrants:

> It seems to be generally agreed that the flow of immigrants from the Caribbean to this country in search of employment is likely to continue for a long time to come and we have been wondering whether there was any contribution that the BBCs Caribbean Service could make by way of explanatory broadcasts for prospective immigrants.[17]

Within the aforementioned memo addressing the creation of the programmes, and accompanying booklet, D.P. Wolferstan also wrote,

> We would go out of our way in both the broadcasts and in the pamphlet to make it clear that we are *not* encouraging West Indians to come here, but trying to help those who for their own reasons decide to do so.[18]

The British Caribbean Welfare Service had suggested that the BBC offer a series of broadcasts describing in the simplest possible terms what life in the UK was like, in the form of fifty five-minute talks on life in England, with tapes of each broadcast available to interested local services in the Caribbean. In conjunction, an illustrated booklet printed by the BBC would contain a summary of each broadcast. The pamphlet would be fifty pages (one talk to a page, plus a foreword), and it was thought that at least 20,000 copies could be distributed. The BBC suggested that every effort be made to not date the broadcasts and the pamphlets so that the whole project was of more than ephemeral value, and there was a strong reference to the BBC not giving out information about prospects of employment in any particular industry. It was regarded as a worthwhile undertaking, the successful accomplishment of which would reflect considerable credit on the BBC. As discussed in this chapter, the text was designed in many ways to dissuade immigrants from the Caribbean.

The BBC, academics, and immigration issues

Academic voices signalled a further concern over racialism and hostilities against West Indians, as noted during a London Council of Social Service conference at Oxford in September 1961. The subjects discussed indicated a move away from issues of adjustment by the immigrant 'newcomers' in the mid-1950s, and more toward sociological analyses of racial hostility and stereotyping. Contents for an episode of BBC's *Tonight* for the following month included a segment from Alan Whicker about West Indians returning to 'their own country'.[19] Meanwhile, a concerned ENCA initiated discussions on the content of *Panorama* in the light of the reputation it was acquiring for exposing problems, yet showing bias against conservative views on immigration issues.[20] Subsequently, two distinct discourses arose regarding these efforts: those involving 'colonial' West Indians anxious for acceptance as 'black English', and Asians with a 'strongly cohesive family-based culture that resisted complete assimilation to British culture and mores'.[21] Harman Grisewood later told J.A. Camacho (the Head of Talks and Current Affairs, Sound, involved in the development of the show) of a 'highly reputable piece of field research work into racial relations in Notting Hill', referring to Pearl Jephcott's forthcoming book, *A Troubled Area*. The author arranged for the BBC to receive an advance copy 'and/or to meet the principal people concerned', as a roster of academics doing field studies of coloured people in Britain was included in the programme. They all worked in the Department of Social Anthropology at Edinburgh University with Kenneth Little, including A.T. Carey, who researched relationships between colonial students and British students, accommodation, and colour prejudice, while Sheila Webster undertook similar work on West African and West Indian students at Oxford University. Michael Banton examined colonial immigrants living in the Dockland area of London, and Coloured working-class employment. Violaine Junod's work on the Coloured social elite in London included an 'estimation of the position of educated coloured people in British middle class society', possibilities for leadership roles, and their interpersonal relationships with each other; E.B. Ndem concentrated upon Coloured people in Manchester with descriptions and analyses of their social organisation and 'relations with white people'; and S.F. Collins described the social organisation of groups of West Indians, West Africans, Arabs, and Somalis engaged in seafaring. This examination included adjustments to life in Britain, and 'the role of white women' in the latter respect. Handwritten notes from Camacho suggested that these research efforts and 'Little's book, *Negroes in Britain*', be considered as background research, as should 'Collins' social study in Jamaica', considered 'very relevant' by Camacho, since Collins 'himself [was] a Jamaican'.[22]

A proposal was also accepted by C.F.O. Clarke for a thirty-minute talks feature programme, *Generation of Strangers*, from producer Anne Owen of the Midland Region, about Coloured children in schools. His office requested that the Midland service prepare the programme to broadcast 'well ahead of any programme on Notting Hill'.[23] Ultimately, Richard Hooper, with support from Camacho, produced a project called *Colour in Britain*, creating the radio series and accompanying book.

The Head of Secretariat, A.L. Hutchinson, cites an article from the *Guardian*[24] and a study conducted on Commonwealth students visiting the country. He notes that 'the question of coloured immigration and the adaptation of coloured citizens to British life [are] once again uppermost in the news', and passes on a suggestion received from the Commonwealth Relations Office about the article, and the book *Disappointed Guests* by social scientists Tajfel and Dawson. The book's commentaries from students, and an essay by the Institute of Race Relations, claim that the 'main stumbling block for coloured students in Britain' was the difficulty of 'obtaining and keeping lodgings', and that it 'is hardly possible to exaggerate the immense impact that landladies have on the image of Britain'. However, within the book's epilogue, students were polled on what action should be taken to educate White Britons, and noted was the elimination of stereotypes (golliwogs, minstrels, etc.). Further, the book emphasises the elimination of BBC programmes on 'backward' Africa, and the 'primitive nature of the lands and peoples from which the students came', images not clearly representing 'the developments which are taking place today', and only adding to the 'general ignorance about their countries'.[25]

This was the situation in the country when the BBC acquired a second channel, and a new direction under Director-General Sir Hugh Greene in 1960 ignited the possibilities for a liberalist platform for television programmes on, among other socially relevant issues, race relations.

Greene and the programming of race

As the BBC's charter came up for renewal amid fears of the populist programming on Independent Television (ITV), the government's intentions to authorise a third television channel leaned heavily toward the BBC, which was the preference of the Pilkington Committee.[26] In the days prior to the establishment of ITV, BBC TV as a single-channel operation held a great degree of control over the British population and the cultural production of a nation. When commercial television began on 22 September 1955, following Royal Assent of the 1954 Television Act introduced by the Conservative Government, and despite the controversy surrounding the power of advertisers to potentially affect content, its supervision under the Independent Television Authority (ITA) was firmly established. Much like the BBC's board of governors, the government held the power of appointment as Reithian values of the public-service concept still pervaded broadcasting, due to a more general distrust of what commercial television represented.

At the BBC, concerns had arisen over Cecil McGivern, the Controller of Programmes since 1950, who had been obsessed with programme detail, and, according to Goldie, was prepared to take responsibility for the Television Service as a whole.[27] Many assumed that McGivern would become Director, and appoint a Controller of Programmes; however, he wanted to maintain the authority he had earned and become Deputy Director of Television. In 1957 the BBC eventually chose as the new Controller *Manchester Guardian* journalist Kenneth Adam, who had worked previously for the BBC as Director of Television. Stuart Hood, previous Editor of Television News, became Controller of Television Programmes, and Donald Baverstock, formally of the *Tonight* news team, became Assistant Controller; P.A. Findlay became head of BBC News and Current Affairs in 1958, the same year as Notting Hill and Nottingham, and ridiculed the corporation's television news as lacking style and topicality.

New Director-General Hugh Greene told the Television Service that without any abandonment of BBC standards they must aim at increasing an audience share from its 'lowest ration of 27:73 to 50:50 by the time the Pilkington Committee reported. That was exactly achieved at the beginning of 1963'. Further, he noted,

> The Pilkington Report seemed to us at the time a gratifying vindication of all that the BBC had been trying to do. We had hoped for an endorsement of the aims of public service broadcasting based on a licence fee system and we got it; we had hoped for an endorsement of one BBC, of the advantages of a unified system of public service broadcasting covering radio, television and our external services and we got it; we had hoped for a second television channel which would provide viewers with a genuine choice of programmes and we got it; ... By the early 1960s, many of the old hands in the BBC who thought we were going too fast and too far were leaving. A new and younger generation was in control and there was a remarkable flowering of production and writing talent.[28]

The BBC's efforts under Greene demonstrated the corporation's concerns for a desire to serve all of its audiences, but with more of a grassroots approach toward the average citizen and their tastes, unlike the Reithian tradition of catering to middle-class values. It is also evident that the organisation clearly needed to underscore these efforts and demonstrate to any doubters its commitment to – and involvement of – Coloured people in its broadcasts and programmes. In Greene's push for change and improved services for audiences, issues of race, though not clearly pronounced, are evident. News commentator Richard Dimbleby's work on *Panorama* helped expose the events of the Sharpeville massacre in 1960, when White South African police shot and killed sixty-nine Black South Africans demonstrating against the 'pass laws'. Previously, Greene had praised Christopher Mayhew's *International Commentary* segment on South Africa, produced by Goldie, for its upholding the BBC's impartiality and balance in its analysis of the system of apartheid, without claiming tolerance for racialism.[29] Smith, in his work on apartheid and Sharpeville, notes Greene's address, entitled *The Conscience of the Programme Director*, to the International Catholic Association for Radio and Television in 1965. In a presentation rife with acknowledgments of clergy, autonomy, and basic standards of broadcasting, Greene also explained that though the BBC aspires to remain impartial in its treatment of news and current events, 'there are some respects in which it is not neutral, unbiased or impartial', such as the events of Sharpeville, and the policies of the South African government.[30]

Harman Grisewood, Chief Assistant to the Director-General, had already forwarded information to Greene regarding proposals to interview Oswald Mosley and neo-Nazi advocate Colin Jordan on *Panorama* and a Midland Regional programme respectively. Greene expressed concerns, and though freedom of speech could be supported through recordings of fascist meetings, it would 'not be right to offer a platform to Sir Oswald Mosley, Colin Jordan or other fascist leaders by arranging special interviews'. He recognised that, in the case of television news, reporting a press conference through a subsequent interview was necessary provided the result was no more than reporting, and used for news value only.[31] Notes from a Controller's meeting of 6 February 1962 indicate that neither Mosley nor Dr Alan Nunn-May was a suitable subject for the *Face-to-Face* programme.[32]

On 20 April 1964, the BBC2 TV service began, considered by the dominant press to be the most important event since the BBC began broadcasting again following World War Two.[33] The London television market was considered the most important sector, and the south of England now had a choice of three channels – BBC1, BBC2, and ITV. Michael Peacock, former producer of *Panorama*, headed the new channel, and considered BBC2 'younger than the rest', offering a choice of alternative programming.

Peacock also felt that the fresh blood encouraged by Greene could help BBC2 'give talented young people a chance that BBC1 or ITV cannot give', and the channel would take risks, provided there were few mistakes, and his staff 'learned from them'. As he stated in an interview with the *Evening News* in 1963:

> No matter how big the minority interest, [the] Service has to first consider filling peak hours to majority taste. They dare not cater to minorities because BBC1 would lose audiences to ITV and the object is to hold the audience … but we in BBC2 will be able to appeal to minority and majority audiences and give them all kinds of shows.[34]

Also noted in the article was a reminder from Director-General Greene that BBC2 would open officially on 20 April, which was also Adolf Hitler's birthday. Though noting nothing significant about this coincidence, he did anticipate a possible sketch on *That Was The Week That Was* (*TW3*).[35]

Initially, a fire at the Battersea power station interrupted the first night of broadcasting, and BBC2 had attracted fewer than one million viewers, who then tuned in for less than one hour a week.[36] Within four weeks, a harsh criticism published in the *Daily Mirror* came from 'an anonymous television chief' who attacked Peacock and BBC2 for faulty planning, and a flawed broadcast policy. The critic noted that the 'once mighty monopoly' was 'running scared as it realized that its two channels are competing with each other for the minority audiences ITV had left them'. However, Richard Sear, the *Mirror*'s TV critic, disagreed, noting that BBC2 still had to find its audience. Whilst he agreed that the eight million pounds spent on broadcast as conversions was not worth it at that point, he felt it would be eventually. He noted that BBC2 would extend the range of television, offer viewers an alternative, cater to the minority audience, and 'stick spurs into the flagging horse of BBC1 and ITV'.[37]

The new BBC channel began to emphasise that each night of the programming week would have a different theme. Peacock's staff released a programming table that offered grand occasions programmes such as opera on Sundays, humorous shows on Mondays, and educational programmes on Tuesdays, whilst Wednesday nights would be reserved for repeats of successful programmes that had run on either BBC1 or BBC2. Thursdays were for leisure, including hobby programmes and sports, and Fridays offered dramatic fare. Saturdays would present 'contrast' shows, or various forms of entertainment.[38] The basic approach to programming was also becoming clear. Peacock's original intention had been to maintain the original programming schema for the first eighteen months of service. However, within the first year, BBC2 scrapped its original programming in an attempt to gain more viewers. The emphasis would shift away from 'the old, rigid pattern of devoting each night to a single type of programme'.[39] Scrapped was, as David Attenborough called it, the 'Seven Faces of BBC2' for fear of losing viewers for entire night's worth of shows.[40] This change was to coincide with the broadcasting of BBC2 from Birmingham as well as London. However, BBC2 was yet to incorporate a plan for programming to ethnic audiences.

After his appointment to Director-General, Greene began to encourage talent and more unconventional ways of approaching the onus of public service and education as mandated by his colleague, Reith. By 1962, the year of the BBC's fortieth anniversary and two years before the birth of BBC2, Greene was credited with helping to green-light programmes considered controversial in their depictions of class considerations and urban life. This, of course, incorporated issues related to Blacks and immigrants. The BBC also sought to incorporate more light entertainment, including gritty dramas such as *The Wednesday Play* (1964–70), which, with its offerings of *Up the Junction* (3 November 1965), *Fable* (27 January 1965), and *Cathy Come Home* (16 November 1966), proved highly controversial in the eyes of the public, notably clean-up-TV campaigner Mary Whitehouse. The programmes *Steptoe and Son* (1962–74) and the considerably irreverent and self-reflexive *TW3* (1962–63), also broadcast and adapted by NBC, drew upon Greene's love of cabaret-influenced entertainment.[41] These programmes, along with the highly popular *Monty Python's Flying Circus* (1969–74), became a sign of Greene's intent to increase audiences and reach out to the public.

Another in this series of more populist programmes, *Z Cars* (1962–78), had originally been produced by the documentary department, and the realism the programme brought to television screens gave it even more credence, illustrated in the immigrant vs. landlord misunderstanding of the 'A Place of Safety' (24 June 1964) episode featuring Johnny Sekka and Alaknanda Samarth. A problem with late rent and a gruff bailiff causes Sekka's Adigun Sadik to attack the process server with an axe, to the horror of his Asian wife. Ultimately PCs Smith (Brian Blessed) and Weir (Joseph Brady) become involved, as does Detective Chief Inspector Barlow (Stratford Johns) and Detective Sergeant Watt (Frank Windsor). In a famous sequence of scenes, Sadik is within his cell that night, alone. His children lay awake at home, staring at the ceiling, concerned about their father; as Weir and Smith drive his wife home, she condemns them for not showing more compassion. As they eventually drive away to answer a call, the policemen express relief; relief over the opportunity to deal with a flat-out crime, not an issue surrounded by grey areas of social misfortune.[42] The problematic circumstances and subsequent discourses surrounding immigrant families are represented by a Black male (thought to be African or West Indian) and Asian female (probably Pakistani).

It is seemingly ironic that the most popular programme during these early years to regularly engage with race was Johnny Speight's *Till Death Us Do Part* featuring Cockney bigot Alf Garnett, played by Warren Mitchell. This character's utterance of prejudice and xenophobia served as a double-edged sword within contemporary popular culture. There were viewers who loved to hate him due to his ignorance, and those who loved the character as a representative of traditional Britishness. One episode 'In Sickness and in Health' (BBC 1, 13 February 1967), found Alf visiting his regular doctor, only to find that he's away on holiday and has been temporarily replaced by a 'blackie', prompting a waiting room full of patients to leave. Alf reacts with such shock and horror that his sore throat becomes immediately worse, and he completely loses his voice. Before the scene ends, however, the doctor provides relief for an appreciative Alf, who blames his regular doctor for hiring the replacement, stating that he should have known the doctor would not fit in. He remarks, in a moment of imagined insight, that most of his neighbours 'think you still live in trees, all your lot'.[43]

During this time of change, it remained apparent that programming such as *TW3* represented a stronger platform for the critique of government policies as related to race and immigration, though these topics may have challenged Greene's administration. As suggested by Goldie, Donald Baverstock and Alasdair Milne provided tremendous contributions to the shaping of the programme.[44] The men had worked together closely on *Tonight*, and hoped that *TW3* would operate within similar editorial guidelines as the news magazine; instead, however, the programme's mockery of politicians, particularly John Profumo, the monarchy, and religious values created more difficulties in the long run than many could have envisioned. It is difficult to understand how a programme like *TW3* did not see an opportunity to critique race relations from a satirical perspective, but it is difficult to recall any episodes that did and difficult to find any research indicating this effort.

As the 1960s progressed, civil rights continued to become a highly publicised issue in the USA. The BBC drew upon these struggles as a source of topical information. Race riots had already taken place in London and around the country, partly as a reaction to the increased presence of West Indians. Yet, in an attempt to address the issue of civil rights, the service presented programming that examined Black life in America. The programmes featured on BBC radio, slated as a 'sudden burst of programmes about the Negro' by the London press, offered a series of specials on the Third Programme.[45] One programme in eighteen episodes, entitled *The Negro in America*, investigated contributions by Blacks to American life. Later in this same week, however, BBC2 featured *White Man's World*, a documentary that investigated Coloured and White relations in

Britain. Discussions included West Indians, with an emphasis on the problematic circumstances that surrounded their arrival, and language barriers
confronting Asians.[46]

The presence of others, and programming concerns

In January of 1965, Russian-born journalist Taya Zinkin wrote a series of
articles published in the *Manchester Guardian* addressing how immigrants,
particularly women, could assimilate into English culture. In one that
addressed non-English-speaking Indians, she noted that

> The most rural of immigrants have transistor radios, most immigrants
> dwellings have a television set. The BBC finds time once a fortnight for a tele-
> vision programme for the deaf and dumb; it should find time, at least once a
> week, for a programme in Hindustani (understood by both Indians and
> Pakistanis).[47]

Postmaster General Anthony Wedgwood Benn forwarded this article to
Greene, and two others, with a letter addressing Bedford's Italian population, and Zinkin's concerns over a sense of xenophobia among Britons.
Greene thanked Benn for his efforts, and noted that discussions about
programmes for immigrants had taken place at a recent meeting of the
General Advisory Council. Opinions about the desirability of special
programmes as discussed in Zinkin's article were evenly divided, 'but some
of the people closest to the problem through their daily work were doubtful
about the wisdom of doing anything which might tend to emphasize the
apartness of coloured immigrants'.[48] Greene wrote to Phillip Mason of the
Institute of Race Relations about the same possibility, and expressed the
same concerns as he did to Benn, yet Mason was in favour of such broadcasts, particularly for Pakistani and Indian women. However, Greene
expressed a need to gather data on location, and available viewing and
listening facilities for audiences, and to continue discussions about this
problem with the Institute of Race Relations. He also expressed a desire to
get more advice from them, and to keep Mason in touch with the BBC's
ideas as they developed. He suggested that the BBC had already done a
special series of informational programmes to the Caribbean Service
addressed to immigrants intending to come to Britain. He felt that this effort
fit in with the desirability for training *before* people go to live in a new
environment.[49]

When considering the intent to educate these immigrant audiences on life
in Briton, the Head of Northern Regional Programmes (HNRP), G.D. Miller,
reported that the Education Officer, North West, had produced a report on
Adult Education interests, and found that the 'old-style adult education is

old-hat and out of date'. People were not interested in international affairs, or extra-mural education offered via sound, but immigrant groups were supposedly more interested in things at a much lower, less sophisticated level; issues that related more to 'their homes, children', and such. Therefore, he believed in a serious examination of programmes for immigrants since integration, as a social problem, was becoming more acute.[50] Yet, in a memo from television secretariat Colin Shaw, a suggestion was made that was far from racially sensitive:

> Have you ever considered the possibility of mounting a regular programme for West Indians in this country? It is not possible that combination of West Indian rhythms and news from home would be a useful service to provide and might interest other listeners. While there is some danger that such a programme might underline the separate status of West Indians in the British community, it is questionable whether more harm than good would be done. (It might be called Spades are Trumps.)[51]

A number of organisations wrote letters to BBC management critical of programming choices. A major complaint was that race programmes simply did not go far enough to stress the similarities of cultures as opposed to problems in assimilation. Director-General Hugh Greene, at a meeting with Regional Controllers in March of 1965, had expressed concerns that special programmes for coloured immigrants should not emphasise the 'apartness' of the Coloured community, reemphasised this concern to the BBC's Regional Controllers.[52] In agreement was famed West Indian cricketer Sir Learie Constantine, who also served as a member of the BBC General Advisory Council, but other members of the General Advisory Council were less convinced. From the meeting notes with Hugh Greene, it is clear that Robert Stead, Controller of the North Region, also stated that it was doubtful whether immigrants would listen to such programmes, 'judging from the evidence already in hand to the lack of initiative many immigrants were showing toward helping themselves acclimate to British life'.[53]

Constantine, through the General Advisory Council, had already requested that the BBC strongly consider more employment of Coloured people, in the External Services in particular.[54] The Controller of Staff Training and Appointments, L.G. Thirkell, requested a copy of minutes from a recent board of management meeting in which Constantine's suggestion was considered 'hardly practicable'.[55] Greene asked that Sir Learie be made aware of the on-going recruitment of non-White programme staff for domestic services. However, Director of Administration (DA) J.H. Arkell, in a memorandum to Greene, expressed no knowledge of any specific plans to train non-White programme staff, other than an attempt by the BBC to hire a Coloured announcer.[56] Concurrently, a report from Assistant Head of

Appointments Gillott compiled the employment of Coloured people in the BBC. In a report to the DA on the employment of Coloured people in External Services, and the BBC generally, examined four groups: Africans, West Indians, Indians, and Pakistanis. The division reportedly employed 76 Coloured people, made up of 35 Africans (25 Programme Assistants, two Monitors, eight secretarial); 18 Indians (10 Programme Assistants, one Monitor, one Studio Manager, one assistant in Audience Research, five secretarial); 14 West Indians (three Programme Assistants, one Monitor, five secretarial, five Newsroom Attendants); and nine Pakistanis (eight Programme Assistants, one secretarial). The Central Services Group (CSG) employed 83 Coloured staff members, not including a considerable number (mainly Nigerians) recruited casually each day for work as kitchen porters in catering.[57] These included 42 West Indians, 33 Africans, and eight Indians and Pakistanis, 35 of whom worked in catering, 38 in manual posts and 10 clerical. The Engineering Division reported 25–30 Coloured men in manual posts in various departments. The report noted that a few (perhaps six a year) applications were received from Coloured people for engineering posts, but 'none of them have been well enough qualified to be serious candidates'.

In Television, one Pakistani Director on Grade B1 was employed, whereas there were three Indians in the Film Department (two Assistant Film Cameramen and one Assistant Film Editor; all in C posts). There were five Coloured secretaries (including two Production Secretaries) and one Dressmaker. It was again noted that the 'DA will be aware that DTel. is considering the employment of coloured people in Television Presentation'. Finance employed 12 Coloured staff, mostly in secretarial/clerical posts, but including 'one African in a Grade B post in Internal Audit'. A scattering of other areas reported four or five Coloured people in secretarial/clerical posts in Publications Management and one Indian secretary in Appointments Department. The Secretary A Division had two Coloured people in posts on secretarial grades and an Indian, who hoped to obtain professional qualifications, had been selected for a clerical post in Club Accounts.[58] In April of that year, Jamaican born Eric Abrahams was touted by the *Sunday Telegraph*, as the 'first coloured person to have been accepted by the Corporation at this level [a TV reporter]', prompting a note from Thirkell to the Editor that Abrahams and fifty other Coloured employees were on grades roughly equivalent to that of trainee reporters.[59] In a proceeding memo, Thirkell called the notice hardly 'worth a reply', since the television group 'hardly appeared at [its] best' when trying to correct misconceptions in the paper.[60]

It was also during 1965 that the *Colour in Britain* radio series on the BBC's Third Programme was receiving critical acclaim for providing a balanced look at race relations within the country. In addition, the BBC planned special broadcasts for the immigrant communities of the north-west (such as *English by Radio*, programmed for Indian and Pakistani immigrants). These programmes underscored a belief by Greene that management should re-examine educational programmes about racial relations and, more importantly, cultural assimilation. In a report cautiously entitled *The Immigrant Problem*, Greene described a meeting with Maurice Foley, Parliamentary Under-Secretary of State in the Department of Economic Affairs, who had special responsibility for coordinating the work of the various departments concerned with Commonwealth immigrants. Greene and Foley were concerned with what role BBC radio and television could play in the assimilation of all immigrant groups, but primarily West Indians, Indians, and Pakistanis. Foley emphasised the urgency of the need for language teaching for Indians and Pakistanis, and advice to immigrants about many aspects of life in Britain. Greene advised him of the correspondence with Mason and the Institute of Race Relations, who agreed that the problem was most acute in London, the Midlands, and Yorkshire. Foley felt there was evidence that Indians and Pakistanis relied more on television than on radio partly because they so often had little or no knowledge of the English language. Greene explained the daunting financial problems involved in the production of special television programmes as well as sound broadcasts; therefore, the experimental efforts on radio in the London, Midland, and North Regions would provide some guidelines before the use of television began. Greene further explained that, to formulate the plan, the BBC would host two separate conferences. Leaders of the Indian and Pakistani communities would attend the first, whilst people concerned with the West Indian communities would attend the second conference. Also invited would be social workers, directors of education and a representative of the clergy. Learie Constantine would attend both conferences as an observer.

At the first conference, the BBC featured sample recordings of *English by Radio* lessons prepared for Hindi- and Urdu-speaking audiences, whilst at the second conference audiences heard examples of Overseas Services programmes giving advice to West Indian immigrants. Greene also discussed making 'suitable films' in the BBC Television Enterprises catalogue available to immigrants curious about life in England. Greene felt this was a natural connection to the special series already offered by the Caribbean Service, and he expressed a desire for some degree of feedback and advice on what each community felt about the corporation's efforts.[61] The efforts of the BBC within the Asian immigrant community directly addressed the challenges of assimilation through an understanding of the English language. However, concerns for the West Indian community clearly incorporated marked cultural differences between their lived communities and the British public.

'How can we help you?' Sir Hugh and the Coloured conferences

In July of 1965, the Press Officer of the Television Service sent a message to several news organisations announcing a series of planned conferences in which BBC management (including Director-General Hugh Greene) would meet with selected 'coloured guests' to discuss immigration issues. A press announcement from the BBC Evening Press Officer, Dulcie J. Marshall, was distributed to the Press Association, Exchange Telegraph, Jewish Telegraphic Agency, Reuters (UK Desk), and the United Press International's Television Department. The first conference on the sixth would specifically discuss the problems of Indian and Pakistani immigrants.[62] The second conference on 13 July in the Council Chamber at Broadcasting House would be with representatives of the West Indian community as 'the guests of the BBC'.[63] The meeting, led by Greene, welcomed representatives from more than twenty Coloured organisations concerned about the impact of immigrants in London, the Midlands, and the north. Joining Greene was Chief Assistant O.J. Whitley; H.G. Campey, Head of Publicity; D. Stephenson, Head of Overseas and Foreign Relations; F.G. Gillard, Director of Sound Broadcasting; and others trusted with the new direction of the corporation.[64]

The Asian conference

In attendance at the first conference were various members of the Asian community, including Dr D.R. Prem, Activist, Liberal Parliamentary candidate and Birmingham's first Asian Labour councillor; Tassaduq Ahmed, prominent community leader, and associate of the Centre for the Study of Minorities; and educator, activist, and scholar Mrs Hansa Mehta, among others.[65] In an effort to serve these people, BBC management discussed further development of the programme *Make Yourself at Home*, touted as a new BBC service for Indian and Pakistani immigrants. The segments would run on radio and television and were planned for transmission beginning 10 October 1965. In a report filed by Producer David Gretton, the programme is described as a 'simple *English by Radio* series in basic Urdu/Hindi', and 'compiled to take account of the everyday situations in which immigrants find themselves in this country'.[66] The approach involved radio broadcasts early Sunday mornings on medium wave (for the north, Midlands, and London) on the Home Service, and each programme included lessons in English. Featured were the characters of Mr and Mrs Chaudury, along with their family and friends, and the problems immigrants might meet in their daily lives. Listeners would meet the Chaudury family on the first broadcast *Mrs Chaudury goes Shopping*.[67] Also included was popular music from current Indian and Pakistani films as a means of drawing audiences. Much like 'The Immigrant Saga' in American radio programming, as discussed by Hilmes, the BBC's efforts to personify the immigrant Chaudury family and their attempts at assimilation would create an interest in the programme. Whilst clearly not designed for a more general audience, and not the same kind of creative narrative inspired by Gertrude Berg's life and family, the programme could potentially do what *The Rise of the Goldbergs* sought to do: teach immigrants how to belong. As Hilmes noted:

> Early scripts of *The Rise of the Goldbergs* concerned themselves explicitly and intimately with an immigrant Jewish family's assimilation into American life. Just as Berg chose to begin her 1961 autobiography with the story of her grandfather, Mordecai Edelstein from Lublin, Poland, and his worship of America, Christopher Columbus, and assimilation into this new world, so these elements are emphasized in the lives of the Goldbergs: Molly, Jake, Sammy, and Rosie.[68]

The programme, planned for repetition on Wednesdays at 12.25 p.m., invited Indian and Pakistani listeners to forward questions, and problems, to the BBC Broadcasting House in Birmingham. General Talks received copies of selected letters and questions, and arranged for research and translation for broadcast.

Meanwhile, on BBC1, a programme Gretton called a 'combination of *Can I Help You* and *News from Home*'[69] would run on Sunday mornings, from 9.00 a.m. until 9.15 a.m., in which guests speaking in Hindustani would discuss 'common difficulties, and answer questions about life in Britain'. The programme also featured a weekly newsletter script in Urdu/Hindi, read by a local anchor in Birmingham. Additional news items of special interest came from news sources in London and the regions, which were then forwarded to the area. Occasional interviews with distinguished guests, well-known musicians, and film stars were also included in the show's content.

Since Whitley's office had identified the main concentration of immigrants as living in London, the West Midlands, and Yorkshire, Greene and BBC management decided that these programmes should be organised under the direction of Midland Regional Controller, Patrick Beech, and produced in the Birmingham studios.[70] With support from the Midland Region headquarters, and via the input of many invited to the Indian and Pakistani meetings with Greene earlier that year, the BBC set up an advisory committee to discuss programme content, as carefully detailed in a press release to many of the same organisations alerted to the immigrant conferences.[71] In the minutes of the Controller's meeting for 6 September 1965, the Director noted the good press coverage of the BBC's plans for programmes for immigrants, 'which had been achieved without a press conference'.

An Advisory Committee for Immigrants' Programmes was created, with noted author and scholar Philip Mason, the Director of the Institute of Race Relations, as Chairman.[72] The Advisory Committee planned to meet in Birmingham, about three times a year, with the first meeting to take place in November 1965 – after members had an opportunity to see and hear the first series of programmes.[73] However, after the Editor of News and Current Affairs Donald Edwards expressed the need for editorial discretion in the reporting of topical items, it was noted that the newsletter portion of the proposed programme would likely be dropped, due to concerns over specific materials being too controversial. Diretor-General Greene agreed, noting that content only included educational material, music, and language instruction. This followed a request by the Eastern Service to arrange an interview with President Radhakrishnan of India, forcing a decision whether or not to arrange a talk by President Ayub Khan of Pakistan for political balance.[74]

The West Indian conference

The conference held with leaders of the Indian and Pakistani communities had helped the BBC to recognise that their problems were, in many ways, *different* from those of West Indians. The focus of the West Indian meeting seemed highly encouraging in that Greene stated the Service recognised that the problems of West Indians were unique, and that the main purpose of the conference was to provide an opportunity for the BBC to learn from those present what the West Indian problems were and how the BBC could help. The BBC had held a list of societies and organisations identifying Coloured groups in the mid-1950s as important sources for televised interviews and talks by management.These included the popular West Indian Students Union, the Stepney League of Coloured People, the Anglo Caribbean Club, and the League of Coloured Peoples.[75] In preparation for the West Indian conference, O.J. Whitley, had sent a note to Greene as evidence of the 'BBC's interest in coloured people', and of the frequent representation of them and their views. He suggested that the DG mention the programmes *Our God Is Black* (BBC1, 6 July 1965), *Frankly Speaking* with Prime Minister of Uganda Milton Obote on the Home Service (9 July 1965), and the Reith Lectures on race relations, by author Robert Gardiner, entitled *A World of Peoples*. Also suggested was mention of the appointment of a Jamaican as a Home Service announcer.[76]

The Director-General noted there were 'two sides' to the BBC's problem. One was to decide how the BBC should make West Indians feel at home in the UK, and the other was to educate public opinion, both in general and in the particular communities in which West Indians lived. With regard to the second part of the problem, it was unfortunate that there was no system of local broadcasting, because this could prove an excellent way of reaching the communities, and discussing their day-to-day problems. As it was, the BBC had to depend on its existing regional and national services in radio and television, not forgetting, however, the External Services whose Caribbean service made a useful contribution. For those who were interested, there was available a booklet, *Going to Britain*, which was based on a series of talks given in the Caribbean Service to prepare would-be immigrants for the life they would meet. He stated,

> The information that we seek from you this morning falls under two main headings: first, what can we do for immigrants in our broadcasts; and secondly, what can we do about immigrants directly or indirectly to improve the climate of public opinion; and, beyond that, how can the BBC's efforts, which must necessarily be to some extent limited, be integrated with what the central Government is doing, with what local authorities are doing, with what local education is doing and what local welfare organisations are doing. Then there is a lot of detailed information which would be helpful and which, I hope, will emerge during the discussion: what, for instance, are the listening and viewing habits of West Indians in this country, if it is possible to generalise at all? Do they prefer television, or do they prefer radio? Are there any arrangements for group listening or viewing or any organised form of further education especially directed to West Indians? Those are some of the points, which, I hope, will emerge.[77]

Within the proceedings, attendees had the opportunities to express concerns over the Service's plans for future race-related programming. Among the many suggestions made were that there be more documentaries to give the other side of the West Indian situation and that 'programmes giving the historical background of the link between Britain and the West Indies would be useful'. It was suggested that educational programming by television and radio should focus upon educating the *British* public in accepting West Indians as *citizens* – not just *educating* West Indians to be citizens. Representations of West Indian life and subsequent customs and behaviour were also principal issues. Cited by R.E.K. Philips, Chief Welfare Officer, Office of the High Commissioner for Jamaica, was a BBC programme about life in Jamaica *A Little Bit of Madness* (BBC, 1965), produced in conjunction with the Jamaican Broadcasting Company. Philips felt that the documentary showed a very small aspect of life in the islands, yet helped to spread the idea that every 'black man in the street' was uncivilised and had lower ethical standards. Philips noted that one of the 'principal roles, whether it be sound or television, must be in the interest of helping to build the right climate of relationships in this society'. His further concerns included a matter of education via radio or television, 'of the British public into acceptance; into recognising that the differences which they might claim on the basis of stereotype, do not really exist'. Philips explained to Greene and other managers that the BBC had already received concerns over the programme, yet ignored the concerns. He notes,

> It was pointed out to the BBC that this was an unfortunate programme. They disputed it, and we had a further slap in the face by a repeat of the programme. I do not think that this is very helpful to the situation. I raise the matter at this stage because I should sincerely hope that we are not just here to discuss things because this is the done thing, but that we are here because there is genuine interest in arriving at some way of dealing with these situations, that any comments we make will be regarded with a measure of weight and that, so far as policy will allow, these words will be taken into consideration. I assume that I will speak further in the discussion, but at this stage, I merely wish to have this assurance.

Greene disagreed with Philips, citing the programme as a 'brilliant documentary, made in association with the Jamaican Broadcasting Corporation', which seemed to provide some measure of authenticity, and 'an accurate picture of a certain aspect of life in Jamaica. It had pretended to be no more than this, and any unfortunate side effects could have arisen only through misunderstanding of its aim.' He also noted the important point that, as a single programme, it did not represent BBC policy in any way. Philips retorted,

> I do not question the brilliance of the documentary. I do not suggest that anything false was stated in the film. This is something which I have no objection to being shown to people who can relate it to the rest of the society, but different results are to be expected when you show this as a mass thing when people already have false notions of families which live in the street because they are coloured – 'Out you go, because you lower the standards' – and yet, if you closed the door of the house, you would never realise that the occupants were West Indian people and children.

Another speaker, J.E. Fraser, formerly of the West Indies Commission, said the primary concern of those present should be to improve relationships between the English people and West Indians. It would be necessary first to realise, however, that there were differences which the mass of people were not, in his view, 'capable of accepting'. He felt that the BBC should avoid 'excessive condemnation of what West Indians did' in the UK, and should not be condescending. The guiding aim should always to put the 'other side of the picture when dealing with subjects concerning West Indian immigrants'. In conjunction with previous concerns expressed, Fraser noted,

Alongside what Mr Philips has said, I should like to say that before we begin to think seriously about improving relations, West Indians and others concerned with this problem must first accept that there are differences. What are the things, which appear to trigger this increase of racial feeling? One point that stands out to my mind is the desire on the part of, possibly, the Press and, possibly, even the BBC unconsciously perhaps to condemn excessively … in my view, any approach which suggests an attitude of condescending to tolerate West Indians would not get very far.

Mrs P. Crabbe, Welfare Secretary for the National Council for the Unmarried Mother and Her Child, said it would help greatly if West Indians or Africans could be 'used more in programmes simply as people in their own right and in their own jobs', highlighting representations that stressed normalcy. She felt that the BBC could 'get away from the tendency of thinking of coloured people who appear on programmes only as entertainers'. She noted that, because she is West Indian, this would be one of the ways of helping with liaison and getting day-to-day acceptance. The Director-General entirely accepted this point, yet proudly reveled in the appointment of a West Indian BBC announcer. Greene explained how the BBC had appointed Dwight Wyley, and another West Indian, Mr Eric Abrahams, who would shortly join *Panorama*. Mrs Thirlwell, Adviser to the Paddington Overseas Students and Workers Committee, regretted that the BBC had publicly announced its appointment, noting that it should have been unnecessary to draw attention to a perfectly natural event. She notes,

> For example, it is fine that we have a West Indian announcer, but probably you should not have said, 'We have appointed a West Indian announcer'. When Stuart Hall, for instance, was appointed to the Youth Council or whatever it is called, he was described as a lecturer in Richard Hoggart's department at Birmingham University; they did not say that he was a West Indian. When a child in Smethwick got typhoid, why not say that a child in Smethwick got typhoid instead of saying that it was a West Indian child? She may have been born here.

Philip Mason of the Institute of Race Relations also expressed concern over the highlighting of difference. He discussed his appearance on *Panorama* years before, after which he had received letters describing his participation on the programme as 'the same, old BBC brainwashing, putting across the fact that immigrants are just like anybody else', further,

> Because there had been shown an educated West Indian and this was described as untypical and brainwashing. This is the danger, obviously, if you put across a message too strongly. I should, therefore, very much like to second what Mrs Crabbe said about making it natural and not too much of a message.

Mason discussed the possibility of a programme that provided a history of Britain's relationship to the West Indies, but concerns arose over the past colonial relationship. He noted that 'it would show that we in Britain owe a debt to the West Indies and this would almost be bound to show the West Indies in the slave days and the arrival of people from Africa'. Despite this, Mrs Jeffrey felt a series of programmes could help to provide history as to why slavery developed, and other myths 'which one has to kill'. Mason suggested that a highly educated audience would get the best out of the programme. Philips stated that balance of representations of social issues was essential. He felt that the press and television alike fell into the same rut of approaching issues with a degree of sensationalism and 'anything to incite'. Philips notes,

> It is no secret, for example, that on Monday night on *Gallery* you had [the] Ku Klux Klan [on the programme], and by Wednesday night you had crosses being lit in Leamington Spa. It is all very well to talk about a lunatic fringe, but what is inciting this lunatic fringe and making them believe that these are the accepted and done things – and that they are in order is that this is what we are showing.

A highly important issue raised by Leeds University lecturer E.D. Butterworth was the continued onus on the BBC to educate the populace about subsequent race misunderstandings. He stated that, on the question of prejudice, it was wrong to assume that people would automatically make the right judgements if presented with the facts about the constructs of race. He reminded Greene and other attendees that there was a need for education of the leaders of the community, the intellectuals, and the public in the reasons for the British attitude to race. Butterworth further noted that if the BBC could show 'West Indians and other migrants in the position of human beings exercising their civic duties and responsibilities and facing up to the various local situations', it would help social conflicts considerably. Similarly, Mr G.W.R. Lines, Director of Education, Wolverhampton Borough Council, addressed ways in which children could be educated to see that colour is immaterial. If documentaries concentrated on various children playing together and in school, it would produce aspects of racial understanding acceptable to 'both sides'. Greene noted that programmes of this sort 'had been done, from time to time'.

Other suggestions included niche programming that addressed specific audiences within the West Indian community, particularly mothers. *Woman's Hour*, as mentioned by Greene, could be a programming block in which subjects of parenting and unwed motherhood, for example, 'would fit in very naturally'. Crabbe noted that Sound broadcast many programmes regarding unmarried mothers, adoption, and so on. However, she was concerned that a programme at 12 o'clock midday is a 'great favourite, though social workers never listen to its content', losing an opportunity to learn more about immigrant mothers. Greene reassured Crabbe, noting that people with whom the social worker worked would be at home and 'might turn to listen to it'. Miss I. Harrison, Westminster City Council Welfare Officer, noted that a problem of the future 'will be the acceptance of coloured English by our own communities, which means that we have to place emphasis on the English children, who are coloured but who speak like other English children'. Greene concurred, citing comments made by Crabbe and others. He then asked R.S. Postgate, Controller of Educational Broadcasting, to address education on the BBC. He noted that many programmes currently produced were those than concentrated on teaching English, as discussed in the previous conference.

However, Mrs M. Dimes warned Postgate that, when considering the content of these kinds of programmes, the West Indians issue of assimilation and acceptance was different. She felt the BBC would go wrong if programmes featured the West Indies as too exotic and desirable, causing audiences to note, '"This is where they come from. That is where they belong. Why don't they go back to that sunny land? Why do they come here?" We do not want to [highlight West Indians] as being different from anyone else. We should be careful to guard against showing anything which perpetuates the difference between us [as citizens], which I should like to see got rid of.'

Yet, Mr W. Knight, Managing Editor designate of Concord, said he would like BBC documentaries to show how culture, music, and the arts in the West Indies had developed throughout the years. People tended to associate the West Indies with Jamaica and Trinidad, and knew very little about the other islands, and when the BBC sent a team to Jamaica footage should show people doing 'worthwhile jobs', to help the people. Sir Learie Constantine noted that in the past the only pictures of the Colonies had shown only the huts and shanties, no pictures of the 'nice buildings in which the doctors and the lawyers lived'. It was important now, he argued, to project the successful man holding his place in the 'Western circle', but equally important for West Indians to contribute in a way that would help to project 'a new society'. He noted that the BBC had a tremendous job to do, and, with regard to the treatment of West Indian history, he saw no purpose in hiding the facts of slavery, for any discredit would fall on those who had made people slaves, and 'not on those who had been enslaved'. Mr A.G. Bennett noted that there was frequently disagreement and animosity between Africans and West Indians and between West Indians from different islands, and that the BBC might be able to help in bringing them together in discussion. Constantine disagreed that this was a serious problem, and Philips noted that it was particularly unimportant compared with the main task of helping West Indians 'find their feet in society'.

Dimes asked whether consideration had been given by the BBC to doing programmes about multi-racial projects undertaken by people in areas where there were integration committees, as, for example, Sparkbrook in Birmingham. Butterworth said it would be wrong to assume a national pattern for immigrants' problems. The position, in terms of prejudice, changed between different areas. Butterworth did note that enough publicity was given to positive contributions. He did not, however, think that there could be much lasting effect from getting people together to resolve differences and understand one another, nor could the BBC do a great deal to change public opinion. He did feel that the BBC might do something to explain the strains and stresses of moving from one country to another. Featured could be programmes that stressed the contribution of all immigrants, as could an exploration of common assumptions about jobs and housing. Such subjects could be highlighted within 'education programmes or in a tough kind of documentary like *Tonight* or *Panorama*'.

As the discussions concluded, the Director-General said it appeared that West Indians, and Indians and Pakistanis had differing sets of priorities. For West Indians, the problem of integration was fundamental, in that many of them wished to settle in Britain and become British. Asians, on the other hand, intended to go home eventually to their own countries. The overall group roundly disagreed, stressing that it was impossible to speak that generally about the issue. Greene noted that some Asians had told him and other BBC managers that they had 'a different attitude toward integration. The idea has come up here, that [West Indians] are English children of another colour, did not come up with the Indians and Pakistanis; so to that extent there is a dilemma.' Mr Bennett said it often did not please West Indian parents when their children lost contact with the home country.

Constantine said he welcomed the idea of West Indians as Black Englishmen. This was, in his opinion, a sign of successful integration. He regretted the housing difficulties, which caused many West Indians to rent from other West Indians, forcing them to reside in ghettos, and preventing them from moving into 'wider circles and achieving integration'. He noted that there was the question of whether a West Indian ceased to be a West Indian when he wanted integration:

> I know where to go and where not to go. I have lived here 28 years and am quite content. I am more contented here than I am in my own country. That may be a reflection on me, it may be a reflection on my own society, but I beg them to make their contribution in fields other than the immediate circle in which they live. This would be a better way of advertising the fact that a West Indian has moved. If you keep to your own immediate circle in the face of opposition,

of prejudice and of antagonism, how will you educate the rest of the world that we are making progress in London, in Liverpool or in Manchester?

Mr Fraser said that although he agreed with Sir Learie, when touring schools he had been astounded to find racialism among the young. In the north, younger children under the age of eleven were less prejudiced, but in the higher age groups resistance to integration was hardening, and in the Midlands it was worse. Even in London and in the south, children showed very little interest in Coloured people or the way they lived. One puzzling trend was that of children aged between six and nine taking on the prejudices of their parents. It was felt by many that the BBC could contribute by avoiding nursery rhymes such as 'Ten Little Niggers' in children's programmes, and by directing programmes at parents to correct the attitude of their children. Mrs Dimes said similar arguments could be applied to religious broadcasts in which imagery was based upon notions of 'white was pure and evil things, dark'. Sir Learie agreed that the problem really started because of adult influences, and that prejudice would have to be 'broken down in the adult world, not in schools'. When speaking to over 5,000 students, his aim was to help the child to stand up against a prejudiced parent.

Mr R.D. Chapman said his own experience led to a similar conclusion. There was a need to educate the English toward integration; however, there was a need to educate West Indian communities of their responsibilities to the larger community in which they lived. This was vital because in areas where there was 'bad behaviour due to lack of understanding, prejudice was the result'. Two-way education was needed. Mr E. Irons agreed with both speakers, noting that in Nottingham there was progress toward getting immigrants to identify with the larger community, and that it would be a great step forward if the BBC's programmes could emphasise that West Indians had to decide what role they were prepared to play in the community.

However, the suggestion made by many attendees was that the service should 'not be thinking in terms of special programmes addressed to West Indians, whether immigrants or people born and long settled in the United Kingdom. Instead, programmes should take into account that White and Coloured people were living in a mixed community, and would be listening and into watching those programmes together. It was on this basic concept that the BBC would have to build. Crabbe and others realised, however, that the mass media alone could not overcome all the problems. The Director-General thanked those who had attended, and noted that the discussion had given the BBC many individual ideas to follow up. As Mr Lines had said, the occasion would have influenced the BBC's thinking, and this was perhaps

one of the most important things of all. When asked, the West Indian participants felt that the conference was helpful, but the events had not led to any
specific commitments from the corporation. The representatives were
highly concerned, however, that once again BBC programmes in general
should lean toward integration rather than emphasising racial differences,
something the Service had done throughout history in its constructions of
West Indian culture and ethnicity.[78]

Going to Britain

The BBC participated in the authorship and publishing of a booklet for the
hopeful immigrant, written specifically to provide information to West
Indians about immigration policies and life in the UK. *Going to Britain* was
also a complete guide to altering cultural behaviour to fit into the British
way of life. The booklet provided advice that informed the West Indian as
though he or she were ignorant of the UK's basic social policies, but many
of these islanders had already come to understand British cultural practices
via their presence as soldiers and pre-war citizens.[79] Whitley and Gillard
suggested to Greene that the booklet be distributed at the West Indian
conference:

> The book would be placed near the door for interest, as example of something
> done by the BBC ante-migration, which is a pointer to the kind of thing that
> might be done post-migration. (I thought it best to keep this on the sidelines
> for the first Conference at any rate, since the pamphlet is for West Indians).[80]

The foreword to the *Going to Britain* booklet states that the publication does
not 'set out to dissuade or persuade you; it merely tries to give the facts about
the difficulties which you will encounter in the United Kingdom', a clearly
negative subtext. The foreword indicates that the booklet and talks discuss
the difficulties one might encounter, including racism and xenophobia.
These issues are framed as a natural part of the immigration process, not
criticised or deconstructed within the booklet for subjective thinking.

The Honourable Sir Grantley Adams, Prime Minister of the West Indies,
wrote the foreword to the publication. Garnet H Gordon, Commissioner for
the West Indies, British Guiana, and British Honduras, wrote an introduction that reminds West Indians that migration to the British Isles had grown
to such a large extent that it was worthy of more than just 'casual attention'.
Gordon tells the reader and listener that migration from the West Indies,

> is, of course a matter of personal individual choice and that the decision to
> migrate will not affect you alone, but many others ... there must be clear
> purpose. In other words we hope that after you have read this booklet you will
> not casually travel to England as so many others have done in the past, but

undertake the adventure, if you so decide, with a better chance of making it a success.

Questions are then asked of the reader that revolve around

1. Where one plans to study;
2. Who the reader's contact is;
3. Whether the reader can find support for their studies via their employer;
4. Issues regarding rent and food.

Nowhere in the introduction does it mention any aspect of permanent settlement.

The Adviser on Community Development to the Commissioner for the West Indies, British Guiana, and British Honduras, E.N. Burke, authored the next section of the booklet, called, 'The Journey'. A warning of scarce jobs and the fact that the UK offered very little employment to unskilled people again reinforces a frightening premise of failure. A section on living accommodations briefly reminded the reader they would probably end up living with a White proprietor or landlady (who was possibly racist) as opposed to a West Indian. On the following page under the section 'Remember the Rules of the House', the reader is told that some property owners 'welcome coloured people, others turn them away'. This point is a first of many that seem to suggest tolerance of racism on the part of West Indians. Later in a section called 'Keep Smiling', the immigrant is encouraged to accept expressions like 'I work like a black' or 'nigger in the woodpile'. The narrator says that those racist utterances were

> accepted expressions in England and are not meant to be insulting so do not be over-sensitive and take offence. However, there will be workers who do not like West Indians and may well make nasty remarks. The best thing to do is to ignore them, or try to show our good sense of humour, which we boast of possessing.

In addition to limited job and economic opportunities in England, social problems, sparse living conditions, a limited job market, and other factors, the booklet strengthens the BBC's historical voice of authority. The choice of prized West Indian authors as narrators situated within colonial patronage again reinforces the strategy of White British discursive authority to know what's best: by example, no less.

Days before the meetings with West Indian leaders, 100 copies of the booklet were found for distribution.[81] Anthony Martin, Programme Organiser for Caribbean & Colonial Services, External Broadcasting forwarded a note of thanks to the Overseas Publicity Officer J.R.T. Hopper for notification of about 1,300 additional copies of the booklet held by the

BBC. Martin suggests that extra copies are useful, since 'requests are always trickling in, and we could easily dispose of them to Jamaica, for instance, before the Immigration Bill becomes law'. Whilst he determined that basic information contained in the booklets was 'still valid', he suggested the issuance of a supplementary leaflet to go with the booklets giving the fundamental requirements of the Immigration Act.[82]

Further feedback on racial initiatives

In a report on race relations and the BBC submitted by the Leicester Campaign for Racial Equality (LCRE) during October 1965, the organisation applauded the provision of special programmes for immigrants on television and radio.[83] They were particularly pleased that BBC was not concerned over beliefs that special treatment for immigrants encouraged separatism from dominant culture. That praised the corporation's efforts, noting that overcoming the language problem helped with the integration effort considerably, and avoided racial tensions. They noted that producers of the programmes would 'take care to exclude any suggestion of a patronising approach or of condescending attitudes in the tone and presentation of these programmes'. They cited the damage this would cause given the present mood of the immigrant communities, and that 'any trace of such an approach or of such attitudes may well nullify a great deal of the positive good that these programmes can do'. The organisation also expressed a desire for the BBC not to confine its work in this field simply to programmes intended for immigrants, but instead to draw upon its duty to society to provide more programming. Criticised by the committee was the preponderance of stereotypes in the media, reinforcing tensions and difficulties for people of colour. A prevalent stereotype noted was that of the 'coloured person as a dirty, illiterate and unskilled labourer' despite a presence among 'managerial groups, doctors, dentists, university lecturers, nurses, technicians and white-collar workers'. The organisation noted that very few BBC programme producers adhered to 'criteria of accuracy and verisimilitude, in that they should bring their casting in line with the presence of coloured people in many of the occupations and roles portrayed'. The organisation noted that the appearance of Coloured people in non-typecast television roles were 'marginal':

> Whereas audiences may see a coloured person flitting across the screen in a crowd scene, or a hotel or airport lobby, it is extremely rare to see a coloured person at the centre, not only of the screen, but also of the relationships presented in the programmes. Again, simple realism demands that coloured people [should] be seen sometimes in central, rather than peripheral, roles.

By comparison, some American television shows broadcast during these years, such as *Perry Mason* (CBS, 1957–74) and *Slattery's People* (CBS, 1964–65), included Coloured faces in the line-up and featured episodes in which 'a Negro' was 'assertive, even aggressive, and above all defiantly individual', and who figured as 'a central character in the plot'. The organisation noted that the only programme on British television that appeared to have recognised the validity of both these foregoing points was *Emergency Ward 10* on ITV (1957–67). The LCRE noted how it was now commonplace to describe Coloured people in the UK generically as immigrants, despite family histories. Unless White Britons 'accept their presence, not only de facto, but in their conception of what British society is like, there can be no significant advance towards integration'.

True integration of the immigrant would involve absorption of many of the different cultural patterns that the immigrant communities brought with them into the texture of life of the entire community, not the eradication of their different social and cultural backgrounds. A major effort for race relations should reflect a social education for a positive acceptance of cultural diversity, not seen negatively as differences from present and superior norms, but an enrichment of social and cultural lives, thereby defining a genuinely multiracial society. The report noted that the BBC had not 'risen to this challenge', or had risen to it 'only inadequately', prompting their criticisms and suggestions.

First cited was how the BBC and other mass media sources treated issues that highlighted conflict as newsworthy events, rather than focusing on positive events meant to successfully integrate neighbourhoods and organisations. Stories regarding race stood against a 'background, largely built up by the mass media, of hysteria, extreme prejudice, hatred and violence'. A related concern involved the failure of public institutions to influence race relations positively through declaration. The reasoning, as noted, was that anything to do with race relations was seemingly framed as controversial, and that strict neutrality was leading to a failure of the press, the churches, political parties, and public figures to speak for decency and humanity. These concerns for balance in racial relations and conflicts created platforms for racists and fascists to reinforce messages of hate, and further problematised racial integration.

Mentioned was an occurrence in which a cross-burning took place in the Midlands, prompting a report on the BBC programme *Midlands Today*. The person suspected, Mr Robert Relf (a one-time member of the fascist National Socialist Movement), was told he would be allowed to state his point of view if he contacted the BBC. The LCRE had sent a telegram expressing its concern at this proposal. The following evening, Mr Relf stated his anti-immigration stance, whilst a telegram from the LCRE was read aloud on air. The latter group claimed that free publicity was given to 'rabidly racialist propaganda' that harmed harmonious race relations greatly, adding that publicity of this kind was moreover very often 'precisely what groups of this sort want'. The implication by the BBC that expressions of racial hatred of the 'totally irresponsible and ill-informed kind propounded by Mr Relf' represented a serious and considerable point of view was therefore harmful to race relations despite issues of free speech. The LCRE further queried whether the BBC would, noting pre-war 1930s xenophobia and American racial problems, allow anti-Semitic ranting as a counterbalance to those who reject these views. The organisation offered these two suggestions,

> It seems to us that the BBC must decide whether these views are to be given serious and proportionate coverage in its programmes. We feel that since we do not, as a community, tolerate the right to pollute the atmosphere or the right to poison one's neighbours, there is no good reason why the pollution and poisoning of men's minds should be defended on the grounds of freedom of speech ... This is an obligation that seems to us implicit in Lord Reith's original vision of the BBC.

Within a society in which racial prejudice and discrimination are considered a grave problem, as noted by a editorial in *The Listener* of 2 September 1965, the LCRE rejected the view that television must reflect these particular standards, but instead that it should not aspire to reinforce attitudes of racism and social dystopia, and should seek to change them. The committee also noted that they looked 'forward to the day when either of the two channels can put on a serial dealing with the life of a coloured family', but in a fashion that was realistic 'in all their humanity and human diversity'. They further noted that the BBC and mass media should present Coloured people as members of society, as 'ineradicably part of the English landscape, not as "dark strangers", not as "the dark million", and still less as people who are perennially involved in unpleasant incidents and conflicts'.[84] The committee also cited how these suggestions were in keeping with portions of the Pilkington Report on the purposes of broadcasting. The group presumed that television was, and would be, a main factor in influencing values and standards, and stated that, by its nature, broadcasting must be in a 'constant and sensitive relationship with the moral condition of society'. Broadcasters were, and should be, involved; this gave them a responsibility they could not evade. Further, 'television does not, and cannot, merely reflect the moral standards of society. It must affect them, either by changing or by reinforcing them'.[85] The report went to Sir Hugh Greene from the committee and to Dipak Nandy, one of the founding members of the Runnymede Trust. Letters of acknowledgement and thanks went to the organisation from

Whitley on behalf of Greene, and Patrick Beech, then Controller of the Midland Region.

However, on 13 June 1966, BBC2 elected to run a programme that dealt specifically with the difficulties West Indian immigrants continued to face in Britain. The show *Minorities in Britain: The West Indians* examined housing, job opportunities, and cultural assimilation. The programme, produced by Michael Bunce, would run as an educational show, with an emphasis on children and families. In February, Director of Further Education Television, Dianne Farris, began her research of the West Indian community by contacting an Oxford sociology professor, Ceri Peach. In a letter to Farris, Peach suggested that a basis of a programme could be the conflict between economic and social desires, highlighting how the demand for labour led to what Peach called economic integration, yet a housing shortage led to social rejection, and a dislike of strangers, especially 'visible ones like West Indians'. In citing an article she had written for *Race* (the journal of the Institute of Race Relations) in July 1965, she noted how housing shortages, and distrust and dislike of West Indians by the local population made it very difficult for West Indians to get digs in White people's houses. Peach suggested that interviews with most West Indians would support this point, as would discriminatory advertisements in newspapers. Further she noted that when West Indians were 'thrown back on the limited housing resources of the coloured community ... overcrowding often results', suggesting the producers simply interview public health inspectors for more evidence. Peach further noted how Whites would become aggravated as West Indians tried to 'get away from the centres of settlement' as there was 'great resistance from estate agents who do not want to "spoil" areas'. She also suggested a number of people to interview, 'whose experience on this point is quite enlightening'. Other points worth examining, in Peach's opinion, included a frustrated love of Britain, frustration with religion, British style, and how West Indian society tends to be more matriarchal or mother-orientated for a number of reasons, leading to poor discipline of their children.[86]

That May, an editorial by Peter Simple (aka Michael Bernard Wharton) from the *Daily Telegraph* cited a pamphlet from the Bow Group think tank on immigration that advocated the dispersal of immigrants around the country to avoid the heavy ethnic concentrations seen in Brixton, Notting Hill, and other urban areas. The *Telegraph* article criticised the systematic movement of immigrants away from places where they were concentrated at that time to other urban and rural districts, with the desire to ensure that 'every New Town would have its quota'. The author compared this dispersal to similar social engineering and 'lunatic schemes discussed in Hitler's "Table Talk"', in which he proposed moving the population of Holland to the Urals of Russia for the benefit of the future frontier of Nazi Europe. The author suggested that, if people needed to be dispersed, instead of Radnorshire, Harrogate, or the Highlands of Scotland, they could instead be sent back to the Commonwealth countries from which they came, asking 'would they not prefer this themselves? What West Indian in his senses would want to move from rainy Birmingham to rainy Lincolnshire if he could move to Jamaica?'[87]

The next month, Farris arranged for the participation of local families in Brixton, the International Language Club, the West Indian Community Centre, nursery school, the Council for Unmarried Mothers, and the cultural theorist Stuart Hall to participate in *Minorities in Britain*. Filmed sequences also included a local record shop that catered to West Indians.[88] Bunce sought to provide balance by requesting that a Trinidad-born physician, appear on the programme, hoping to outweigh the majority of publicity, which tended to give the impression that West Indians were exclusively in lower-skilled or unskilled occupations.[89] The filming schedule for the programme indicated 30 March was for shooting West Indians at Croydon, and a factory location;[90] ultimately, Farris did not include planned footage that featured a group of young West Indian children from a local school. After the broadcast, many of the West Indian participants criticised the programme; for excluding footage of their organisations or offices, and for a far too sanitised approach to a far too serious problem. Dorothy Case, the Matron of Cowley Day Nursery in London, criticised Farris and the BBC:

> A number of my friends watched the programme and we all found it rather disappointing. We thought that the way the interviews were presented made it monotonous as there were so few illustrations it might as well been given over the radio sound. If you would like to pass on to the BBC some of the criticisms I received, they might find it useful for similar occasion.[91]

Farris responded to Case by writing that she found most of the criticisms interesting and that she agreed with the point 'about showing the West Indians in various activities. If I [Farris] counted up, money-wise how much this would have cost, you would realize the main reason why we were not able to do it'.[92] Despite these limitations, the programme did feature an introduction by Stuart Hall. Programming notes and scripting noted that the opening shot would show a West Indian labourer stating 'I do feel a longing for home, do sincerely feel a longing for home … ' This image as a production of this citizen's cultural position constructs him as an outsider not truly at home in this new land. Hall also goes on to give a narrative that addresses history and possible inclusion:

> The majority of West Indians are descended from West Africans who were uprooted and forced to work on the Caribbean estates as slaves. Not only did

they lose their own language, customs and culture, but also they were forced to accept a British pattern of life – first by the slave owners and then by the colonial administration. The West Indian immigrant, then, looks upon coming to Britain rather as coming home, and may not realize how great the adjustment required of him is.[93]

The message is one of resilience within the shadow of colonialism. Yet this narrative is a warning, perhaps a foreboding, to those expecting to maintain a sense of autonomy whilst creating postcolonial agency. Though possible, this allegation within the introduction seems to remind the subject of the inescapable consequences of immigration, including xenophobia and racism. Within the narrative of the introduction is the challenge of establishing place when already othered by the normative. The introduction continues:

To the British, West Indians, like most foreigners, tend to look the same, and they are grouped together and stereotyped. This leads to an oversimplified picture of what the West Indian is actually like. The people in this programme may not conform to your image of the West Indian, but they are quite ordinary people; the men are skilled or semi-skilled workers, the women are a social worker, a nurse, and two factory workers.[94]

The next month, however, Carmen Neckles wrote a letter to producer Michael Bunce on behalf of friends who saw the programme, expressing concern that the importance of acceptance and integration was lost in the production, and that the programme was broadcast on the fledgling BBC2 instead of being available to the BBC1 audience:

Just to say (rather belatedly) that we found the series very interesting. Some of our friends labelled it too tame. My one criticism, however, is an obvious one; any programme or series which sets out to show people as people and not as easily-digested caricatures, shouldn't really be restricted to a minority channel: and I, for one, sincerely hope that the immense effort you and your colleagues put into the making of the series, will eventually be seen and appreciated by a much wider audience.[95]

The programme was repeated, but was limited to running on BBC2 again. Beech had asked whether regular programme space on BBC2 was available for programmes for immigrant audiences, mainly Indian and Pakistani, but no additional resources were allocated to a new programme, allowing for only a repeat. The Advisory Committee asked for an extra programme, and an evening slot,[96] but the controller David Attenborough felt that the effort would be a waste of resources and time. He wrote to the Controller Manager:

I am afraid I cannot accept the idea of repeating the immigrant programmes on BBC-2. I should doubt very much if any large proportion of the intended audience are BBC-2 viewers with the appropriate sets and serials and my off-air time is likely to be occupied increasingly with colour tests of one sort and another.[97]

There seemed to be reluctance to broadcasting the programme again due to an assumed failure at reaching the intended audience, though it wasn't clear who this was.

West Indian narratives, presence, and the problematic

The popular BBC television current affairs programme *Tonight* (BBC, 1957–65), hosted by Cliff Michelmore featured a segment on 'West Indians' on 21 August 1963, narrated by the novelist and poet George Lamming. Originally created to fill the 'Toddlers' Truce' between 6.00 p.m. and 7.00 p.m.,[98] *Tonight* covered current events, topical issues, and the arts. Credited with the feel of the programme were producers Alasdair Milne and Donald Baverstock, including its set design and informal approach to interviews, many of which were unscripted. The show also became famous for its inclusion of Cy Grant, who sang calypso melodies for audiences. Directed by Jack Gold, the piece provided a sketch of life for immigrants in Britain, who despite many commonalities with Whites – such as football and a desire for a better life – still underwent incidents of racialism and resentment. Gold became a director after having served as film editor, which allowed for a degree of autonomy in the structure of *Tonight*. He stated that 'if a good idea came along, it could be expanded into a segment'.

The West Indigan segment had been prompted by an earlier newsreel of West Indians arriving at Southampton that Gold had seen. He had been 'intrigued by these people in their summer clothes arriving in bleary old England', and the segment reminded him of his own grandparents, who were immigrants from Russian Poland. Gold received complete support on the idea and the ultimate segment, since *Tonight* 'was an extraordinary programme. They allowed you to do things like that. They encouraged it.' The output of the *Tonight* programme was 'so tremendous, being on five nights a week, they could afford to take chances', on material considered meaningful to audiences. Further, had he read Lamming's work and was deeply impressed, and though there were other writers available for the project Gold felt that 'this was a West Indian story'. Therefore, Gold explained, 'Lamming wrote [the] commentary and read it', whilst Gold chose the project. Lamming's reputation as writer and cultural icon made him a natural choice.

Gold's explanation of the structure of the programme was that, in 1963, West Indians were 'playing a series of test cricket matches in England. There had already been a series of stories about racial troubles, housing and the like.' He thought it would be interesting to use the match as a backdrop for a study in racial relations as 'Black batters play white Britons; meeting on equal terms, on Lords' Cricket field.' He was particularly taken with the players who were 'stylish and extroverts – very extravagant in their batting and bowling, [and] in their music'. As the camera scanned the stadium, Gold said one could 'sense there was exuberance with the West Indians watching the match, smiling, and seeing their countrymen coming to England, being very successful, and often beating the English'. He found a 'West Indian sitting next to a white guy' as shown in the film, sharing the experience. As Lamming's commentary began, the images of the Black fan served as a 'narrator link' to the narrative that followed: the experiences of West Indians in London, beginning with an attempt to find housing. New changes in technology such as smaller film cameras and radio microphones allowed Gold's crew to secretly film and record audio portions of the man's quest for a room. A radio mike hidden under a newspaper carried by the man allowed Gold to hear the 'very polite, yet firm refusals' from White landlords 'who turned him away'. The film continued with other vignettes of West Indians living in the poor, near-squalid conditions in Notting Hill, highlighting limited employment opportunities, and what Gold called 'the lower end of the scale as busmen, orderlies in hospitals, dishwashers, cleaners', and assorted other positions. These images of West Indians and their tasks also featured a quest for employment at the labour exchange, with 'an astute commentary by Lamming' framing each image. As the camera's eye returned to the football match, Gold focused on West Indians enjoying the bravado of the Black players, 'intercut with the brief shots of West Indian life in London, it was sort of cry of defiance, if you like, stating this was their achievement, was quite where they were coming from. Every strike of the ball, or bowl of the wicket was the way they could show equality or even superiority.'[99]

The Colony (16 June 1964), directed and produced by Philip Donnellan, provided an opportunity for working-class West Indians living in Birmingham to explain, in their own words, the challenges of living among White Britons (Figure 11). The documentary programme was novel, in that these hopeful settlers engaged in a pseudomonologue styling, eager to clarify points of contention, using no commentary or narration from others, particularly not the White producer. Interviewed was Jamaican bus conductor Victor Williams, in his home, whilst British Railways signalman Stan Crooke was at work, carefully switching trains as he provided personal insights for the audience. Their perspectives highlighted during the programme led to an open discussion among West Indians about their experiences in England, thus far. They openly disagreed on specific issues of inclusion and assimilation, providing a cross-section of ideological perspectives and avoiding any notions of essentialism.

Figure 11 The documentary programme *The Colony* was novel, in that these hopeful settlers (Victor Williams and Stan Crooke) spoke without the voiceover of a narrator, eager to clarify points of contention. There were several as each had a differing perspective of life in England. This diversity of opinion demonstrated how varied these men were, despite the encompassing label of 'West Indian'.

One of the most controversial Black-themed programmes transmitted during the Greene years was the *Wednesday Play* instalment of *Fable* (27 January 1965), written by John Hopkins (who also wrote the *Z Cars* 'Place of Safety' episode), during the height of apartheid. The narrative, directed by James MacTaggart and produced by Christopher Morahan, examined a Britain in which a Black-dominated government ruled with an iron hand, providing a socially inspired reversal of South African political practices. Whilst the play contrasts the experiences of an oppressed White couple, Len and Joan (Ronald Lacey and Eileen Atkins) with the charmed lives of the liberal, Black, middle-class couple, Mark and Joan (Thomas Baptiste and Barbara Assoon), the harsh oppression of Whites was paramount. Concerns of its impact were so disconcerting that the BBC delayed transmission until after a key by-election in East London involving a candidate who had previously run a racist campaign in Birmingham. Concerns arose that the programme would frighten viewers into believing that Blacks would indeed come to engage in the same racist practices as Whites if given a chance. Those directly involved in the project did not consider the teleplay controversial; Producer of *The Wednesday Play* James MacTaggart considered the project timely and important to race relations.[100] However, the BBC regarded the programme as troublesome, and was concerned it might seem that a side was being taken before a highly controversial, and racially bated, election. Head of Television Kenneth Adam discussed the issue MacTaggart, advising him the show's delay by at least a week. MacTaggart protested against the decision and complained to Head of Drama Sydney Newman. Newman in turn contacted Adam regarding the decision, who responded via memo that he was sorry if the producer viewed the decision as a mistake, but the 'the DG would have come to the same decision'. Furthermore, the decision had:

> only been strengthened by the news later last night that a new candidate standing on the racial issue has come forward ... Now it is possible that if the racial issue heats up even further in Leyton, and one had only to see the *Panorama* item last night to realise how ugly it is already, a play that is 'stark, explosive and contemporary' – our own words in *Radio Times* – might, shown the very night before polling, be *deemed* by one candidate (any one) to have affected his chances by persuading voters to support another ... It is therefore perfectly possible that a number and it could even be a significant number of Leyton voters might indeed, in the mood of the moment, misunderstand this play, and taking it simply on face value, vote anti-black as a result ... I do not want the message of FABLE [sic] to run any risk of being obscured by a squalid and contrived outbreak of racialism in one corner of London.[101]

Potential pressure from the press and the possible reaction of voters had caused the service to make an editorial decision in its programming. This was not the first time, as this research has shown. However, Hopkins as a writer had a solid reputation for creating thought-provoking material that had received critical and public acclaim. He blamed the press to a great degree for creating the type of pressure that had caused the service to second-guess its public-service directive in lieu of less controversy. In an interview, Hopkins stated:

> And so *Fable* was pulled, and – as often happens when clever people make decisions that they think will service their own purposes – it caused a great deal of trouble because the papers picked it up. In those days, the press was in the habit of picking up things that I did. I had previously written several controversial episodes of *Z Cars*, for which the BBC had to make public apologies. So, because of these experiences, the press was ready to pounce again. I remember one of the tabloids doing a centre-page spread with a big picture showing a scene from the play – an act of violence against, I think, Ron Lacey, one of the white characters. Underneath this, there was a brief list of my credits up to that point, and the naughty things that I had done in the past, like upsetting the public. So, in their eyes, I had obviously become totally insane, because I had written a play where there was a black ruling minority and a white slave majority, and everybody knew it wasn't true![102]

When the BBC telecast the play after the election, the BBC ran a disclaimer stating that the show was 'not meant to represent a situation that could happen any time in the future, or one that has happened at any time in the past'.[103] Hopkins told interviewer Pines that he would have preferred it if *Fable* had affected the public as Orson Welles's treatment of *War of the Worlds* did in 1939, 'when everybody in America believed that Martians had landed in Upstate New York and were killing people'. But the play was highly regarded by viewers, and Hopkins felt that it was 'an interesting illustration of how wrong authority can be'. He continued:

> In their efforts to try and avoid embarrassment, they merely drew attention to the play, which, in the end, served our purpose. I knew, of course, what I was doing. I wasn't an idiot. I knew that they would be outraged when they saw scenes like the white husband being beaten up by the black police. You have to remember that this was 1965, long before the appearance of the extraordinary films that are being made today, like *Boyz N the Hood*, which portray that kind of violence, *Fable* was fairly innocent compared to what we see today, though it was profoundly upsetting nevertheless.[104]

In one particular scene, a pair of Black police officers comes to the home of a liberal Black British author who employs a White woman and her husband. The, male according to policy, should have been home in another section of town before dark. The police begin to question the two and insist that he leave for a distant part of town as a penalty for not abiding by the governmental rules. Horrified that her husband will be taken away from her and their family, the White woman reaches out to touch the arm of an officer in an appeal for leniency. He immediately shoves her away, and she careens into a bookcase (Figure 12). White viewers were outraged at the violence (though it was tame compared to actual violence against Black South African women) and wrote in to the service bitterly complaining, despite the fictitious nature of the show.[105]

A memo from Head of Drama Sydney Newman to all drama group producers, directors, and story editors under the heading of 'Violence, Sexual Relations, and Blasphemy in Drama' warned about depictions of these subjects, following press complaints over recent programming. The new memo refers to a previous one, in which Newman warns writers and producers to avoid 'rocking the boat', and to pay close attention to how sexual relations were discussed, the use of bad language in 'a Christian country', and the portrayal of physical violence. A subsequent section on 'Portrayal of Minorities' notes that a 'main guiding principle is that a minority cannot hit back. Recently, through good intentions, mistakes have been make in which Negroes have appeared in a light, which can only feed the argument of fascists and racialists.'[106] The memo also addressed other issues of content, particularly complaints from the press. Ironically, Newman also called upon these staff to exercise freedom of expression, but with 'responsibility to the public equal to [their] responsibility to television as a creative medium'. In addition, the memo addressed the reaction of 'anti-BBC hounds' to programming content.[107]

Voices of contention and the BBC

As the service attempted to incorporate programming that addressed ethnic issues, political controversies continued to arise. In 1967, the BBC had decided to interview a Black American activist, Stokely Carmichael, in a segment of a popular newsmagazine. At the time, Enoch Powell was serving as a Conservative Tory MP for Wolverhampton South West. It was in April of 1968 that Powell made the infamous 'Rivers of Blood' speech, when he told the residents of Birmingham that they as White British must be 'literally mad' to allow '50,000 dependants' to immigrate into the country each year. His reference to 'wide-grinning piccaninnies' merged with the haunting memories of the Nottingham and Notting Hill riots. The BBC had come under fire from Powell and his constituents for broadcasting the Carmichael interview: Mr Powell had complained that the interviewer, Patricia Philo, 'went out of her way' to ask Mr Carmichael what 'we black people in Britain should do to liberate ourselves'. In a letter to Powell, John Crawley, the editor of news and current affairs, said 'In the light of the re-examination of all the

Figure 12 In *Fable*, Joan (Eileen Atkins) is horrified that her husband (Ron Lacey), may be taken. She reaches out to an officer (Rudolph Walker) in an appeal for leniency. He immediately shoves her away, as she careens into a bookcase. White viewers were outraged at the violence from the black man to the white woman, despite the fictitious nature of the show.

circumstances … we have decided that the occasion of Stokely Carmichael's return to New York did not properly justify the inclusion of this interview'. The service later gave a formal apology to Enoch Powell for an 'error of judgment'.[108] The press also highlighted Mary Whitehouse, an outspoken critic of BBC television and its immorality. In 1967, Whitehouse published her book *Cleaning Up TV: From Protest to Participation*, which addressed 'improper' images for the public, particularly children. When Carmichael's interview ran, Whitehouse immediately wrote to the BBC and several papers as well, stating that the interview was damaging to the psyche of the public morale.[109] These events followed the appearance of Malcolm X on *Tonight*, in which he discussed a new, Black-themed newspaper, the *Magnet News* that was starting up in Birmingham.[110]

However, political candidates such as Powell were not above criticism by BBC writers. As a not-so-subtle reference to the horrors of British xenophobia in Parliament, the teleplay *Election 70*, commissioned for BBC's *Wednesday Play*, based upon a mythical constituency and dystopic by-election in the near future, created a warning of racial intolerance, as the politician and his campaign become racist and ultimately violent. After acquiring broadcasting rights to the programme, BBC management delayed its broadcast date, and then rejected the television play. Author of the play Stuart Douglass accused the BBC of political censorship in their rejection of the script. The BBC denied the charge and claimed that the script did not meet the required artistic standards. When asked to address the issue, Gerald Savory, Head of Television Drama, denied there had been any political censorship. He claimed that the play's content was not the issue but that the BBC 'couldn't really make up' their 'minds about it', so they released the script. Normally the service would retain television rights over scripts for two years after their initial acquisition. Douglass told the press that this had been the third script held and dropped by the BBC reflecting controversial issues.[111] Again political concerns created pressures within the service that limited its creative licence and critical ability.

Favourites like the *Black and White Minstrel Show* were also highly criticised by the press, but more importantly by those called upon to provide assessment of BBC programming. Barrie Thorne, author of a lecture and essay on the BBC's finances and cost control, wrote a series of letters to Kenneth Adam in 1962, regarding the racist content of the *Black and White Minstrel Show* (BBC, 1958–78). First, he wrote to inform him of his membership in the Urban League and support of the National Association for the Advancement of Coloured People. In reaction to a letter written to *The Times* about Sunday night programming, and the return of the popular programme to the line-up, Thorne wrote,

> It is not the news that the *Black and White Minstrel Show* is to return on Sunday that is in any way distressing but that it is to return to the screen at all. The Uncle Tom attitude of the show in this day and age is a disgrace and an insult to coloured people everywhere. If black faces are to be shown, for heaven's sake let coloured artists be employed – and with dignity.[112]

Further, he expressed concerns over actor Ron Moody's portrayal of Fagin in a West End production of *Oliver*, and how, despite the voices in 'loud in praise of his performance', Thorne found the anti-Semitic themes 'distressing', noting that the performance 'could never be played like that in New York', a city with a large Jewish population. Thorne reminded Adam that 'Moody was dropped from the American production for this reason'. Racial insensitivity and ignorance was highlighted further, as Thorne noted that the BBC might also be equally to blame for continuing 'the resentment the era of the minstrels', and other stereotypic constructs stemming from the 'deep [American] south'. Thorne acknowledged the show's popularity with British viewers, but wrote that, despite this, and the detrimental affect its absence might have on Associated Television (ATV) and BBC's 'Sunday night supremacy, I do so hope that it will not be renewed after this season'.[113]

Adam's response, whilst defensive of the show's historical and theatrical value, seemingly took an air of personal concern:

> I am sorry to say I find myself in complete disagreement with you that the *Black and White Minstrel Show* represents 'racial guying' in any way. I yield to no-one in my detestation of apartheid and the Little Rock philosophy. But to suggest that to continue a perfectly honorable theatrical tradition of the British music hall is a 'disgrace and an insult to coloured people everywhere' is, I submit, arrant nonsense. I have indeed hinted at this in the foreword I have written for the book, which is due shortly on the Show. I have discussed the subject with one or two of my coloured friends, and I find them much less sensitive in the matter than their well-meaning white friends.[114]

Five years later, when it was suggested that the programme incorporate Black minstrels into the cast, Adam retorted to T.J.H. Sloan, Head of Light Entertainment,

> Introducing genuine Negroes into the *Black and White Minstrel Show* was thought by Board of Management yesterday to have been an unjustifiable breaking of the coon convention, which has been our defence against the growing attacks upon the show. See this week's Tribune for a particularly nasty article some of the strictures however are deserved in this case. Please see that it does not happen again.[115]

In a handwritten response, Sloan noted that he planned to 'review a copy of the Tribune from the Library. One or more B&W to be transmitted in this series – contains no coloured artists'.[116] His concerns were in response to criticisms from Elisabeth Thomas, who had reviewed the show for the *Socialist* magazine. Whilst she raved over the brightest spot in the evening's entertainment, the 'magnificent programme *Till Death Us Do Part*', she indicated that she nearly did not watch the programme, angered by the BBC's *Black and White Minstrel Show*. The programme had put her in 'such a frenzy of rage' that she was near to vowing 'never to watch the square box again'. Her concerns, however, were less about the representations of Black people and obvious social caricature, but more fearful of Black retaliation:

> We are going through the long hot summer. American Negroes are boiling over with feelings of resentment and impotence which none of the platitudes of the white liberals can subdue. Their only answer is violence against the white man and the advocacy of Black Power. And the signs of unrest here are obvious and disquieting. Yet our dear old fuddy-duddy BBC goes on putting out this coon programme ... the continuance of *The Black and White Minstrels* makes one give up hope that any real understanding of the standards they owe to their viewers will ever get through to their smug minds.[117]

A London viewer expressed further complaints over discriminatory practices, though in a less reactionary fashion than Thomas. Katherine Wadleigh of London openly accused the BBC of limiting the representation and involvement of Coloured actors in television programming. Her concerns were intentionally sent to Wheldon 'instead of the Tories', she wrote, because 'publicity would kill [the effort]'. Her belief was that few, if any, Black people were cast in meaningful roles or as presenters, and that a kind of positive propaganda could be quietly spread by simply casting Blacks and Asians as everyday citizens, thereby 'fighting racial prejudice in the country'; however, it would 'have to be done without being seen as done'. If Coloured people were cast in programmes where their colour had no relevance, the viewing public might be unconsciously persuaded to accept them in such roles in real life. She notes that viewers 'expect to see immigrants as nurses, bus conductors, tube staff, and waitresses; they do not automatically accept them as accountants, secretaries, PR men or newspaper reporters'. She suggested that an Indian or African expert or zoologist 'might offset the "native bearers"'. In closing, she wrote that the BBC should practise integration of their programmes 'without pointing it out', and thus in a more 'subliminal' manner.[118]

Huw Wheldon, Director of Television reacted by arguing that the BBC already did a 'good deal' to counter racial discrimination. He noted that the organisation employed 'a considerable number of coloured staff, including a coloured radio announcer, coloured characters frequently appear in plays, and the whole subject of racial prejudice is often discussed in current affairs programmes like *Panorama* and *24 Hours*'. He noted that the BBC was 'currently considering for scheduling a serial revolving round a mixed marriage' (probably *Rainbow City*, given the year), 'although the mere hint of this in the press has already brought complaints from people who do not share your enlightened views'. Wheldon considered the idea of 'casting coloured actors in plays in professional jobs, as reporters, public relations men, accountants and so on, merely because they are coloured', objectionable on many counts. He noted:

> In the first place, our plays usually aim to reflect real life and it would go against our whole policy to show a world which every viewer will know does not exist. In the second place, this would itself be a form of discrimination on colour grounds and unfair to white actors. In the third place, it would undoubtedly provoke very strong resentment among a large part of the viewing audience and would stir up the very feelings you are anxious to lessen. And in the fourth place, the number of good coloured actors is in any case very small.[119]

Rainbow City

Heralded as an iconic, new six-part series about a 'Jamaican lawyer and other immigrants living in and around Birmingham' by the *Radio Times*,[120] the programme *Rainbow City* (BBC, 5 July–9 August 1967) was considered a bold experiment by the BBC and author/producer John Elliot. The six twenty-five-minute episodes were the first regular British television drama series to place a West Indian actor (Errol John) in the leading role. John played barrister John Steele, and British actor Gemma Jones played his White wife, Mary. The programme examined the challenges he personally undertook, and his cases, some of which involved cases of racialism and police misconduct. In the episode 'Beards and Turbans' (26 July 1967), Steele successfully helps an Asian student (Renu Setna) keep his flat after being threatened with removal for complaining over rent prices and filthy conditions (Figure 13). The episode underscores a multiethnic solidarity among immigrants, as an Irish tenant (Shay Gorman), who considers the property owner friendly, testifies on the student's behalf, helping to win the case. The episode ends in a celebration with all the tenants and Steele.

Steele's marital relationship was portrayed as nearly ideal, yet with Mary's father (Arthur Pentelow) nonetheless doubting whether they could endure the pressures from their White neighbours. Before the programme was transmitted David Porter, Head of Programmes in the BBC's Midland Region, remarked that he and others at the BBC 'wanted to do something' that addressed racial problems in England. The programme would show that '[John Steele] and other immigrants have the same recognizable egos and psyches, hopes, fears and difficulties as the rest of us, plus a few problems of their own: these are the bases of our stories'.[121]

Figure 13 In the 'Beards and Turbans' episode of *Rainbow City* (26 July 1967), Steele (Errol John) successfully helps an Asian student (Renu Setna) keep his flat after being threatened with removal (by Robin Wentworth) for complaining over rent prices. The episode underscores a multiethnic solidarity among immigrants, as an Irish tenant (Shay Gorman) testifies on the student's behalf.

One of the episodes than ran, 'Always on Sunday' (9 August 1967), high-lighted a confrontation between Steele and his liberal-minded father-in-law described, as '100% Brummy' by Elliott himself.[122] The focus of the discussion was the issue of Steele's interracial marriage, and his father-in-law's acceptance of the family and their plans, including their biracial child. Despite an ongoing subplot that examined the tensions their mixed marriage brought about, historian Stephen Bourne remarks that Steele's character as the husband of a White British woman actually helped to legitimise the presence of West Indians to White British audiences. Bourne stated:

> A programme featuring a Black family would have been too real – too radical. Even though it was a radical time in television – in the 60s – and a groundbreaking time, it still wasn't a place for the black family. Television makers as a whole had anxiety about putting a Black family on television. [It] wasn't so much that the audience [might have] a problem with it. I think was the television makers who didn't – and still don't understand – about cultural differences … The BBC's concerns were still clearly with white audiences and their perceptions, despite the organization's well-intentioned liberal stance at the time.[123]

Newspapers were quick to discuss the controversial programme, and television critics such as Stanley Reynolds of the *Guardian*, Philip Philips of the *Sun*, and Peter Black of the *Daily Mail* each addressed the impact of the Black-male-with-a-White-wife phenomenon. Philips noted that there was great concern and uncertainty as to whether the BBC would transmit the show, whilst Black was certain that the programme would 'drive the loony minorities into frenzy', indicating continued concerns of sexual miscegenation, the very issue that allegedly began the Nottingham riots.[124] In an interview with the *Radio Times*, Errol John stressed that the programme was 'not about a mixed marriage. To make an issue of this aspect only is to distort what the series attempts to say. It oversimplifies, states the obvious, and, living is a very, very complex business'.[125] In a retrospective critique of the programme, Stanley Reynolds of the *Guardian* wrote a cryptic review that accused the BBC of taking the programme off the air after only six episodes when it had kept programmes on that had far less potential. The organisation's decision was considered 'a bit unchivalrous' by Reynolds, and the show should have been 'juiced up'. He wrote that the programme could have featured:

> Scenes of West Indians flashing teeth and rolling eyes … with shockeroo shots of Errol John … in bed with Gemma Jones who plays his white wife – and why not? It might have been a bit better than proceeding so half-throttle towards these legitimate aspects of a mixed marriage in a Jamaican community – and then reversing quickly.[126]

Whilst this was obviously a cynical criticism of the effete nature of the programme, the desired engagement with racial and sexual eroticism as a selling point for racial understanding and tolerance was brutally evident.

Good Coloured actors abound – 1960s and 1970s programming

A 1968 report filed by Robert Silvey (Head of BBC Audience Research) and the Current Affairs Group discussed BBC television programmes about social, political, economic, and industrial affairs, specifically regarding race relations. This included daily news programming from *Panorama* and *24-Hours*. In accordance with the BBC charter, which requires 'information, education and entertainment', the Current Affairs output was to stimulate public interest on matters considered important, and to present them on television in a manner that was as interesting as possible. An 'immediate problem', according to the report, was race relations. Noting that racial tensions in the USA and possibly in the UK would make headline news, 'the voice of Black Power' may become louder than ever. Silvey charged the Current Affairs group with putting events into perspective without invoking sensationalism. His Current Affairs Group wanted to avoid undesirable side effects, such as increasing racial tensions. However, despite positive audience responses, Silvey's report noted that Current Affairs race-relations output was unlikely to affect change in those whose opinions were already set, and would be most likely to reinforce them, whether 'liberal or reactionary'. Yet Current Affairs race-relations programmes could contribute to the fortification of attitudes of those who saw the problem as important but had 'not yet taken entrenched positions about it'. A programme that featured Black extremists calling for a 'kill whitey' campaign would be likely to create shock and horror, yet it was safe to predict that the secondary effects would vary. On some viewers, secondary effects could drive the need to remove the causes of racial tension, while others could develop stronger anti-colour attitudes, 'sowing the seeds of prejudice'. Silvey further noted that a large proportion of information about racial attitudes was 'scrappy, partial, half-baked or just plain wrong', and that this misinformation was 'staggeringly high' despite various discussions about the issue of race, 'in the mass communication media ad nauseam'.[127] It was perhaps these feelings of concern that drove the organisation to green-light more programming related to race, particularly Black issues. As a backlash against racism in America reached the news media in the UK, a degree of concern grew among Whites, fearing Powell-like images of racial Armageddon, and young Blacks, seeking a means to fight back against the faceless monster of racialism.

When considering the issues of Black identity and the popularity of these notions with Black British audiences, the BBC began to offer more programmes that addressed issues related to Black people. Among other programmes featuring Black Britons during the late 1960s and early 1970s, a *Man Alive* segment featured 'Some of my Best Friends are White' (BBC2, 12 October 1966), an analysis of six Black women and the 'educated American Negro' who, despite middle-class trappings and aspirations, still endured prejudice.[128] The *Thirty-Minute Theatre* offered the teleplay *Go Tell It on Table Mountain* (BBC2, 1 March 1967) featuring Calvin Lockhart, followed in the same year by an episode of *Panorama* (BBC1, 3 April 1967) that addressed the growing middle class of Black people in England. Of particular interest was a programme entitled *We're Only Human* (BBC1, 11 February 1968) an episode of the *Meeting Point* series. Within the programme, a new generation of West Indian teens addresses problems and issues related to life in the United Kingdom. The opening sequence featured a West Indian boy noting how 'they' say Black boys are bad, as they run up and down the streets, but he expresses his discontent with this slur, saying, 'how long can you take it? Because we're only human. We're bound to fight back eventually.'[129]

Man Alive offered *Black Power In Britain* (BBC1, 27 February 1968), a programme considered inflammatory by management, and that served no useful purpose, according to audience Reaction Indexes, but offered no sentiments not heard 'almost daily in Hyde Park', according to Desmond Wilcox.[130] The *Cause for Concern* series ran *Equal before the Law* (BBC1, 26 July 1968), an episode that addressed the often-strained relationships between the British police and Black people. On *Scene*, *The Dark Immigrants* episode (BBC1, 26 September 1968) highlighted how West Indian immigrants were faring in the 1960s. The *Wednesday Play* featured Errol John's teleplay *The Exiles* (BBC1, 23 April 1969), a drama that revolved around the lives of Trinidadians and their lonely, near exile despite living among Whites in Britain. The *Play for Today* offered *In the Beautiful Caribbean* (BBC1, 3 February 1972), a drama by Jamaican Barry Reckord about the effects of Black Power in Jamaica. With what could easily be considered an all-star cast of actors from the region, the teleplay featured poet Louise Bennett, Horace James, Thomas Baptiste, Carmen Munroe, among others. *Long Live Our England* (BBC1, 20 March 1972) was a three-part series that chronicled Britain's Black community and its attempts at assimilation and survival. In a similar vein, *In Mother Country?* (BBC1, 20 March 1972) allowed post-war Caribbean settlers to tell their stories, while in *A Tale of Black Families* (22 March 1972) Caribbeans openly discussed their views about the English. *Young and Black* (23 March 1972) included interviews with young, British-born Blacks and their lives in an ever-changing multicultural UK. *Full House* (BBC2, 3 February 1973) was noted by historian Stephen Bourne as the first Caribbean arts programmes made for television, and offered the work of various West Indian writers and filmmakers. *The Black Man in Britain: 1550–1950* (BBC2, 15 November 1974) featured five documentary films which explored the historical impact of Black people in British society. *The Centre Play* offered *The Museum Attendant* (BBC2, 2 August 1975) written by Michael Abbensetts and featuring Horace James. Also in that same year was Abbensetts' *Black Christmas* (BBC2, 20 December 1972), with Carmen Munroe as a mother determined to bring her family together for a joyous Christmas, but with bittersweet results.

A diversity of immigrant culture, and *Empire Road*

Perhaps the BBC's commitment to racial balance within televisual texts was never more pronounced than the green-lighting of the drama series *Empire Road* (BBC, 31 October–28 November 1978; 23 August–25 October 1979), written and developed by writer Michael Abbensetts and producer Peter Ansorge. The programme, made at BBC Pebble Mill with location shots filmed around the Handsworth area of Birmingham, revolved around the lives of citizens living in a Birmingham West Indian community (Figure 14). *Empire Road* featured the well-known Norman Beaton as Everton Bennett; Corinne Skinner-Carter as his wife, Hortense; Joe Marcell as well-intentioned brother-in-law Walter; Wayne Laryea as Marcus; and Nalini Moonasar as his Asian love interest, Ranjanaa. Rudolph Walker was nemesis Sebastian Moses, and established thespian Thomas Baptiste was Herbie. Other leading actors, such as the popular Julie Walters, also appeared on the programme in varying roles. More importantly, the series was the first written by a Black Briton of West Indian descent, Michael Abbensetts.[131] He began his involvement with the programme after writing 'a number of one off TV plays'. He then came up with the idea for the TV series that he called *Empire Road*. When asked about any challenges in getting the programme commissioned, Abbensetts stated,

> To tell you the truth, I did not have too much of a problem getting the series commissioned. Two people helped, a young BBC producer called Peter Ansorge and the Controller of BBC Two, a youngish upper- middleclass Englishman called Brian Wenham. Ansorge had [already] commissioned some one-off TV plays of mine. One day, I said to Peter and later to Brian, 'I've written a TV series idea.' I told them I'd based the main character on an uncle of mine who had a wicked sense of humour. I showed some of the script to both Brian and Peter. They both loved it. It was surprisingly easy to pitch and sell the project.

When asked about some of the reaffirming measures taken by the BBC as the show was being considered, Abbensetts explained that even before series one

Figure 14 *Empire Road* featured Everton Bennett (Norman Beaton), his wife, Hortense (Corinne Skinner-Carter) and his well-intentioned brother-in-law, Walter (Joe Marcell). Class issues are evident as Bennett often ridicules Walter for a variety of reasons, notably his underclass status and inferior business skills.

of *Empire* was shown on BBC, 'Brian Wenham commissioned a second series from me! Not only that but he introduced me to some of the other heads of BBC TV.' Abbensetts expressed shock at the sudden death of Wenham, noting that 'whilst the 2nd series was still being made, Brian Wenham died. I lost a great Controller of BBC Two, but even more important I lost a friend as well.' Abbensetts considered many stories of West Indian or Black British families in contemporary England, but chose these particular storylines and subsequent developments because of his personal knowledge of the cultural affectations demonstrated in the series. He noted: 'I write about what I know. Always have.'[132]

In the world defined by Abbensetts, the area in which Beaton's character lived was inhabited by West Indians and Asians, leading to storylines that included an interracial relationship between his son Marcus and an Asian woman, much to her father's concern (Figure 15). The romance was not the familiar and arguably more acceptable union of a Black female with a White male, as *Mixed Blessings* had highlighted. *Empire Road* became known as 'the Black *Coronation Street*' (ITV, 1960–), and fell within the genre of 'dramady'. It featured a range of directors, including Horace Ové (*Pressure, Playing Away*), and was considered to be one of the BBC's first efforts at providing a Black-themed drama, with tinges of comedy, written from the perspectives of Black Britons. Ové later work on the controversial *Play for Today, A Hole in Babylon* (BBC1, 29 November 1979) and continued to establish his ability to relate the frustrations of both first- and second-generation immigrants, particularly Black Britons. Ové originally was interested in working on *Empire Road*, and stated 'Frankly, I did not like the first lot that went out very much. But I got interested when I read the new lot: they dealt with real life up to a certain extent.' His concern, expressed by many Black Britons working in the British media, was the absence of true cultural values. Ové explained that 'when West Indian actors go on television they react, clean up their accents, and lose out on their rhythm and style. English directors will tend to suggest English motivations to them, and they create something else out of it.' Ové credited his West Indian heritage as the principal reason actors felt comfortable evoking ethnic stylings in their work. Corinne Skinner-Carter felt more relaxed in her own 'body as opposed to the way the English make you work', as Beaton felt Ové 'was in touch with all the unwritten lines in Abbensetts' world', noting that 'it was a joy working with a West Indian director'.[133]

Producer Peter Ansorge began the project with Abbensetts whilst serving as script editor at BBC's drama department at the Pebble Mill Studios, Birmingham. Ansorge had already worked closely with Head of the Department, David Rose, 'a very enlightened man who had a strong track record in producing drama series for the BBC'. They had previously worked

Figure 15 Marcus (Wayne Laryea), and his Asian love interest Ranjanaa (Nalini Moonasar) deconstruct the standard trope of interracial romance, by removing the binary construct of black and white, yet complicating it further with Eastern and Western cultural affectations. This matters little to Bennett when he discovers Walter has lent his flat to a pair of Rastafarians (Trevor Butler and Vincent Taylor).

to develop *Gangsters* (BBC1, 1976–78) at Birmingham, a programme not without its critics for its violence and racial stereotypes, based on the local underworld, and featuring 'a host of Black and Asian characters'. Ansorge script edited the series, and found the work 'stimulating and inspiring', particularly since 'nowhere else in television drama was multiracial Britain being so directly reflected'. After the programme, Ansorge thought the unit should continue to 'mine this new vein of drama'. He had known Abbensetts from his theatre work at the Royal Court in London, and one day met him on Oxford Street. He asked Abbensetts if he 'might have a TV idea for us at Pebble Mill', and Abbensetts 'came up with a one-off drama called *Black Christmas*' (BBC2, 20 December 1977), a film featuring the interactions and bittersweet emotions of 'an ordinary black family at Christmas in Birmingham'. Director Stephen Frears cast Norman Beaton as the father, whose portrayal became the inspiration for the character in *Empire Road*. The special *Black Christmas* was considered a success within the BBC by Ansorge and others, because

> There had never been a successful drama about normal black life on television. Invariably previous attempts had centred around racism and criminality. *Black Christmas* avoided those routes. So, Michael and I talked about extending this idea to a series. That's how *Empire Road* was born. Later we walked around the Handsworth district of Birmingham and began discussing characters and storylines.

Ansorge talked to David Rose about the project, a budget was developed for scripts, and the writing began. The first run was five episodes, whilst the recommissioned second series ran for ten episodes. Ansorge's promotion to producer from script editor by Rose provided his first credit as producer. Wenham, who Ansorge says 'moved it out of early evening and into primetime' as a means of helping the programme's success, intentionally rescheduled the recommissioned series for 8 p.m.,

> To up the profile and audience, He supported it through trials, and it got the cover of the *Radio Times*. Viewing figures went up too. The ratings actually increased during the second series. It was heavily promoted when Wenham switched it to primetime. Audiences of two million were – and are – very respectable for BBC2.

During the time of former Head of Radio Sir Ian Trethowan as Director-General, Ansorge and Rose held the responsibility of selling programme ideas to the Controllers of BBC1 and BBC2, a task Ansorge says Rose was 'very adept at'. His involvement helped to keep the production team away from 'any intrigues or rivalries taking place at Television Centre in London'; Rose and Abbensetts also considered Brian Wenham 'a big supporter of the show'. However, Ansorge explained that he did not 'want to give … the idea that the BBC in those days was the Garden of Eden, but the biggest challenge was to produce a successful show'. When developing the show, Ansorge found reactions from within the BBC to be mostly more ambiguous, noting that, when the series was announced to the press, a colleague from the 'drama department in London rang to tell me I was crazy'. Further, he told Ansorge that 'a black soap opera would never work. There were very few good black actors in the UK, and those that were [acceptable] would never turn up in time for rehearsals.' Ansorge added that 'to this day I pinch myself and ask whether this conversation ever really happened, but I'm afraid it did'. Many of the technical crews and support (design, make-up, camera, etc.) that Ansorge worked with were suspicious of *Empire Road* as a 'project for propaganda reasons' rather than a quality drama. Most of the White people working on the crews 'lived locally, but outside the inner city of Birmingham', and most were suspicious, with very few 'black or Asian friends'. Yet Ansorge noted that it 'was fascinating to watch the crews begin to warm to the actors as we began filming and studio recordings'. Ansorge credits Norman Beaton with helping to bridge differences, by talking to the crews, joking with them, and impressing them 'with his skill, wit, and brilliance as an actor. Norman was the nearest thing we ever had to a Cosby, and *Empire Road* brought out the best in him.' In another comparison to Bill Cosby, Ansorge believed that *Empire Road* did, like *The Cosby Show* (NBC, 1982–94), help to overcome some aspects of White prejudice, with 'a similar ripple'.

When considering the many stories of West Indian or Black British families in contemporary Britain, Ansorge and Abbensetts chose to develop a narrative that did not present the characters as problematic; they instead chose to frame them as 'real West Indians, but for everyone to identify. We wanted to use humour and soap opera techniques to get people on our side, whether black, Asian or white.' Ansorge and Abbensetts didn't want to be seen as 'taking a leftish political stance', and instead made Beaton's Everton 'a rather conservative character' whose views shocked many of Ansorge's White liberal friends. However, Ansorge and Abbensetts did not want to exclude social issues entirely, and as the series went on they began to tackle controversial matters, 'but always from the point of view of characters which the audience had come to care about and engage with'. Ové's direction of the final three episodes helped considerably, according to Ansorge. In 'Kalaloo Sunday' (20 September 1979) – in which two characters, Miss May (Rosa Roberts) and Skinner-Carter's Hortense, visit two separate churches, Baptist and Anglican, respectively – Ové's direction not only showed a study in cultural contrasts, but evoked a sense of nostalgia for Hortense's Sundays 'back home' in the islands. 'Streets of Thornley' (25 October 1979) proved his ability to work on location, and placed 'Michael's characters in the real life of the inner city'. Ansorge noted how in the episode when a White gang attacks the sweet shop of Mr Kapoor (Mellan Mitchell) and later threatens Marcus and Ranjanaa, the fight was shot with a hand-held video camera, providing a more realistic point of view for the audience. For 'Wedding' (1 November 1979), Ové brought in a host of Black actor friends 'to participate as extras', giving the episode 'an extra dimension'.

Ansorge found it difficult to know how Black, White and Asian audiences reacted to the programmes specifically, because the BBC refused to carry out audience research with specific minority groups. He reportedly

> Begged them to but they said – no, the audience is the audience, we don't distinguish between white and black. However, it became clear as time went on that black audiences were watching in great numbers ... A teacher in a London Comprehensive school had asked his class (mainly black kids) to write in. What was moving was that the letters were addressed to the characters in the show, not the actors. The teacher explained that they had identified to an extent that he'd never experienced. I knew then we were in with a chance.

Ansorge also noted that Africans and Asians reacted to the characters on the show quite differently. He found that Asians loved it, due to a Bollywood-style tradition of 'loving film and soaps', and 'liked the Romeo and Juliet storyline' between Marcus and Ranjanaa. Ansorge's next-door neighbour was a strict Muslim who 'never allowed his wife to speak to mine', he explained, yet 'loved the show'. He laughed about the 'black man in *Empire Road* falling in love with the beautiful Asian girl'. He'd never permit it, of course, and neither would his friends at the mosque – 'but we all watch your show, Peter!' He noted, however, that the reaction among Africans was less clear, citing how the Head of Nigerian TV saw several episodes involving conflict between parents and their teenagers, and was 'appalled' by the behaviour of teenage upstarts Desmond (Trevor Butler) and Royston (Vincent Taylor). 'No African child would dare to speak to his parents like that', he told Ansorge. The reaction of White audiences was mixed, according to Ansorge: some reportedly loved the programme, while some hated it, yet 'they watched it'.

In an audience survey conducted for the new, recommissioned programme, which began on 23 August 1979, the estimated audience was 3.9 per cent (2 million) of the UK population. On BBC1 during this same time of 8.05–8.30 p.m. was the comedy *Citizen Smith* (BBC1, 1977–80), viewed by an estimated 30 per cent of audiences. ITV was blacked out because of an industrial dispute. The reactions of audience polled, based on 103 question-naires completed by 6 per cent of the viewing panel, were generally positive. This sample of the audience provided a Reaction Index of 57: in weeks 44 and 45 of 1978 the programme had Reaction Indexes of 54 and 61 respectively. When asked if they had seen any of the first series, most viewers (65 per cent) replied 'no'. Divided were reactions to the first programme in the new series of the programme, and the episode *Shark* (23 August 1979). Most respondents 'actively liked than disliked the programme' and those to whom it appealed felt that it promised to be 'an enjoyable series', since viewers felt the characters had been 'believable and the storyline interesting'. They noted that apart from the serious topic of slum landlords it had hilarious touches of comedy. Of those to whom the programme did not appeal, some commented that it was 'neither original nor interesting', and they 'cared for neither the characters nor the story'. However, viewers did agree that the acting was of a 'high standard', with a cast that 'evoked amusement, sympathy, and dislike', and was therefore 'successful'. The production created an 'air of authenticity' with 'excellent scenery, effects, and camerawork'. When polled as to whether they would continue to watch the series, 20 per cent responded 'yes, definitely', whilst 31 per cent said 'probably', and 19 per cent felt that they possibly would. Under the category of probably or definitely not, 30 per cent responded negatively.[134]

Other popular Black-themed shows such as *Love Thy Neighbour* (ITV, 1972–76) and *Mixed Blessings* (ITV, 1978–80) were clearly sitcoms that drew upon the convention of racial difference and social tensions to produce humour. *The Fosters* (ITV, 1976–77), which drew liberally from America's *Good Times* (CBS, 1974–79), centred upon a Black family living in a tower block flat, struggling to maintain 'good times' whilst urban blight, poverty, and racism surrounded them. The British show starred Norman Beaton as the father, Isabelle Lucas as his wife, and, fresh from the *New Faces* comedy variety show (ITV, 1973–78), Lenny Henry. The programme, like *Good Times*, had an ongoing theme that no matter the circumstances, these families could endure, allowing for an absence of guilt or blame on the part of any hegemonic system that helped to create the poverty these Black people so valiantly endured. Controller of programmes Cyril Bennett reportedly said that the show would have 'no racial overtones', and ITV's London Weekend Television (LWT) made an additional twenty-six half-hour episodes.[135] However, *Empire Road* clearly offered a dramatic text as well as moments of comedy, without a laugh track. Television critic Sylvia Clayton wrote in the *Daily Telegraph* that the programme had 'a complex web of family and business relationships'; something White programmes had done for years. This type of genre, show called a 'dramady' in American television, was similar to American shows like NBC's *The Days and Nights of Molly Dodd* (1987–91), CBS's *Frank's Place* (1987–88), and *Hooperman* on ABC (1987–89). Often each episode began with a humorous scenario, but they sometimes ended with angst and concern, driven by the narrative structure of an episodic serial drawing from radio. Another advantage

Clayton saw was that BBC2 decided to 'spread the story out, half an hour at a time, over 10 weeks' later expanded to fifteen. However, it was felt that viewers might have 'easily become involved in the everyday life of the Bennetts featured on the programme, if 'the family album were opened more frequently'.[136] The BBC only ordered fifteen episodes of the show, which was considered a short run by British television standards. Clayton felt that it seemed 'a pity' that the BBC showed inflexibility in its scheduling.[137] Perhaps the multiple personalities and relationships that seemingly existed outside of the normative construction of whiteness caused its failure. As suggested by Clayton, perhaps had the family album been left opened a bit longer, White audiences of the BBC2 would have recognised some of their own images.

When considering the importance of diverse representations of ethnicity on television, management was convinced to accept the cultural practices demonstrated in *Empire Road* via the 'ambition' that drove Ansorge, Abbensetts, and Rose, 'not management's reactions to the idea'. At the time, Ansorge says the BBC provided opportunities 'to do something like *Empire Road* without editorial interference'. However, he noted to others working in drama that programmes like *Coronation Street* had no Black characters, yet 'the real Coronation Streets throughout Britain' were changing, and this was not being 'reflected in our television drama'. Ansorge considered the primary responsibility to belong to him and David Rose. He explained that the department 'had a brief to find and produce new writers for television'. *Empire Road* used up the series budget for BBC2, and had a third season been produced, other 'new work – such as the Alan Bleasdale series *Boys from the Blackstuff* (BBC2, 1982) would have been impossible. Ansorge also noted that 'Michael [Abbensetts] had written fifteen episodes in eighteen months', and 'longer running soaps depend on a team of writers, which Michael wasn't keen on for *Empire Road*'. The programme could have continued if the BBC had allowed for additional funding. However, as Ansorge suggested, the UK 'was going through an economic crisis at the time and the BBC was looking to cut back expenditure. I don't think BBC internal politics played any part in the decision.' Perhaps one of the most rewarding moments came for Ansorge at the end of the first series, when a big party was given for the cast, crew, and management at Pebble Mill. He called it 'a heady occasion', at which he gave 'a speech quoting James Baldwin. Everyone – black and white – cheered.'

In 2005, the Barbican in London held a retrospective of Ové's work. Ansorge was part of a packed audience that was 'ninety per cent black' for a Q and A with the director. Answering an enquiry about *Empire Road*, Ové pointed him out, telling the audience that it 'was all due to "that gentleman" sitting at the back'. The audience erupted into applause, which Ansorge suggests showed that 'the show had stayed with that audience some twenty-five years after transmission. That says something.' Ansorge later added, 'I think part of the black audience was disappointed when *Empire Road* came to an end. There had been nothing like it on British TV before – or, alas, since.'[138]

Community voices and an *Open Door*

The BBC approved, as an experiment, thirteen weekly programmes of a new community series, *Open Door*. The programme would show at a non-peak hour on BBC2, Mondays at 11.30 p.m. beginning 2 April, each programme lasting for 40 minutes. The BBC agreed to provide technical facilities, studio, and cameras, and offer professional advice and assistance if it was wanted, but the groups taking part would decide the content and style of the programmes.[139] A selection committee chose contributors, with Rowan Ayers, former Editor of Presentation Programmes, as editor of the new production unit. Ayers began as a freelance writer between 1950 and 1953 and worked on features with the Amalgamated Press, before creating two plays broadcast by the BBC. In April 1955, he became an editorial assistant for the *Radio Times*, and was later appointed Television Editor. In November 1972, Ayers began preparing the *Open Door* series for airing in April 1973. Following the success of the first thirteen programmes, Ayers became Editor, Community Programmes, in February of 1974.[140] The programme was created in response to a desire for community groups to receive access to television, a political cry from those who felt, according to Stanley Reynolds, that the traditional formulae and attitudes of broadcasting media needed to be questioned by ordinary people. Yet Reynolds criticised the BBC for staunchly determining which groups were responsible, a condition he felt 'stalked the project closely'.[141] Over 300 applications for programme slots had arrived by February of 1973, including one from an unnamed illegal organisation.[142]

Ayers was responsible for recommending which groups should be offered airtime, but he was not alone: a committee – chaired by BBC Director of Programmes, Alasdair Milne, ENCA Desmond Taylor, and BBC2 Controller Robin Scott – considered recommendations. Press releases noted that the committee would have power to co-opt, influence selections, and decide the length of time allocated to each contributing group. In a reference to concerns raised over the approaching meltdown of race relations, Milne noted that 'cynics dismiss this kind of programme as no more than a useful safety valve. Enthusiasts claim that they bring a freshness of attitude and style, which can be achieved no other way. This experiment may establish which is true.'[143] Since the programmes would be live broadcasts, specific directives and an established code would manage certain aspects of content, mainly:

I. Programme time may be offered to any group association, organisation, community, or consortium of individuals with views or activities which are not represented on the air in the course of other programming, and whose purpose is not to represent or promote a political party or group, or to pursue an industrial dispute.

II. Such groups should make application for airtime and submit sufficient information about their activity, argument, purpose, or identity to satisfy the Programme Unit that the application can be granted.

III. Before being granted air time, the groups must give an undertaking in writing that they will not use their air time:

(i) for financial gain or commercial advertisement;

(ii) to make personal attacks;

(iii) for obscene speech or display;

(iv) to infringe the laws affecting broadcasting, e.g. defamation, contempt of court, copyright, and the Representation of the People Act.

If there is any doubt on the interpretation of these undertakings, the BBC Programme Unit will advise, and in the event of dispute, the BBC decision will be final. Any infringement of these undertakings will make those concerned liable to forfeiture of their airtime.[144]

On Thursday, 15 February 1973, Scott and Ayers held an open Q and A about the programme to potential participants and others at Television Centre. The two also shared programme details with attendees that encouraged programmers to use the services of the Community Programme Unit (CPU) if they chose, drawing upon their expertise, offering 'as much or as little help as you want'. The budget was set for each programme, yet participants could use their own funds to supplement the effort. Colleagues or specialists chosen by programmers were welcomed to assist or participate, if those involved felt they were qualified to take on the responsibility. The BBC would not pay for these professionals, and negotiations would be between the group and the individual invited. The studio area for the programmes was small, so live discussions were strictly limited to seven participants, yet pre-recording would be available to allow a variety of interviews to be included in the programme. Participants could arrange for live calls to be taken, if arrangements were made seven days in advance. Scott and Ayers strictly noted that any individuals or groups doing shows for Open Door were liable 'to the same rules and regulations that are faced by any broadcaster at any time. If you commit libel, you will be liable to be sued under civil law. If you commit a criminal act, you will be liable to be prosecuted under criminal law.' Whilst applications for airtime would be taken, the BBC could not guarantee that everyone would have the opportunity to do a programme. Guidelines, in addition to those listed above, further noted that there should be no incitement to riot, or to violent or unlawful action of any kind, and there should be no racialism or attempts to incite racialist feeling.[145] Ayers stressed the importance of these guidelines due to the live nature of the programme, adding that in an extreme case, for example if a group misled the BBC and used the time to 'shout obscenities', control room personnel and management 'would have the ultimate veto of cutting them off from the gallery'.[146]

One of the groups taking part in the programme was the Black Teachers' Group, featuring those who expressed their feelings about the English education system as it affected Black children (16 April 1973), particularly during a time of unease over immigration. In a press release issued to TV preview writers, the group expressed their differences in political viewpoints and organisational memberships. Yet each was Black and an educator, with highly similar viewpoints on their roles in the school system and the plight of Black children. They suggested that if Enoch Powell's predictions of inner cities completely occupied by immigrants by the end of the century were to come true, then it 'will be revealing to see how this group [Powell's supporters] views the prospects for multiracial education in the future'. Also noted was what the teachers called the 'frequently degrading representation of black people in contemporary culture', which included an Oxfam poster featuring a starving African child, reinforcing notions of overseas aid as paternalistic gifts from above.[147] In a report the day after the show, the BBC's automated answerphone took in scores of calls, among them many from Oxfam members who agreed with the criticism of the advertisement shown and who noted 'their intentions to have it withdrawn'.[148] Subsequent discussions of the group and their concerns included social activist Dorothy Kuya and writer Mike Phillips, who suggested more than 'white Liberal help and sympathy' was needed when considering changes in education systems within the country.[149] Television critic Reynolds called the programme the best so far.[150] The discussions were very different from the publicity surrounding Yvonne Conolly, who became London's first Black headteacher in 1969.

Other programmes of a controversial yet decidedly pro-social nature included a show on *Immigrant Workers' Rights* (25 March 1974) featuring a 'strong attack by Indian immigrants on the lack of support provided by the Trade Unions in Great Britain for coloured workers', shot on film and mainly in Nottingham. *Black Feet in the Snow* was presented that April (8 April 1974); a musical drama made by a group of West Indians, called the Radical Alliance of Poets and Players (RAPP). The play told the story of Jahn-Jahn, a young West Indian who emigrates to Britain, and other immigrants from 1960–65. Regular players at a club in Essex, The Nite Blues Steel Band (29 September 1974) told 'the history of the West Indies through steel band music'. The Standing Conference of Asian Communities in the UK (28 April and 5 May 1975) were given two successive weeks in which they discussed and examined solutions to difficulties faced by Asian communities in Britain. As noted in a memo, Senior Features Producer Paul Bonner suggested to Edward Rayner that a host of other groups were chosen for the programme as well, including the British Campaign to Stop Immigration, chosen for a segment to run on 28 February. The organisation had been considered along with several applications from anti-immigration groups, yet the others had 'a more overt National Front flavour'. A separate, hand-written notation read, 'not *for ousting*'.[151] Other programmes covered students' rights, spiritualism, community action projects, educational and medical projects, religion and ethics, and the environment, yet not allowed was any programming that espoused party positions.[152]

The *vox populi* of protest

In a move that represented growing Black British solidarity, a letter was written to the BBC regarding the programme *Till Death Us Do Part* (1966–68; 1972; 1974–75) protesting against the character Alf Garnett's 'racialism'.[153] Despite the fact that the programme had been a source of displeasure to Black and Asian audiences since 1966, the character had gained a huge following among many audiences. The concept for the infamous programme had begun earlier in the decade as part of BBC's *Comedy Playhouse* (1961–75). Thomas Sloan, who served as the Head of BBC's Light Entertainment division in the early 1960s, had inaugurated the show. *Comedy Playhouse* had served as a launching pad for many British situation comedies, particularly those written by the team of Alan Simpson and Ray Galton.[154] The actual programme, written by comedian Johnny Speight, featured the racist Alf Garnett (Warren Mitchell), who constantly complained about foreigners of all ethnicities. The same programme became a template for Norman Lear's *All in the Family* (CBS, 1971–91) a few years later.

This complaint, made through formal channels, was referred to the executive committee of the actors' union Equity. Black British actor Roy Swire served as the Equity shop; he and others wanted the union to press the BBC for an inquiry into the nature of the racist comedy used in the show. Swire had said in an interview that he and other 'coloured workers in London would consider further action if the BBC did not offer an apology and promise an inquiry' by later that same week. The complaints referred to character Alf Garnett's remarks about 'coloured people and heart trans-plants'. The BBC publicly disavowed the complaint.[155]

In a move that surprised many viewers, the show (called the 'BBC's most popular programme') was to be shown for the last time,[156] as scriptwriter Speight had told the BBC and the press that he was not going to write any more of the programmes. Sloan had reportedly planned to ask Speight to suspend *Till Death* scripts anyway. He had already spent a great deal of time 'defending Johnny Speight', who criticised the BBC for undermining his creative freedom to develop the Garnett character. Sloan cited Speight's complaints as 'absolute rubbish' and maintained that savage censorship did not exist at the BBC. Sloan stated that if he made occasional changes in Speight's scripts, it was because he had gone 'beyond the very broad tolerance given to a writer of his talents'.[157] The service could no longer avoid these other voices of contention.

In 1973, a group of actors of colour (called 'Asian and African', not ethnically British, by the press) organised a march on the BBC Television Centre in the West London area of White City, London against racism in casting. Christopher Kum, the organiser of the protest, told the press that he represented about 400 Chinese, Indian, African, and Arab actors and actresses through his work for a casting agency, and stated '90 per cent of them were out of work'. He considered the BBC's attitude in the matter to be insulting and apathetic. He told the *Daily Mail*, 'all we get is glorified walk-on parts with no lines'. Kum stated that in a situation that smacked of minstrelsy, 'the BBC would rather have an English actor in pain for two hours being made up to look like a Chinese or Japanese than use one of us'.[158]

While the BBC continued its racial balancing act, the press and the service covered another conference addressing racial issues that took place in London. The meeting, financed by the charitable Gulbenkian Foundation and chaired by Dr David Pitt, invited 100 West Indian and Asian community leaders to discuss immigration and xenophobic attitudes among White Britons. One of the principle issues discussed was that 'the long held ideal of cultural assimilation should now be pronounced dead for the foreseeable future'. As a participant, theorist Stuart Hall felt that 'Assimilation is not considered either a realistic or indeed a desirable option. Any policies for the future will have to reckon with this fundamental break, this establishment of a radical difference between the migrant and the host communities.'[159] Hall emphasised that the institutional racism of the country had resulted in a segregated society that reflected disaffection among second-generation immigrants. Racial tension in ghetto areas and the deterioration of relationships between 'law-abiding black communities and the police' was another major concern.[160]

While tensions seemingly continued to increase within the country, an attempt began to bring diversity to television, as a pilot episode of the UK's first all-Black television sitcom was shown in 1975. The series was called *The Fosters* (ITV, 1976–77) and centred on a Black family living in a tower-block flat. The programme was based upon Norman Lear's *Good Times* (CBS, 1974–79) from the USA. Like the Evans family, the Fosters lived in a ghetto tenement complex and struggled to maintain 'good times' while urban blight, poverty and racism surrounded them. The show starred Norman Beaton as the father, Isabelle Lucas as his wife, and Lenny Henry, fresh from the *New Faces* (ATV, 1973–78), where he had made his name mainly by doing a series of 'off-beat impersonations', which appealed to audiences and led some members of the press to label him a 'schoolboy'.[161] ITV's London Weekend Television (LWT) made an additional twenty-six half-hour episodes of *The Fosters*. London Weekend controller of programmes Cyril Bennett was reported to have said that the show would have 'no racial overtones'.[162] Like *Good Times*, the programme had an ongoing subtext that, no matter the circumstances, these families had 'good times' to pull them through; a notion that deflected issues of poverty and economic disparity, drawing instead upon valiant endurance.

Despite this depiction of a tolerable ghetto life on television, a feature in the *Daily Telegraph* of 31 May 1976 warned that the young Black community in Britain would 'explode' one day, leading to continued conflicts with the police. The feature described a group of young West Indian men addressing the Select Committee on Race Relations and Immigration explaining how police 'deliberately provoked' them through 'false arrests and general harassment'. The memorandum written by the group contained allegations that the police used racial epithets like 'Black bastards' and 'niggers'. One officer reportedly told one young Black Briton that his father 'never fought a war for Black Bastards like you'. Other concerns included police brutality behind closed doors at the Gypsy Hill Station, and that many young Blacks were the victims of mistaken identity. Also mentioned were feelings of societal rejection, a lack of job skills, no positive self-image to enhance a sense of dignity, and a lack of self-respect. They also reportedly stated that 'trying does not make sense' and that 'crime is exciting'. Witnesses to the hearing stated that the young men had not 'benefited from Britain's educational system' and had not been 'equipped with social or academic skill'.[163]

The same issues appeared in the *Guardian* newspaper of that same day, yet with a different emphasis, as Anne McHardy wrote of the obstacles young West Indian men faced. The findings of the committee were emphasised, particularly the issue of historical perspective. It was felt that the educational system should teach more Black history to provide the 'security and confidence to fit into British society'. Clive Anderson of the Community Relations Commission agreed with the young men, who felt that Black studies would give many of them 'the confidence to go forward'. A young Black woman that addressed the committee felt that both White British and West Indians immigrants needed to 'know more of black history and culture' that that there was too much emphasis on the fact that West Indians' ancestors were slaves. She cited that her generations' parents 'had to be bus drivers or nurses', but they wanted 'something more than that'.[164]

Two years later, in 1978, suggestions were made by Black, Brown and White actors at the Edinburgh International Television Festival about a need for integrated casting. At a session on television dramas, the action was called for almost unanimously. The originator of BBC's *Z Cars* (1962–78) and a contributing writer for *The Sweeney* (ITV, 1975–76, 1978), Troy Kennedy Martin said that 'positive discrimination' and 'tokenism' was needed to rectify past discriminations. He reminded audiences 'there are no non-whites in senior management posts; perhaps two or three programme makers, and only a handful of reporters, researchers and technicians'. The scope of writers was considerably limited, again with Whites constructing representations and cultural notions of Blacks. Kennedy Martin stated that 'only two non-whites' had written regularly for any British television channel and that 'white writers' wrote 'monotonously' and 'lazily', relying on stereotypes and codified imagery. These writers demonstrated an 'ignorance of black life' in their 'inability to turn out convincing black parts'. Broadcasters Margaret Walters and Sue Woodford authored a paper given at the session criticising the lack of opportunities for ethnic minority actors and producers, but did agree that newer programmes, such as LWT's *Mixed Blessings* (1978–80) and *The Fosters* did represent 'some progress'.[165] Yet in 1973 the University of Manchester Department of Extra-Mural Studies released the proceedings of the fifth symposium on broadcasting policy for *Broadcasting and Society*. The study specifically examined the attitudes of the BBC and independent television producers to issues of race, and still found representation woefully one-dimensional and shallow.[166] Prince Charles placed part of the responsibility for racial healing on television, stating in an interview that television 'could help to resolve Britain's racial difficulties'. He felt that the BBC and other channels could provide an 'ideal way of helping to dispel fear, resentment, and prejudice', which were essential if the UK were to exist successfully as a multiracial society. He also made a plea for more ethnological programmes that could expand knowledge interracially. He had stated that prejudice existed primarily through 'ignorance of the way in which other people live, work and worship' and that 'television [was] an ideal way of transmitting knowledge and information to millions of people in a relatively painless fashion'.[167] There was clearly a need to continue addressing race and representations on television, yet multicultural casting lagged behind these efforts.

'Black affairs' programming

As the 1980s began, frustrations over continuing unemployment and racial tensions worsened already tense situations in several cities. The New Cross fire that took the lives of thirteen Black youths at a house party in south-east London was thought to have been caused by a petrol bomb thrown at the residence by members of the National Front. The Black community accused the Metropolitan Police of covering up the attack, and in March 20,000 people marched from Fordham Park to Hyde Park to stage a peaceful protest, despite reports from the *Sun* that riots ensued. Later that month, Enoch Powell again spoke out, warning of racial civil war. Through the year, disturbances took place in which frustrated young Britons of colour, mainly second generation, violently protested against a government and police force they saw as biased and overly suspicious of them. Disturbances began in London's Brixton in April, followed by Handsworth in London, Chapeltown in Leeds, and Liverpool. Perhaps as a means of providing insight to these conflicts, or mere placation, the BBC scheduled more race programmes throughout the coming years.

By early 1982, two TV programmes marketed specifically for Black and Asian audiences appeared on Channel 4 and BBC2 during the autumn season. Thanks to a remit under the Broadcasting Act of 1980, Channel 4, the fourth television channel, began broadcasting on 2 November 1982. The station, which was created to compete with BBC2, was encouraged to be highly innovative and experimental in the form and content of programming. Early programming, some of it controversial, included the Royal Shakespeare Company's production of *Nicholas Nickleby*; *Walter*, a drama that revolved around mental patients; a current-affairs programme called *The Friday Alternative*; a popular soap opera that ran twice a week called *Brookside*, and the hour-long Channel 4 news. The channel received disappointing early viewing statistics and a mixed reception from audiences. Eventually, however, Channel 4 would receive critical acclaim for its commitment to ethnic programming.[168] One programme that was to appear on Channel 4's late night schedule was a news magazine featuring Black and Asian hosts reuniting LWT's *Skin* (1979–80) team of Samir Shah and Trevor Phillips. The weekly one-hour programme, *Black on Black* (1982–85), was originally to run for forty weeks of the schedule, with the intent to address issues that affected Asians one week and African-Caribbeans the next. Whilst initially the show would concentrate on African-Caribbean audiences, the producer John Shearer's intent was 'to win a general audience'.[169]

Black on Black presented news, opinions, and events from Black communities around the country and the world. What began as nine or ten journalists were soon limited to two or three. The programme was widely watched by non-White audiences.[170] However, Black British media critic Paul Boateng wrote in the *Sunday Times* that the Black community's response when *Black on Black* came on the scene was 'predictable and varied. About time too.' Boateng wrote that the programme was 'just another little box they've put us into'. Critical statements from Black viewers were 'they'll never let them say anything worth saying' and 'so; they've discovered that we exist at last'. Boateng felt that Black British now existed 'in TV terms, albeit as minority tastes doomed to Channel 4 once a fortnight, alternating with *Eastern Eye*, and BBC2, with *Ebony*, a once-a-week programme for two eight-week series'. As Boateng challenged the programmes to cover a diversity of issues with a commitment to more than placation and tokenism, he noted that the channels 'had better not forget it either, if they are ever to amount to much'.[171]

Other programming at this time included *The Promised Land* (BBC2, 22 July 1982), which revisited the *Question of Colour* segment from the 1950s, and later featured two other segments on Asian and Italian immigration during the 1940s and beyond. *Black* (BBC1, 1983) attempted to provide a personal look at the lives of younger, second-generation African-Caribbeans and their frustrations with racialism. *Ebony People* (BBC2, 2 June 1989) offered a chat programme in which issues related to the Black community were examined, along with a spotlight on Black contributions to popular culture. Within a year, *Ain't no Black in the Union Jack: 25 Years of Race Relations* (BBC2, 20 August–4 September 1990) ran its three-part series to critical acclaim.

Race and recruitment efforts: changes from within

In 1984, the first professional organisation of Black journalists and broad-casters launched a campaign to attract more Black people into television. The Black Media Workers' Association planned to address concerns of unfair employment at the BBC, Channel 4, and other terrestrial channels. Media unions examined issues of Black employment within television, whilst news bureaus challenged inaccurate reporting about race and Third World countries. A Black journalist working in the newsroom of one televi-sion company said: 'I'm the only black among about 100 other workers here and in the two years since I've been here not another black has been hired.'[172] Black Britons of African-Caribbean decent surveyed about the current state of broadcasting discussed a series of issues, including representations. In a study conducted by the Commission for Racial Equality, more information emerged about the desire to see more African-Caribbeans on the screen. Occasional appearances on regular programmes were not enough; those surveyed wanted more television programmes that 'cater[ed] to Afro-Caribbean tastes'. Mentioned often was a desire for more programming that led to increased White understanding of Black culture. Since Black Britons were forming a sizeable proportion of the population, it was essential to acknowledge their contributions to the economy and the nation's 'essential services'. Many cited that fact that it was a 'living memory that British governments actively encouraged their immigration, and therefore the country should acknowledge and continue to educate whites about these cultures'.[173] Earmarked for enforcement were equal-opportunity policies put in place by the Commission on Racial Equality. Arguments abounded during the mid-1980s over how representations should avoid segregating Blacks into their own programming. Cultural critic and broadcaster Beverley Anderson had suggested in both the majority and minority press for ethnic programming to mainstream minority cultures within their discourse. She argued that Blacks, like any other immigrant group, 'want to be part of majority television', and that it was the 'responsibility of the BBC companies to put them there'. Black British people could not always look to ITV news anchor Trevor McDonald or Lenny Henry. Anderson considered Henry so 'sexy, and funny that only a complete dunce could overlook him and no doubt the BBC is guarding its treasure with fat cheques and large dogs'. However, the routine representations mattered to Anderson, not exceptions. She suggested that Black people should be on game shows and soaps, and in roles that have nothing to do with race relations.[174] Ethnic programmes that constituted only a couple of hours a week did not provide a realistic reflection of the country's true community. Accused of showing communities miraculously devoid of a true ethnic mix were the popular soaps *Crossroads* (ATV, 1964–88) and *Coronation Street* (ITV, 1960–). The plot lines of these programmes had worked for decades without a significant Black presence, and since Black audiences watched the programmes, the formula was not changed. One of only a few West Indian actors Thomas Baptiste did appear in episodes of *Coronation Street* in 1963, but was not included when the programme celebrated its thirtieth year in 1990.[175]

The BBC provided the public with a view of its own failures in diversity when broadcasting a landmark documentary in 1986. *The Black and White Media Show* (1986) ran in two parts. Using excerpts from BBC and ITV programming, it transmitted on BBC1, as opposed to the alternative-themed BBC2. The programme addressed how many Blacks working in news had experienced dissatisfaction at portrayals. Other editorial dilemmas arose from White perspectives on the depictions of minorities within the television news and current affairs section at the BBC. The programme's producer – John Twitchin of the Continuing Education department – said the documentary was made in a 'spirit of self-reflection', and he hoped that the BBC news staff, management, and viewers would ask themselves 'whether they are sensitive enough to black people's interests and perspectives'. At the end of the documentary, Director of Programmes Michael Grade made comments about the issues discussed. His hope was that 'the show will be debated by the black communities, the wider audience on BBC1, and by department heads'. He also added in an interview with BBC's *Aerial* magazine that 'the clear solution to the problem of racism on television lies in more black people being employed to make programmes'. He stated that the 'more there are, the more sensitive we will all become in a less formalized and trained way – it will become instinctive, and that is what we have to achieve'.[176]

In a desire to rectify issues of racial inequality at the BBC, a recruiting drive began to get more Black people working within the service. Head of Television Bill Cotton said he felt that the service should take the responsibility to react to racial inequality, and that the problem had been that 'there are a lot of Blacks' in the country 'and they are not on telly'.[177] Cotton did agree that the BBC should re-think its policies, yet he stated in an interview that he did not consider the service racist, but that, 'like the rest of the country, there is a degree of ignorance'. He said BBC bosses were so worried about the underrepresentation of ethnic minorities that they were prepared to introduce a quota system. Cotton felt that the market should reflect the persona of the BBC and its broadcasts. He said, 'in an area where there are a lot of Black people', a qualification for working on television there 'would be being Black'.[178] Other areas should also reflect the market and audience, whatever the ethnic minority. Cotton also said, however, that the BBC would probably recruit 'already successful blacks in their 30s and 40s'. He felt that younger trainees would become 'too BBC' and 'lose their value in relating to the black community'. As opposed to becoming 'too BBC' these recruits would be most likely to bring a newer perspective to the service. Should these individuals only sample these cultures, it would still allow for a better degree of contemporary Black Britishness discourse. Older Blacks that the company spoke to could be more likely to maintain a continuance of the cultural attitudes already present within a society dominated by Whiteness. Cotton called the involvement of Black people in BBC programmes 'crucial', whilst revealing that the *Black and White Minstrel Show* was not part of the BBC's fiftieth anniversary celebrations 'because it would be offensive to Black viewers'.[179] How Cotton could determine this issue for Black audiences is unknown, but given that the service had received numerous complaints through the years, they now had an opportunity to rectify the issue.

Within a year, the BBC budgeted more than £200,000 on attracting more staff from ethnic minorities and recruiting women. The BBC's Equal Opportunities Officer Cherry Ehrlich called for the monitoring of all staff to determine the make-up of ethnic groups represented. Her office also recommended the appointment of equal opportunities officers in all output divisions, and new training courses in film, management, and engineering, especially for women. Her research determined that of 170 posts at senior management level, only 11 were held by women, and of 79 trainees hired for news and production courses in the previous two years, only four were Black. Of 8,899 people interviewed for BBC jobs in the preceding year, only 602 were Black, with fewer than 150 selected for interviews. The BBC planned to provide positions for six Black reporters whilst training 10 other people from deprived areas in television techniques. However, she stated that the service had 'ruled out quotas for women or ethnic staff'. The service also applied to the European Social Fund for a grant to help recruitment among disabled people.[180] There was also a programme designed to employ more female and Black presenters under the watchful eye of the new BBC1 Controller Jonathan Powell. Besides recruitment efforts, Powell ordered a survey of his BBC1's programmes to determine how presenters 'break down according to race, class, sex, and age'. He said that the results regarding the service would show that most BBC1 presenters were 'white, middle-class male' and that BBC1 'should strive for a greater mix'.[181]

In late 1989, the BBC launched the 'Step Forward' programme, designed to allow more Black comedy-writers to gain positions in television. The idea was a combined effort between controller Powell and comedian Lenny Henry. Henry had considered the effort some time before when 'turning up for the first script readings' of a comedy pilot, and finding that out of '90 writers in the room, not one of them was black or Asian'. He added, 'There were only a couple of women there, too, come to think about it'.[182] The issue of *The Times* that reported this also suggested that Step Forward would not live up to its 'heady promise of its accompanying press release – to determine the kind of broadcast comedy to keep the nation laughing into the 1990s'. The author of the editorial suggested that the mere suggestion of this programme was ironic, because whilst Lenny Henry remained Britain's only famous Black comedian, 'the writers who benefit from his initiative will probably spend most of their career providing laugh lines for white performers'.[183] A more important consideration would be the reinforcement of the comedic representation via Blacks, and a far more encouraging scenario would be an effort by the BBC to employ Black writers throughout the service, scripting programmes for all genres. Henry had told the *Guardian* in 1990 that his plan was to assist writers to work in all facets of TV and radio. Yet the comic's film production company, Crucial Films, and BBC television sponsored a two-day comedy workshop aimed at writers 'who will reflect Britain's multicultural society'. Henry stated, 'Black people are often misrepresented on television and that's because there are very few black writers'.[184]

Despite the BBC's intent on working with Henry, the dominant press elected to criticise this effort as patronising. Certain writers also assumed that these new writers would automatically compose jokes and storylines with a racial or racist overtone. An anonymous writer with the *Telegraph* suggested that the incorporation of comic writers like Lenny Henry to work with the BBC was 'no laughing matter', claiming the last time the 'BBC decided to make a joke of race they came up with the immortal character of Alf Garnett', as discussed earlier. The concern was that the BBC had created a racist monster that the public loved for his blatant racism. The article stated that racial separatist Enoch Powell had made racism respectable, but in 'creating Alf Garnett, the BBC deserves to be taken to task as the true culprit. Now they are up to their old tricks again.' However, there was no indication by Henry or Powell that Black writers would script any particular show, much less one with a racist intent. The article then took a different tack in its criticism of Henry's programme, stating that a special programme launched to recruit humorists from their ranks would 'hurt Blacks', making a comparison to East End Cockney humorists who 'never needed a special recruiting programme, nor did Lancashire or Scottish humorists'. After all, the article says, their jokes 'grew naturally'. The author felt also that 'a comedy writer who has to be patronized' is not very funny. Furthermore, 'in any case, any truly good black humour would soon be bound to run up against the Race Relations Act'. The insistence that these writers could evolve in the same fashion as any White comic (despite class and ethnic difference) was not only ludicrous, but a distraction from the concerns over a programme aimed to help Blacks by a Black. Again there was the fear that jokes from Black writers might take aim at Whites. Based upon these writer's concerns it would seem that some degree of guilt had developed a concern over a reverse in discrimination.[185]

For Black Britons, working within the BBC as writers and producers was an important development for the negotiation of place. However, the ultimate authority and power of the BBC to educate the dominant public on issues such as racial equality was far too reliant on principally White writers and White audiences, as surveys indicate, and on the dominant press, as represented by memoranda addressing their concerns. Minority papers such as the *Voice, Weekly Journal,* and *Calabash* criticised the BBC for its lack of commitment to diversification, other than Jan Oliver, a Black Briton who would go on to rise to one of the highest positions in the corporation.[186]

As a counter-measure to the inability of the BBC to affect these types of changes, collaborative efforts of Black British people within the media became a means to an end. More importantly, to many it seemed the only way to improve representations of Blacks on British television. It was felt that this would only be achieved if Black actors, writers, producers, and directors formed their own independent production companies. As suggested by Alby James, artistic director of a Black theatre troupe, 'real change' could 'only be implemented through the independent sector'.[187] Speaking in April 1992 at a workshop on ethnic representation at the prestigious Royal Television Society, Alby reminded actors and media professionals of colour that 'the more of us who have experience in working in television … can move to that stage of forming independent production companies', the more it would be possible for change and autonomy to come about. He spoke of Asian acting troupes that did 'the work, training actors, directors, and writers' and that this effort helped them to 'move further into the mainstream'. Alby stated that 'screaming at the BBC or Channel 4 or anybody else' would not help. Taking the power into their hands, as professionals, would be essential in the development of opportunities.[188]

The independents

Independent producers had also expressed concerns over limited representations and opportunities. A famed White producer of comedies, Charlie Hanson, stated in a BBC documentary that more Black central characters were needed in not just sitcoms but also in dramas. He had been responsible for a host of comedies featuring Black actors when their presence of television was very rare, having worked on *Desmond's* (Channel 4, 1989–94) featuring West Indian actors Norman Beaton and Carmen Munroe and the more contemporary *Chef!* (BBC, 1993–96) featuring Lenny Henry. The BBC had also featured Hanson's beliefs in an in-house training project *Race in the Frame* (BBC, 1993). In the video (designed for White comedy writers) Hanson reminded the viewer via an interview 'Black humour should be only one aspect of Black life'.[189] He suggested that there were varying degrees of the Black experience and each needed to be told with dignity. He also stated that a funny script written by Black writers just might have a primarily White audience.

However, in another interview British Indian writer Farrukh Dhondy, at the time Channel Four Commissioning Editor for Multicultural Programmes, told the press that the question of writers and their audiences was irrelevant. In his view, there was 'already too much substandard work by Black writers on our screens, which has been put there only to assuage the guilt of liberal commissioning editors'.[190] When Channel 4 did Black comedies, he told *The Times*, it was because they were funny. If his channel managed to draw viewers of all races into understanding a different experience from the one they knew, 'then they will have achieved something'. He stated that the goal of Channel 4 was 'not to create positive images of Black people, but to say something culturally significant'. The only way to increase the number of Black dramas or comedies on television, Dhondy said, was to have people like himself, who were culturally self-critical, making the decisions; 'The other channels and producers would only make decisions on a guilty basis'.[191] This view was problematic in that it positioned any attempts to rectify previous disparities as insincere. As the research indicates, the BBC had been involved in the recruitment of Black writers long before it was popular. The notion that Channel 4 did comedies merely because they were funny does not justify racist depictions or shallow White production of West Indian imagery.

His successor was Yasmine Anwar, who took over his post in October of 1997, having worked previously at the BBC as an Executive Producer of Cultural Programming. She addressed issues of racial representations and writing when stating that the biggest challenge for Black programming was to 'pull off the kind of series which can make the kind of impact that probably only three or four other programmes that feature black people have done in the last 50 years'. She mentioned the favoured *Desmond's* as one of the shows. Her concern as a programmer was to find a programme that can be 'shown in the country in [which] a Black lead [is] actually crossing over into a primetime mainstream'.[192]

Trevor Phillips had been well known and respected throughout British television for years. As a producer, he had also been (and is) an outspoken critic of policies and procedures that limit the possibilities for Black people to work within television. Phillips felt that a large part of the problem was that 'few TV programmes have Black producers'. At higher levels where key decisions made about issues of financing and scheduling affected programming, he wrote, 'British broadcasting remains whiter than the pre-revolution'.[193] In 1994, Phillips identified six minority executives out of the 'several hundred' who ran British television; by 1996, there were four. Phillips felt that Black audiences had a different programming preference from White ones, and therefore needed to be catered to, by Blacks preferably. Phillips wrote in an editorial for the *Guardian* that many Black people were 'lukewarm about police and adventure dramas – and not just because we are always the villains – and they dislike holiday and travel programmes'. He wrote that Black viewers preferred health programmes, and religious shows. His notion was expanded to suggest that Black communities (which were younger) had different ideological notions from White Britons. 'Just think back to the OJ verdict', he wrote; 'most white folk saw it as unjust. The universal black reaction was relief, tinged with exhilaration that one of us for once had beaten the rap. Our experience is different, and our perspectives are different.'[194] There was a perceived need for Black British involvement from within the walls of the BBC and others, as well as the possibility of independent productions.

As the next chapter highlights, interviews held with Black Britons working within the television media showed similar opinions about these issues. They also acknowledged the importance of the BBC in shaping the future for Black Britons working within media. There were obvious concerns about the BBC's lack of opportunities for minorities, yet hope for new programmes and leadership emerged, at first.

Notes

1 Rich, *Race and Empire in British Politics*: 145.
2 Notes of the General Purposes Committee, 28 June 1956, T/16/175, BBC WAC. All references BBC WAC unless otherwise noted.
3 Kathleen Paul, *Whitewashing Britain: Race and Citizenship in the Post-war Era*. Ithaca, NY: Cornell University Press, 1997: 148.
4 Programme as Broadcast Record, 17 January 1955, *BBC and Pathé News*.
5 Paul, *Whitewashing Britain*, 149.
6 McCall to Norman Swallow, 29 December 1958, T16/175/2.
7 Salter to CPTel., 31 December 1958, R51/92/1.
8 Hunkin to Swallow, 1 January 1959, T16/175/2.
9 Further Education, 21 November 1956, T16/175/2.
10 Jackson to CPTel., 2 January 1959, R/51/797.
11 Barry to CPTel., 2 January 1959, T16/175/2.
12 Baverstock to HTTel., 2 January 1959, R/51/797.
13 Notes on *Panorama* and related programming, T16/175/1.
14 Adams to McCall, 5 January 1959, T/16/175.
15 McCall to Adams, 6 January 1959, T/16/175.
16 Pelletier to HPHS, 8 September 1958, R51/797/1.
17 Wolferstan to the COS and ACOS, 18 November 1958, R51/92.
18 *Ibid.*
19 Controller's meeting notes, 21 November 1961, T/32/1703.
20 Controller's meeting notes, 28 November 1961 T/32/1279.
21 Rich, *Race and Empire in British Politics*: 186–7.
22 HTCA Sound to Camacho, 8 June 1964, R/51/781.
23 Clarke to AHTG (S) 17 June 1964, R51/781/1.
24 *The Guardian*, 24 June 1965.
25 Henri Tajfel and John Dawson, eds, *Disappointed Guests*. London: Oxford University Press, 1956: 156.
26 Crisell, *An Introductory History of British Broadcasting*: 109.
27 Goldie, *Facing the Nation*: 212–13.
28 Sir Hugh Greene, *The Third Floor Front: A View of Broadcasting in the Sixties*. London: The Bodley Head, 1969: 132.
29 Webster, *Englishness and Empire*: 177.
30 Howard Smith, 'Apartheid, Sharpeville and "impartiality": the reporting of South Africa on BBC television 1948–1961', *Historical Journal of Film, Radio and Television*, 13:3 (1993): 251–98.

31 Greene to DSB, ADXB, DTel. and Grisewood, 8 August 1962, T/16/175, BBC WAC.
32 Controller's meeting notes, 6 February 1962, T/16/175.
33 James Green, '10 million will see the new baby!' *Evening News*, 29 October 1963: 3.
34 *Ibid.*
35 Anonymous, 'Not significant', *The Guardian*, 30 October 1965: 8.
36 *Ibid.*
37 *Ibid.*
38 Financial Reporter, 'BBC2: Plenty of plans, but less material', *The Times*, 2 March 1964: 15.
39 Express TV Reporter, 'BBC2 battle to win more viewers', *Daily Express*, 25 August 1964: 12.
40 James Green, 'What are we making of BBC2?', *Evening News*, 20 April 1965: 3.
41 Goldie, *Facing the Nation*: 221.
42 'Z Cars: A Place of Safety', written by John Hopkins, Prod. Colin Morris, Dir. Ken Loach. BBC Television, December 1964.
43 Script, 13 February 1967, T12/1254/1.
44 Goldie, *Facing the Nation*: 223.
45 Anonymous, 'Thanks to the Negro', *The Observer*, 27 September 1964: 12.
46 *Ibid.*
47 Taya Zinkin, 'Women talking', *Manchester Guardian*, 18 January 1965.
48 Greene to Benn, 2 February 1965, N/25/175/1.
49 Greene to Mason, 2 February 1965, N/25/175/1.
50 Regional Controller's notes, 26 February 1965, N/25/175, BBC WAC.
51 Shaw, Secretariat to the CPP regarding a programme suggestion, 17 August 1961, T16/175/2.
52 Minute 41 from the Director-General's meeting with Regional Controllers, 8 March 1965, N/25/175/1.
53 *Ibid.*
54 Thirkell to Pendlebury, 28 January 1965, R/49/1095.
55 Meeting notes, 25 January 1965, R/49/1095.
56 Arkell to DG, 26 February 1965, R/49/1095.
57 Central Services Group was a BBC department in charge of sub-groups including Information and Finance, Hostels, Facilities, Central Premises, and Catering.
58 Gillott to CSTA and DA, 19 February 1965, R/49/1095.
59 Draft notice to the *Telegraph*, 4 May 1965, R/49/1095.
60 Thirkell to CSA, 4/25/65, R/49/1095.
61 Report from the DG, 19 May 1965, N/25/175.
62 A press announcement from Marshall to various press organisations, 6 July 1965, N/25/175/1.
63 Programmes for Immigrants meeting held with members of the West Indian community in London. Present: Mr A.G. Bennett (Blue Star House, MacDonald Road, Highhate Hill, N19); Mr S.P. Bourne (Department of Economic Affairs);

A.B. Burton (Welfare Officer, Reading Borough Council); Mr E.D. Butterworth (Lecturer, Department of Extra Mural Studies, Leeds University); Mr R.D. Chapman (Head of Department of English for Immigrants, Birmingham); Mr R. St C. Charles (Office of the High Commissioner for Trinidad and Tobago); Sir Learie Constantine (Member of BBC General Advisory Council); Mrs P. Crabbe (Welfare Secretary, National Council for the Unmarried Mother and Her Child and member of the Immigrants Advisory Committee, London Council of Social Service); Mrs M. Dimes (Chairman, Wood Green Commonwealth Citizens' Consultative Committee); Mr G.A. Evans (Information Officer, Public Relations Bureau, Hackney Borough Council); Mr J.E. Fraser (Formerly West Indies Commission); Miss I. Harrison (Welfare Officer, Westminster City Council); Mr E. Irons (City of Nottingham Education Committee); Mrs P. Jeffrey (Kensington Citizens Advice Bureau); Mr W. Knight (Managing Editor Designate of Concord); Mr G.W.R. Lines (Director of Education, Wolverhampton Borough Council); Mr P. Mason (Institute of Race Relations); Mr C.E. Maynard (Deputy Head of Welfare Department, Office of the Commissioner of Eastern Caribbean Governments); Mr R.E.K. Philips (Chief Welfare Officer, Office of the High Commissioner for Jamaica); Mr J.F.C. Springford (British Council, Student Welfare Department); Mrs D.P. Thirlwell (Adviser, Paddington Overseas Students and Workers Committee); Mr A.R. Truman (Inner London Education Authority); Mrs M. Winchester (National Council for Commonwealth Immigrants); Miss D.M. Wood (Secretary, Nottingham Commonwealth Citizens' Consultative Committee), 13 July 1965, N/25/175/1.

64 All management in attendance are noted as: Sir Hugh Greene (Director-General); Mr O.J. Whitley (Chief Assistant to Director-General); Mr C.J. Curran (Secretary); Mr H.G. Campey (Head of Publicity); Mr D. Stephenson (Head of Overseas and Foreign Relations); Mr F.G. Gillard (Director of Sound Broadcasting); Mr R. D'A. Marriott (Assistant Director of Sound Broadcasting); Mr A.P. Monson (Chief Engineer, Sound Broadcasting); Mr G.E. Mansell (Chief of Home Service and Music Programme); Mr J. A. Camacho (Head of Talks and Current Affairs, Sound); Mr P.M. Beech (Controller, Midland Region); Mr R. Stead (Controller, North Region); Mr D.F. Gretton (Assistant Head of Midland Regional Programmes); Mr R.S. Postgate (Controller, Educational Broadcasting); Mr D.M. Hodson (Controller, Overseas Services); Mr G. Steedman (Head of Overseas Regional Services); Mr D.G. Scuse (General Manager, Television Enterprises); Mr G. Del Strother (Head of Productions, Television Enterprises); Mr D.B. Mann (Secretariat). Controller's meeting notes, 6 September 1965, E/2/930.

65 Those invited by Greene and the BBC included Mr Ahmad, Mr Tassaduq Ahmed, Mr T.G. Ayre, Mr G.M. Bebb, Rev. P.A. Berry, Mr S.P. Bourne, Sir Learie Constantine, Mr T.F. Davies, Miss J. Derrick, Miss J. Henry, Mr P.S. Khabra, Mrs Hansa Mehta, Mr Niazi, Mr P.M. Nanda, Dr J.S. Nehra, Miss N. Peppard, Dr D.R. Prem, Mr K.C. Sen Gupta, Mr J.F.C. Springford, Mr S.B. Sufi, Mr A.R. Truman, Mr W. B. Tudhope, Mr J.H. Turner, and Miss N. Uberoi. Programmes for Immigrants, 29 July 1965, N/25/175.

66 Gretton to all, 19 August 1965, N/25/175.
67 Press release, September 1965, N/25/175.
68 Michele Hilmes, *Radio Voices: American Broadcasting, 1922–1952*. Minneapolis: University of Minnesota Press, 1997.
69 Fiscal report by Beech, 21 July–4 August 1965, N/25/175.
70 Whitley to all, 21 September 1965, N/25/175.
71 Bayley to several offices, 26 August 1965, N/25/175.
72 Controller's meeting notes, 6 September 1965, E/2/930.
73 Whitley to all, 21 September 1965, N/25/175.
74 Controller's meeting notes, 15–17 September 1965, E/2/930.
75 Further Education, 21 December 1956, T16/175/2.
76 Whitley to Greene, 12 June 1965, N/25/175.
77 Programme for immigrants meeting notes, 13 July 1965, N/25/175/1.
78 Controller's meeting notes, 20 July 1965, N/25/175/1.
79 From British Caribbean Service. *Going to Britain?* London: The British Broadcasting Corporation, 1957.
80 Whitley to Greene on suggested issues for the DG's talk, 7 May 1965, N/25/175.
81 Hodson to COS, 23 June 1965, N/25/175.
82 Martin to Overseas Publicity Officer, 27 November 1961, E40/171/1.
83 The LCRE report to the BBC, 4 October 1965, N/25/175.
84 *Ibid.*
85 *Ibid.*
86 Peach to Ferris, 7 February 1966, T57/162/1.
87 Peter Simple, 'Way of the world', *Daily Telegraph*, 4 May 1966.
88 From Farris to a series of others, 4 May 1966, T57/162/1.
89 Bunce to Maingot, 17 March 1966, T57/162/1.
90 Minorities in Britain schedule, 4–7 April 1966.
91 Case to Farris, 17 June 1966, T57/162/1.
92 Farris to Case, 20 June 1966, T57/162/1.
93 Rehearsal and programme recording form, 20 December 1966, T57/162/1.
94 *Ibid.*
95 Neckles to Bunce, 21 July 1966, T57/162/1.
96 Beech to Attenborough, 14 April 1967, T57/162/1.
97 Attenborough to the CM, 24 April 1967, T57/162/1.
98 The Toddlers' Truce was the early scheduling policy that no programmes would be broadcast between 6 p.m. and 7 p.m., to enable people to put children to bed. It was abandoned in 1957.
99 Jack Gold, e-mail interview, 5 February 2010.
100 Pines, *Black and White in Colour*. 95.
101 Adam to Newman, 12 January 1965, T5/1349/1.
102 Pines, *Black and White in Colour*. 27.
103 *Ibid.*
104 *Ibid.*
105 'Black and White in Colour', Dir. Isaac Julian, Prod. Colin McCabe for BFI TV/BBC Television, 1992.

106 Newman to all, 22 November 1965, T16/162/2.
107 *Ibid.*
108 Anonymous, 'BBC apology on "Black Power"', *The Times*, 23 December 1967: 10.
109 Mary Whitehouse, *Who Does She Think She Is?* London: New English Library, 1971: 212.
110 Meeting minutes, 12 February 1967, T16/746.
111 Harold Jackson, 'BBC not to show play on racialist', *The Guardian* 17 July 1967: 14.
112 Thorne to Adams, 10 September 1962, T/16/175.
113 *Ibid.*
114 Adams to Thorne, 11 September 1962, T16/175/2.
115 Adams to HLEG Tel, 15 August 1967, T/16/175/2.
116 *Ibid.*
117 Elizabeth Thomas, 'Under review', *Guardian Magazine*, 11 August 1967: 10.
118 From Wadleigh to Wheldon, 14 May 1967, T16/562/1.
119 From Wheldon to Wadleigh, 16 May 1967, T16/562/1.
120 'Rainbow City' *Radio Times*, 29 June 1967: 35.
121 *Ibid.*
122 John Elliott, 'End of the rainbow?' *Radio Times*, 3 August 1967: 29.
123 Stephen Bourne, personal interview, 2 April 2005.
124 Peter Black, 'Real trouble hits an illusion called Rainbow City', *Daily Mail*, 6 July 1967: 11.
125 *Radio Times*, 13 July 1967.
126 Stanley Reynolds, 'Rainbow City', *The Guardian*, 10 August 1967: 11.
127 Report: The Influence of TV Current Affairs Output, 19 March 1968, R51/1243/1.
128 Reaction Index, *Man Alive*, T14/2497/1.
129 Programme Recording Form, *Meeting Point*, 11 February 1968, T24/79/1.
130 Reaction Index, *Man Alive*, R19/2073/1.
131 Tise Vahimagi, *British Television*. Oxford: Oxford University Press, 1994: 240.
132 Michael Abbensetts, e-mail interview, 26–28 January 2010.
133 Khan Naseem, *Radio Times*, 18 August 1979.
134 Viewer Research Report VR/52/458.
135 Ken Hughes, 'A black comedy for ITV', *Daily Mirror*, 15 October 1975: 27.
136 *Ibid.*
137 *Ibid.*
138 Peter Ansorge, e-mail interview, 4–12 February 2010.
139 Press release, *Open Door*, T66/15/1, 13 February 1973.
140 Press release, *Open Door*, T66/15/2, 5 February 1974.
141 Stanley Reynolds, 'Access means you get a look in', *The Guardian*, 21 April 1973: 3.
142 Peter Thornton, 'BBC sets date for viewer's own "Open House" TV show', *Daily Telegraph*, 19 January 1973: 5.
143 Press release, *Open Door*, T66/15/1, 13 February 1973.
144 Memo: Community Programmes, T66/15/1, 21 December 1972.

145 Press release, *Open Door*, T66/15/1, 15 February 1973.

146 Thornton, 'BBC sets date', 5.

147 Robin Sharp, 'Oxfam's programme', *Radio Times*, 10 May 1973.

148 Programme log, 17 April 1973, T66/15/1.

149 Chief Assistant to the Head of Publicity, 14 May 1973, T66/15/1.

150 Reynolds, 'Access means you get a look in', 3.

151 Memo, Chief Assistant of Publicity to the DG, T66/15/3, 1 March 1976.

152 Peter Avis, 'Viewers own programmes on BBC: but no politics', *Morning Star*, 16 February 1973: 4.

153 Anonymous, '"Racialism" on BBC: actor wants inquiry', *The Guardian*, 1 December 1968: 15.

154 Vahimagi, *British Television*, 99.

155 Anonymous, 'Racialism on BBC', 15.

156 Vahimagi, *British Television*, 99.

157 Anonymous, '"Till Death" breathes its last', *The Guardian*, 17 January 1968: 22.

158 John Webb, 'Actors "face colour bar by BBC"', *Daily Mail*, 24 February 1973: 6.

159 John Clare, 'Problems ahead for Blacks', *The Observer*, 18 January 1975: 13.

160 *Ibid.*

161 Ken Hughes, 'A black comedy for ITV', *Daily Mirror*, 15 October 1975: 27.

162 *Ibid.*

163 Anthony Looch, '"No hope" Blacks warn MPs of racial unrest', *Daily Telegraph*, 21 May 1976: 17.

164 Anne McHardy, 'Young blacks list obstacles', *The Guardian*, 21 May 1976: 3.

165 Michael Church, 'Integrated casting is urged for TV dramas', *The Times*, 31 August 1978: 22.

166 Bill Jones, ed., *Broadcasting and Society: The Fifth Symposium on Broadcasting - April 1973*. Manchester: 1973.

167 Anonymous, 'Prince sees TV as answer to race tension', *The Times*, 11 March 1978: 5.

168 Barrie MacDonald, *Broadcasting in the United Kingdom: A Guide to Information Sources*. London: Mansell, 1988: 24.

169 Joe Steeples, 'Blacks to get their own shows on TV', *Daily Mail*, 13 May 1982: 12.

170 Anonymous, 'How the Beeb backed off its all-black show', *The Times*, 17 May 1982: 14.

171 Paul Boateng, 'Blacks on the screen: a long way to go', *Sunday Times*, 24 April 1984: C-11.

172 Lindsay Mackie, 'Blacks in media campaign', *The Guardian*, 19 September 1984: 12.

173 Mike Shaft, 'Now we need a black network', *Broadcast*, 29 June 1984: 15.

174 Beverley Anderson, 'Opinion: TV's shades of pale', *Broadcast*, 21 September 1984: 78.

175 Pines, *Black and White in Colour*, 10.

176 Anonymous, 'BBC looks at its ethnic reporting', *Ariel*, 13 August 1986: 10.

177 Avril Connard, 'BBC aiming to put more Blacks on TV', *The Times*, 29 October 1986: 22.

178 *Ibid.*

179 *Ibid.*

180 Harvey Lee, 'BBC drive for women and blacks', *Daily Telegraph*, 6 May 1987: 5.

181 Anonymous, 'The Beeb goes for Black and White', *Evening Standard*, 8 April 1988: 5.

182 Patrick Stoddart, 'A crucial step for black comedy', *Sunday Times*, 28 October 1989: 15.

183 Anonymous, 'A Step Forward?', *Sunday Times*, 28 October 1989: 23.

184 Steve Clarke, 'Lenny looks for wicked new talent', *The Guardian*, 29 August 1990: 31.

185 Anonymous, 'A high price for black humour', *Sunday Telegraph*, 5 November 1989.

186 Kevin Haggarthy, 'The woman from Auntie', *The Voice*, 17 July 2000: 15.

187 Angus Towler, 'Minorities told to organise', *Television Today*, 30 April 1992: 15.

188 *Ibid.*, 16.

189 *Race in the Frame*, Dir. Sukai Eccleston, Prod. BBC Television, 21 April 1997.

190 Alexandra Frean, 'Does television paint Britain too white?', *The Times*, 21 June 1995: 13.

191 *Ibid.*

192 Yasmine Anwar, personal interview, 13 August 1998.

193 Trevor Phillips, 'Are we getting the big picture?', *The Guardian*, 10 June 1996: 10.

194 *Ibid.*

4

A Black eye

Then, there's the other type of programming for Black people, where we are perceived as victims, where we're looking at the crack problem in the black community, single parenthood in the black community. They don't show enough Black people doing well. When we do get success stories, it's quite often the American experience, which is fed into us – and that's all we dream and breathe.

(BBC Correspondent Brenda Emmanus, August 1993)

As the BBC helped to construct post-war British culture as a broadcasting monopoly, policies relating to the representation of race were largely dependent upon management's desires and audience opinion. To disarm the population's concerns about West Indian immigration, the BBC used a host of programming genres to examine integration and its social ramifications. Despite eventual competition from ITV via the Television Act of 1954, BBC television maintained its influence in shaping these issues, yet reinforced cultural differences more often than similarities. This often included the image of the West Indian as a noble, sometimes bitter immigrant, yet these narratives seldom addressed the origins of White racist practices.

Within this chapter, interviewees discuss a multitude of issues previously examined within this study, with an emphasis on contemporary broadcast practices, notably those of the BBC. Interviews were conducted during the period 1993–2010 with seven media professionals, and material from six of these interviewees has been used in this chapter. The initial discussions were conducted in 1993, and a portion then continued in 1997–98 when I again interviewed four of the participants. These four subjects were again interviewed between the years 2000 and 2010. Each of those chosen subjects has worked within the medium in varying capacities, and most are Black Britons. They often reaffirmed the BBC's inability to provide balanced representations of African-Caribbeans. Some link this on-going practice to very few positions behind the camera for those of colour, and a perpetuation of stereotypic, one-dimensional characters within programmes. Despite occasional opportunities such as those created by Henry, Ayers, and Wenham to create fresh, innovative programmes, opportunities for Black Britons to produce, write, and direct remain limited. There are exceptions, but only under the watchful eyes of White executive producers, bound by formulaic texts, and ever-worn plotlines. One interviewee considered this 'white, old boy's network noble in its efforts, yet obsolete'.[1] The Reithian belief that the BBC has a responsibility to educate and mould the masses creates strategies that can benefit, if not promote, alternate voices. In the responses they provided, these media professionals expressed similar solutions to these challenges: more involvement of Black Britons and multi-ethnic media professionals in the production of television programming. When there were contradictory opinions on how this might be accomplished, it underscored the vast diversity of opinions within the Black British media collective, yet with a shared vision. BBC programming policies sometimes incorporated this effort, as programming on ITV, Channel 4 and others helped to increase the televised presence of black Britons, but, as suggested by those interviewed, with woeful results. Those projects written and directed by Blacks, yet sanctioned by White producers, were sometimes criticised for their content, and the manner in which they were publicised. Notable were complaints over the advertisements for the black-themed mini-series *Babyfather* (BBC1, 2001–02) featuring the four main black characters Gus (David Harewood), Johnny (Don Gilet), Linvall (Fraser James), and Beres (Wil Johnson) nude in a shower, reminiscent of slaves at pre-auction. Two White women developed the campaign.[2] The eventual direction of the series infuriated Patrick Augustus, the author of the books on which the series was based, who accused the BBC of reinforcing negative stereotypes, including the usage of drugs.[3] The cultural production of the Black British experience through dramas like *Babyfather*, or the highly controversial *Shoot the Messenger* (BBC2, 2006) held some redeeming qualities, yet still framed the Black presence as fraught with dire problems and a marked dissimilarity to mainstream lifestyles (Figure 16). The notions of sexual miscegenation as a race and class consideration were also explored in these discussions, as analyses of romances between Black men and White women are discussed in conjunction with three highly successful British television dramas, *London's Burning* (LWT, 1986–2002), *Prime Suspect 5* (Granada, 1996) and the BBC mini-series *Holding On* (BBC, 1997).

When the structured polysemy present in these policies and programmes was considered, comparisons were made between comedic portrayals within sitcoms and the autonomy of stand-up comics. Black comics, according to Stuart Hall, operated as resistant agents by giving personal, self-referential tales of culture and adaptation, outside of discourses often constructed by White writers. The inclusion of these voices through stand-up provided

Figure 16 Highly criticised for its depictions of Black Britons, *Shoot the Messenger* depicts Joe Pascale (David Oyelowo) as a teacher driven to despair, and near insanity, by his failure to relate to his students and ultimately other Black people. Germal (Charles Mnene) expresses hostility toward Pascale, creating notions of intolerance between the adult generation of Black Britons, and the young, eager to be as tough as their American counterparts, in the 'gangsta' tradition.

second- and third-generation Black Britons with more contemporary yet homegrown issues to reflect upon. This consideration did not equate to an acceptance of all Black humour, as some interviewees roundly criticised BBC's *A Force* block of Black-themed programmes, including *Blouse and Skirt* (1996–2000), *Brothers and Sisters* (1996), and Channel 4's offerings of *Baadasss TV* (1994–95), and *Get Up, Stand Up* (1994). Each attempted to address trendy, topical notions of Black issues but in a manner considered insulting.[4] Black British involvement in news and public affairs programmes such as *Black Britain* (BBC2, 1996–97), or LWT's *Skin* have been helpful in noting discourses of Black life, yet those expressing opinions about their content perceive chosen topics as of interest to those of colour only, distancing issues from the White consciousness.

Solutions to these challenges, as discussed by the interviewees for this chapter, include seizing opportunities for independent programming, reinforcing multiple representations of Blackness, promoting more discourses on a multicultural UK, and the avoidance of ghettoised programming slots that target Black audiences at off-peak hours, limiting audiences and ultimately success. Another principal issue is the possibility of counter-hegemonic resistance, particularly within public service broadcasting, yet there is also a critique of the first Black cable channel in the UK and its failure. Further, Americanisation and its effect upon the Black Briton's self-image are still prominent within mediated texts, shunting positive Black portrayals and consequent fandom toward African-Americans like Oprah Winfrey or Bill Cosby, and away from Black British talent.

As a means of exploring the opinions and interpretations of Black British media professionals, interviewed were ten participants involved directly or indirectly with media production or criticism between 1993 and 2010 in the UK and the USA. Black as defined to these participants fell within the same definitive framework as this research project: those of African, African-Caribbean and African-American ancestry. Class or socio-economic considerations were not important, in that each considered him- or herself middle class at the time of the interviews, though their economic origins differed. Also addressed was the continuing cultural production by White television producers and writers and the social culture in which they operate, notably the BBC. Despite the diverse backgrounds and ages of the subjects, each had similar readings of Black representations on British television programming. In examining these Black British interviewees from a qualitative perspective, there was no specific notion of a singular ethnic identity, a consideration that would essentialise participants into a singular notion of Black Britishness.

Concerning their backgrounds, three were first-generation British born while the other three immigrated as children: two from Jamaica and one from Tanzania. One interviewee felt that the UK would never accept Blacks and Asians, and could only offer opportunities to learn through their White-controlled media projects. She, though British born, was planning to take her knowledge to a technologically adept location, probably in Africa. Some had similar ideas of Blacks working together, despite any perceived differences, to produce their own media projects. Another felt that race was not an issue when assembling a quality production staff. Each was generally aware that public service efforts within the BBC established strategies to affect public sentiments on a variety of issues, yet television programming allowed Whites to focus upon cultural and racial differences from Blacks. In addition to Michael Abbensetts, Peter Ansorge, and Michael McMillan (whose perspectives have already been partially described in earlier chapters), the other three participants had differing histories with British television, and opinions on life in the UK varied. Each also engaged with queries about whether the television industry in Britain will ever allow more Black participation in mediated cultural production.

Treva Etienne over the years became a familiar face in British television. Having been born in London, he was firefighter Tony Sanderson in the television programme *London's Burning* (ITV, 1986–2002). The programme focused on members of an urban fire brigade, and their personal and professional lives.[5] Produced by London Weekend Television (LWT), it was a spin-off from a successful two-hour film originally shown in July of 1986. Etienne has also appeared in *Desmond's*, *The Lenny Henry Show* (BBC1, 1984–85; 1993, 2003–5) the hospital drama *Casualty* (BBC1, 1986–), and more recently in two highly successful mini-series. In BBC's *Holding On* (BBC1, 1997), he played a security guard involved with a successful White public relations officer.[6] In the science-fiction-themed *The Last Train* (Granada, 1999), Etienne played a self-absorbed thief turned hero.[7] He has also done theatrical and television producing and directing, and has written screenplays and teleplays. Despite his success and popularity on the screen, Etienne and his White female co-star eventually walked off the set of *London's Burning* in protest of the producer's framing of their interracial relationship and its sexual miscegenation as problematic and insolvent.[8]

Actor and filmmaker Neema Kambona was born to an upper middle-class family in Dar es Salaam, Tanzania, the daughter of an esteemed government official. Shortly after her birth, however, political unrest and neo-colonialism issues forced her parents and two siblings to leave the country. They relocated to Europe, where they travelled extensively throughout her middle school years. After settling in London, Kambona later embarked upon a Master's degree in the USA during the early 1990s. Prior to this, she had been a stage and television actor who toured Europe and America. As a stage actor, she enjoyed the live feedback she and her colleagues received when performing as a troupe. Her favourite play *Black Heroes* chronicled the presence of Blacks in British culture from the eighteenth century onward. The troupe travelled to Liverpool, Manchester, and other major urban centres in the UK before coming to New York and Chicago, playing to audiences comprising Africans, Caribbeans, and Black Americans. Kambona has also worked for years on British television for additional income and exposure. She served as a journalist for the *Caribbean Times* and the *Voice*, both prominent Black newspapers in Britain. She has also been an art and media critic for several Black British publications.[9]

British television audiences know Brenda Emmanus as a television presenter and host of *The Clothes Show* (BBC, 1986–2000), a weekly programme devoted to fashion trends and cultural influences throughout London.[10] She was also the on-stage presenter who interviewed Black British actor Carmen Munroe, as part of the *Black on White TV* National Film Theatre retrospective in 1996.[11] In an article published in 1997, Emmanus made her feelings clear when it came to addressing the involvement of Black British people on television. In a *Guardian* article, Emmanus and Krishna Govender, a former BBC producer, discussed how Black ideas for programmes received a back seat in favour of those from White writers. The article, by writer Geoff Small, stated in part that:

> People of colour have enjoyed increasing exposure on British television screens during the nineties. However, increasingly, minority insiders consider calculated pigeonholing an insult to multiracial Britain, and even more so they are offended by television's virtual ostracism of non-white participation behind the camera.
>
> 'We're all part of United Kingdom … but we're not getting a fair crack of the whip', says Emmanus … Similarly, [black and Brown producers] feel [that] broadcasters like Channel 4 don't welcome mainstream ideas from minority filmmakers, but 'encourage white-owned companies to do black programmes'.[12]

Kadija (George) Sesay has been a freelance journalist and editor since the early 1990s, and has written for a number of Black publications in the UK. Most recently, she has written for the magazine *Calabash*, devoted to expressing the views and concerns of Britain's African-Caribbean and Anglo-Indian communities. The publication, called a 'literary magazine for writers of African and Asian descent', gives emphasis to issues of popular culture, film, and literary works. She considers her beat to be issues relating to people of colour in the UK, Africa, and America, and her writing has featured interviews with bell hooks, tips on screen and stage writing, poetry, articles on Black American stereotypes and discussion of local actors and producers. Sesay also serves as managing editor for the publication.[13] When discussing British television, she had no favourite television programme aimed toward Black audiences,[14] but expressed a dislike for certain BBC depictions of Blacks even more. She cited *Babyfather* as a programme that 'almost hit the mark', but got 'it wrong with the marketing', so it 'totally [made] people angry before the programme [had] even been aired'.[15]

BBC's Jan Oliver has worked within British television since the late 1980s. She began as a secretary for London Weekend Television (LWT) working within the network's legal department. She later left the network due in part to blatant sexism and limited opportunities. She went on to work for *Essence* magazine in New York for a short time, and then returned to the UK, where she worked for Granada Television of Manchester. She eventually joined the BBC in 1992 and worked for Mark Thompson, controller of BBC2 at the time.[16] Oliver then worked closely with Greg Dyke, as the Multicultural Development Coordinator and head of the BBC Black Forum, an organisation assisting in the corporation's transition toward a racially diverse future. When asked about a favourite programme as a child, Oliver ironically explained that, because of a very religious background, she 'was not allowed to have, or watch, a television as a child'.[17]

Stuart Hall was a professor of Sociology at the Open University, and 'for a long time' the Director of the Centre for Cultural Studies at Birmingham. He has authored over thirty books in cultural studies, and has often analysed television within his work. He was born in Jamaica, came to England in 1951 as a student, and 'has lived in England ever since'. When asked about his favourite television stars as a child, Hall noted that he was 'old enough not to have television as a child'. He first saw television in England, which he remembered vividly, because when he 'came over as a student', he 'never had much money, and television wasn't commonly available in Britain'. The first time he did, it was watching the Coronation of the Queen in 1953. Hall described limited opportunities to see television until the 1960s, and limited exposure to Black British actors:

> I don't have many favourite black British television actors because black British television actors, on the whole, tend to be concentrated [in] situation comedies. Most of the other television that one sees has occasional black British actors in them, but they don't have careers [that are] solid and secure enough, [to] have established themselves in the way that a Cosby ... has been able to do.[18]

Examples of better programming suggested by Hall seemingly reaffirm the influence of Americanisation within British television.

Writer and cultural archivist Michael McMillan notes the arrival of televisions into West Indian living rooms toward the end of the 1960s, which symbolised the changing nature of the front room into more of a communal space, especially where children were concerned. McMillan notes how

> Televisions then were either usually rented or money had to be punched in a meter at the back for the electricity. And, before colour television, a transparent green plastic covering could be stuck onto black and white television screens, though all the colours were green. As many hadn't seen a colour television before they wouldn't know the difference between one with only green colours and the real thing.[19]

His experiences with television in his living space evoke the fascination of television, and, more so, the appearance of Black faces upon it. Representations of Black faces were appreciated, even if cast in buffoonish and stereotypically racist roles. McMillan notes *Love Thy Neighbour* (Thames, 1972–76), as an example of this, much like some African-Americans watched Black characters on *Amos 'N' Andy* (CBS, 1951–53) *and The Beulah Show* (ABC, 1950–53). Each appearance was an event, and the whole family would leave whatever they were doing to come to witness someone who looked like them. He also suggested the power of *The Fosters* (ITV, 1976–77), to project a West Indian family that he and others 'could identify with, even though we suspected that it was attempting to reassure viewers that black families in sitcoms were just as "normal" as white ones'. Television also altered the manner in which second-generation and/or educated West Indian families saw *themselves*, particularly after reports of the Notting Hill Carnival in 1976 and its disturbances. McMillan notes that 'consequently the intervention of the television into the front room changed it forever, and has become a vital appliance as furniture in the contemporary living room, if not in every room'.[20] With the pleasure television provided came further images of Black Britons, which now hailed each member of the multigenerational family.

Despite opportunities to see more Black faces, Etienne always felt that 'black situations' on television mainly revolved around drugs, police trouble, prostitution, and negative aspects of the Black British experience. When cast as a drug dealer in a BBC production, Etienne nearly refused the role and criticised the script as 'full of stereotypical things' that included usage of cigarette papers ('for rolling "spliffs"') and a feathered hat. He suggested to the director that his character should wear a fashionable suit and express himself more articulately. The day of the shooting, he received a beautiful suit to wear, but accompanied by the hat. Etienne protested to the director yet again that the character looked far too much like a pimp. Therefore, Etienne and the director reached a compromise: he wore the hat when the filming began but immediately removed it so that most of the scene played without it.[21] Having drawn his characters from his experience of 'a life of modest means', Etienne often disagreed with White directors and producers over the manner in which they wanted him to play the role. He suggested:

> I think what has to happen is to present images where we are normal, every day. [We as Blacks] are party going, womanizing, whatever, and we are no different from the White man in that sense. We bleed red. I would say now, that images are improving, definitely. We're not seeing the stereotypical stuff we were seeing in the '70s and the mid-to-late '80s. I think things are slowly turning around and more Black people are aware of how powerful television is and what influence it has on young people … Because of that, I think the accusations of [how] television companies get it wrong are more prominent from Black people. Before, we would just moan at the television.[22]

However, despite these cultural productions of Black Britons by White writers, Jan Oliver felt that these images were better than no representation at all, as White writers try harder to 'get it right'. Oliver also discussed issues of roles as problematic:

> OK, there is a move, a swing to try to reflect [Black] society. But, I will also say that, most of the scripts [and] the way it is, most of our writers are White. What we [then] see is their perception of what it is to be Black. More often than not, they get it completely wrong. I think once they get maybe one or two Blacks [as writers], that could change. However, females, more often than not, are still portrayed as the baby mother, the prostitute. So from a female point of view, I think that we're probably best served [by female writers] than we are from the male point of view.[23]

Popular Black British actor Cathy Tyson further discussed how Black women as whores within British television programming were common. She played prostitutes on the British television series *Band of Gold* (ITV, 1995–96) and in the film *Mona Lisa* (Handmade, 1986) with Bob Hoskins. In an interview with the *Guardian* newspaper, she explained that, far too often, she and other Black women were 'prostitutes or princesses from Africa', and that she desired to 'do something challenging'. Despite this, she too expected things to change, though she's 'not sure that they will'.[24] Tyson spoke to the press in 1986, yet eleven years later bell hooks addressed Black females in British (and American) media in an editorial piece that stated that British films such as *Mona Lisa*, or *Peter's Friends* (BBC Films, 1992) 'portray the black female using conventional sexist/racist iconography'. Further, she suggests that if all Black actors refused to play roles perpetuating the degradation and dehumanisation of Black people, images of mainstream media would change, noting that these performers 'have the power; [but] they could have the glory, too'.[25] Since Oliver too had suggested gender as an important consideration within racial construction, I asked her about whether images had improved overall for Black women since hook's piece,

I know that we feel we deserve a hell of a lot more because we've been here for a while. But, I just think that we have to take it slowly, because [whites are still] growing up with us as Britons; they're our peers, and they're beginning to realise that things have to change, as well. If you don't see a [character who is a] Black bank manager, or Black MD, it's because they can't write about it. They don't know it, believe me. They do not write positive roles for Black men, because they never see it. You don't see any Black people running the BBC'.[26]

Brenda Emmanus had a different spin on representations. She saw some progress in Black representations on British television, but also discussed the context of these images, and the Black community's perceptions:

What I think needs to be looked at now is in the context in which our images are portrayed, and the level of progress of our personal development and career development within the mainstream media. I'm not saying that we want to put everybody [on television] that sounds like Louis Farrakhan, but you know Black people are as diverse as a packet of crisps. We're allowed to excel in music and sport and that's what they'll show on the telly, but there're so many more Black people doing so many positive things that I'm not seeing. [These are things] we don't even get to see unless we read Black newspapers, tune in to the Black radio, and I'm beginning to find that more and more frustrating.[27]

Empowerment and opportunity

Another prominent topic within these interviews was the belief that more Black people could get into work in British television through training programmes initiated by channels such as the BBC. However, along with these opportunities should come the autonomy to produce programming that reflects what Black British culture could be; a notion still under construction. A major advocate of more opportunities was Stuart Hall, suggesting that Blacks in British television could empower themselves and improve their images:

In a number of ways – they could be more vocal, and more critical to the broadcasters and to the broadcasting institutions. Britain has a long tradition of public service broadcasting and even the commercial companies are, in fact, governed by quite strict and careful regulations of a general nature. So if people thought that, as it were, the general images [on TV] of Blacks in British society was not sufficiently diverse in terms of its coverage of the lives, they could, I think, make an impact by being critical of the kind of programmes they see. I think they could make [complaints about] representations to the BBC and the independent companies about the coverage of news stories which affect the lives of British Black people. [These] affect their socio-economic position, their position in housing and jobs and employment and so on, which cover, very much, their kind of social aspects of their position in the society.[28]

Etienne felt that concerns over programmes, policies, and representations could be best changed and improved through more financial independence and creative freedom for Black people working in television productions. When asked what would help to bring hopeful Black artists forward and guarantee opportunities to effect these changes, he replied,

> Money, because there are more creative Black artists who want to produce, who want to direct, and a lot more people coming out of film school are emerging as directors. The problem is that there hasn't been an established policy that's going to allow Black people that. [Some] have [a deal] with the BBC and some are getting commissions from Channel 4, but most Black production companies over here are stuck in documentary because that's where most of the money is. An exception is Crucial Films, Lenny Henry's company, which began with stretching the boundaries [with] drama. If producers and writers have the money, they can produce the stuff on their own.[29]

Lenny Henry's 'Step Forward' programme, sponsored in part by the BBC and Controller Jonathan Powell during its 1989 season, allowed more Black writers to participate in television programmes. As already reported in Chapter 3, Henry felt the concept was overdue: he told writer Patrick Stoddart in the *Sunday Times* that he remembered 'turning up for the first script readings for *Three of a Kind*. There were about 90 writers in the room, and not one of them was black or Asian', and that 'there were only a couple of women there, too, come to think about it'.[30] Henry's affiliation with the BBC continued to encourage Black writers to work on television. He formed the production company Crucial Films, which, along with the BBC, sponsored a two-day comedy workshop.[31] Henry also stated that Black people were often misrepresented on television, 'because there are very few black writers', which he hoped to remedy through the programme.[32] Years later Henry's initiative incorporated opportunities for writers of other genres as well. Henry's attempts to use his comedic authority (along with the BBC) did provide additional outlets for these Black British voices.

In 1994, the Commission for Racial Equality had accused the BBC of racist practices in a report. As a partial response management brought in new guidelines for its Regional News Trainee Scheme for the 1994–95 year. Each year, the BBC received thousands of applications for these writing and development positions, and in 1994 it split its thirteen traineeships into two groups; seven were open to all sections of the community, while for the remainder the organisation would consider only applicants of African, Caribbean, Asian, and Chinese descent. The aim of this initiative was to help writers that would 'reflect Britain's multicultural society'. The BBC responded to concerns of reverse discrimination by reminding the public that the slots were part of their equal opportunity schema, under Section 37 of the Race Relations Act of 1976.[33]

However, the dominant press continued to criticise efforts by the BBC to include Black people within its ranks. Patrick Stoddart in *The Times* wrote that Lenny Henry was Britain's only 'seriously famous Black comedian' and that the writers benefiting from the programme would be most likely to 'spend most of their career providing laugh lines for white performers'.[34] In another article, the programme came under criticism for allowing participants of colour and opportunity to make in-roads at the predominately-White institution. The Conservative government also criticised the BBC for its programme, noting that the corporation practised reverse racism because it supposedly stopped White people from applying for journalists' positions within the 'coveted programme'. Tory MPs felt that the policy would lead to lower standards and damage broadcasting, noting Michael Fabricant of the Commons National Heritage Select Committee, who stated 'I do not see why the BBC should take it upon them to adopt a recruiting policy based on misguided ideals, rather than choosing the best person for the job'.[35] The *Sun* newspaper printed an article on 13 June 1994 in which the BBC defended its programme by citing minorities as underrepresented in radio and television. However, the article accused the organisation of bias in refusing applications from White Britons.[36] By September of that same year, the programme was discontinued after concerns arose that it was unlawful. An article reported that the BBC programme was one of its positive action training schemes, and that it had been 'scrapped'. The service insisted that it remained 'committed to using section 37 where appropriate as part of our overall equality strategy, but it seems unsatisfactory to us that so much of it is unclear and open to interpretation'.[37]

The Pebble Mill unit in Birmingham, developed under the leadership of controller Jonathan Powell, had been created to get, as one writer stated, 'more Black people on the screen and, perhaps more importantly, behind it'.[38] At the inception of the project, African-Caribbean and Asian units had separate budgets for programme creation. The BBC was seemingly pleased with the programming developed by the Afro-Caribbean Unit, yet the Asian unit, under Narendhra Morar, consistently received larger budgets. However, after being merged into a single, multicultural department in 1991, their chances for multiple productions were more limited.[39] The Afro-Caribbean Unit was angered by the decision, but was not allowed to speak publicly about the merger.[40] The unexpected news came to staff members as they completed work on a programme about the positive aspects of the Notting Hill Carnival. The new multicultural department in 1992 had only three African-Caribbean members of staff out of thirty; by 1995, there was just one African-Caribbean staff member in the unit. According to members of the Black British press, the BBC had never been able to commit itself to the multicultural diversity of either group. The only plans the BBC had for future Black programmes at this point in the mid-1990s were more episodes of a BBC2 comedy *The Real McCoy* (BBC, 1991–96) from White television producer Charlie Hanson. The other forthcoming show was a documentary on African-American migration called *The Promised Land* (BBC, 1995), narrated by actor Morgan Freeman.[41]

However, BBC2 controller Michael Jackson announced an expansion of multicultural programme production in London 'to channel existing expertise to serve ethnic minority television audiences better'. Production of Asian programmes would continue under Jackson's mandate at Pebble Mill. The Executive Producer for Afro-Caribbean programmes, based in Manchester, would

> act as a focal point for programme ideas from all corners of the BBC and from independents. We need to give fresh impetus to our programming for Afro-Caribbean audiences and to build on the range of our Asian programmes that have a successful 30-year track record. Separating the focal points of Afro-Caribbean and Asian programme production will enable us to redouble our efforts to meet our ambitions and the expectations of these communities.[42]

Despite these opportunities, early programmes developed by Pebble Mill continued to address the problematic challenges of Black British life. When Blacks at the BBC received an opportunity to produce television programmes, documentaries about race and immigration were common.[43] Slums, crime, labour problems, and the like shaped this new generation of Black-immigrant descendants within the White imagination. The content of the British press during the 1970s and 1980s had primarily covered five topics, relating to the problematic construction of Black British: immigration, race relations, crime, discrimination, and interracial hostility.[44] Now, more documentary programmes reinforced these types of issues while further distancing the Black Briton from the mainstream.

As someone who has worked on the world stage, Neema Kambona had come to understand the importance of current opportunities through varied exposures to media. She felt that positive roles for Black Britons were still clearly missing, particularly at the BBC. Concerning efforts toward diversity, Kambona compared opportunities on BBC1, BBC2, Channel 4, and ITV:

> They say Channel 4's supposed to cover, you know, a sort of ethnic full spectrum. But, I can't remember what they've done. BBC1, BBC2, all of them have done very little because, again, within BBC you had [the] Pebble Mill multicultural sector, and all programming came out of that. But it was very much a sort of ghettoised Black programming. The only features shown are 'this is what Black life is about'. It wasn't [really] covering all aspects of Black life.[45]

Etienne's opinion on the same topic was that most opportunities seemingly came from Channel 4, due to a mission within its creation to provide more minority voices within its programming, which he found hopeful. He also reflected, as did Hall, upon public service as the opportunities this doctrine could provide. However, Etienne also stated that the BBC had the worst record of opportunity. He felt that

> [Opportunities are better through] Channel 4. Because that's part of their remit, that's part of the reason why they got the money to be broadcasted. [In this case] their remit is to broadcast to minorities in all aspects – race, colour, creed, disabled. That's what they do, and they're quite creative. BBC2 come a close second, because they, too, are a minority channel. But because they're also under the guise of the BBC [and its] institutionalised politics. My least favourite is BBC1, because I don't see them doing anything at all to encourage or to promote Black people on their channel. You see Black people doing guest spots or little appearances in their little soaps, or in their little TV shows, but apart from Lenny Henry, there isn't any BBC1 star that has any clout, and there has to be alternatives.[46]

When discussing the most progressive channel, Oliver cited BBC2, but blasted ITV as her least favourite channel. Her answers were more personal than professional:

> I won't watch ITV. [They] don't make any programmes for Black people. I mean, every now and then, they sneakily throw in a couple of characters into a drama or and at the end of the year [when making reports on diversity in programming] they add up how many Black people they've had in a show, and it appears that they're really trying. And, if you've ever watched their breakfast news, they tend to use White, blonde [presenters] all the time. This really pisses me off. I want to see somebody like me![47]

When asked about the channel offering the most opportunities for training and balanced representations of Blacks, Oliver noted that BBC2 had tried to 'tackle the problem' a number of ways. She was particularly pleased with the development of the news programme *Black Britain*. During the 1996 season, the newsmagazine was scheduled to run for eight weeks and address hard and human-interest news stories. However, when audiences saw a trial broadcast, concerns over subject matters caused the *Independent* to ask 'Why focus on another 'black problem? Why are black programmes always about sport? It's good to see them eating Went Indian food, [but] why not show them eating McDonald's?'[48] When criticised, the series producer Patrick Younge told the *Evening Standard* that

> We'll never please everyone. The key measure of success has to be our impact on the main news agenda … Stories we're running are already being picked up by others in the media – if we can keep on doing that, we'll have made a real

change. A ghetto is somewhere people have to live or work because nobody will let you live or work elsewhere. We've chosen to work on black programmes. This isn't ghetto broadcasting – it's classic public service broadcasting.[49]

Oliver agreed, calling the programme 'socially conscious and [rather] sophisticated'. She noted:

I mean, the production teams – they've used their experiences from working on other shows and brought it to *Black Britain*. And it's so classy. [It] looks good, it's pacey. Also, we've commissioned programme ideas and we're trying to make sure somewhere along the line there is, you know, a programme of and about Black people in some other kind of area of programming. So, you know, I'm proud of the channel, and what has been achieved.[50]

I asked Emmanus, as a past employee of the BBC, to make a comparison of the BBC and Channel 4. I inquired how Channel 4 had done a better job and she answered, addressing diversity among Black images on television:

We do see more independent Black films making it onto Channel 4. We have Black comedy programmes because Black comedies never had a problem in getting on television. [Black programmes are] at the mercy of what [White] tastes are, and what the commissioners want. So [then it becomes] a case of us knocking and knocking and protesting and protesting – and then we're perceived as angry.[51]

Americanisation as an influence

Americanisation as a principal influence of British television has historically affected the Black British self-perception, as well. A glaring example of this type of Americanisation took place when Etienne discussed the BBC's 1955 television production of Shakespeare's *Othello*.,[52] when Black American actor Gordon Heath played the tortured ruler despite many talented West Indian actors being available.[53] In 1980, the controversy continued as the BBC cast Anthony Hopkins in another television production of the play. The year before that, the Royal Shakespeare Company and the National Theatre had both put on productions of the play with White actors in Black face (Donald Sinden and Paul Schofield respectively).[54] Shortly after this, the BBC attempted to begin another television production, this time suggesting Black American actor James Earl Jones. Opinion pieces written by actors Rudolph Walker and Norman Beaton slammed the decision, with both men publicly criticising the casting of American actors instead of homegrown talent.[55] Etienne discussed Americanisation, as an 'old and re-hashed standard'. In his assessment, the acceptance of American values has had too much of an impact upon British popular culture:

I think we need to look at different perspectives, with the energies of other nations, of other cultures, of other countries. [There are people] who are living everyday lives, with interesting stories that will entertain, educate, and enlighten. These aren't, essentially, American bubble-gum-chewing, burger eating, car chasing [types]. American culture is too dominating in the world, period. And I think that they have to pull back in order to accept what the rest of the world has to give them.[56]

The influence of American media was also discussed with Oliver, who, when asked about her favourite shows, reflected upon the influence of American programming. When she admitted that her favourite shows were American, she jokingly felt that if her boss, Mark Thompson, knew 'he'll kill me':

With most American shows, you can see positive Black people who are doing ordinary jobs, and it's really not a big deal. They're just part of the story, they're part of the fabric; they are doctors first and Black second, whereas, over here, your colour always seems to be an issue. You know, we have [a medical show] *Casualty* and, they don't have a Black doctor – and they've never had a Black doctor. And I think that's what we've got to try and move away from, doing what we [British in television] do. [If] we just happen to be whatever colour, then we are, you know?[57]

Hall discussed his ideas on Americanisation when asked what impact American television has upon the industry in the UK. He stated that

Well, the impact is enormous, and as with the rest of the world, there are very substantial American imports into British television or the television. I mean, we have a restricted system, [when comparing] the UK with the US. Both cable and satellite are relatively new in terms of bringing in the opportunities to see a wider diversity of programming. American programmes are very slick in terms of their news and production values. British audiences have seen American programmes, which include Black actors or [are] based on situation comedies. They know Black American entertainers. They know Black music. I think the influence of that is by and large good. But if you looked at the way in which Black British public culture has been, transformed in the last twenty years, by Black American popular musical styles, [and] by particular kinds of attitude, as it were, I think probably, there has been an Americanisation of Black British culture, as well as Americanisation of British culture in general.[58]

When comparing American broadcast media vs. the UK's, diversification of programmes and Black imagery was highly important when discussing representations with Stuart Hall. I asked how he would relate these movements to cultural self-production for Blacks, many of whom were attempting to carve their own niches, or tell their own stories with some type of authenticity of authorship. He responded:

They, as it were, are perfectly familiar with British society. They've been to British schools. They've been born here. They know their way around the society. They can negotiate. They know it's a racist society and they're likely to encounter discrimination and so on, but they know their colour and their distinctiveness is not tradable. Nevertheless, they've achieved a certain position, a certain visibility indeed, almost certain envy in public culture. I think things have improved in terms of coverage, certainly in terms of [the] range of images we see. But there's still too little opportunity for what I would call the integrated coverage of people from Afro-Caribbean backgrounds, who [are] in their second or third generations in Britain, yet indigenous to British social, economic, and political life, generally. They're still treated as a very distinctive and somewhat strange minority, with special problems – so they're not treated as a sort of natural part of a multiculturally diverse audience in society.[59]

Concerning an integration of Black presence within contemporary English culture, Hall discussed a television programme and its treatment of multi-culturalism as a fact of British life. The programme *Prime Suspect 2* – the second series of the programme, which went on to run for seven series – was written by Allan Cubitt from a story by Lynda La Plante.[60] In the programme, Jane Tennison (Helen Mirren) plays a serious minded homicide detective who has a relationship with a Black officer named Oswalde (Colin Salmon). Ultimately, the relationship fails, but only after a London tabloid exposes his and Tennison's tryst. As critiqued by *Sight and Sound* magazine, we've 'seen it done before, and better realized'; the story was believed to be clichéd and derivative of La Plante's previous plots.[61] However, despite the problematic framing and coding of the interracial rela-tionship, the presence of this Black detective is important to Hall's notions of a multicultural England that supersedes the trappings of race:

Salmon has a relationship with Mirren's Tennison. Well, you know, this appearance takes it for granted that we live in a multicultural society. The focus is not on race. Race is taken as a kind of lived part of the reality of an increasingly multicultural society. When you come to very serious drama – I mean, 'one-off' plays – which are not part of an established television genre, or not part of a series, [it] gives a particular figure little time to develop a dramatic situation. There you very rarely see a Black figure or Black families or Black woman, given the depth of treatment and the time and space, as it were, to become a centrally dramatically interesting figure. So, I mean, there are two things going on at one and the same time. There's the attempt to carve out a distinctive space in which Blacks can explore, in a variety of genres, and then, secondly, there's a reflection of their presence in a multicultural society, across the broad span of British television coverage as a whole.[62]

Similarly, the BBC broadcast the twelve-part mini-series *Holding On* (BBC, 1997), which featured a series of intertwining narratives about life in pre-millennial London. Most notable was the relationship between Lloyd, a

Black British security officer (Treva Etienne), and Hilary, his white public-relations-officer girlfriend (Lesley Manville). After a theft brings Etienne to the woman's rescue, they bond as victim and protector resulting in a sexual involvement. Eventually this relationship wanes after Etienne's character is forced to lie to the woman's friends about his profession. The embarrassment within the scene highlights an obvious difference in social-economic status as the Black, lower-classed male attempts to prove his worth to the wealthy White woman's friends, one of whom refers to him as 'Denzel Washington' in a moment of sexual desire.[63] They later argue over the charade, and, as the altercation becomes more heated, Manville's Hilary runs to the phone to call the police. It is painfully apparent that Etienne's character perceives her fear as racially motivated. In the next episode, Hilary attempts to reconcile, yet they eventually part at the suggestion of Etienne's Lloyd. Racial difference, though framed as secondary within their subtext, still becomes a problematic issue. Hall spoke of this merger of class and race distinctions:

> You had one story, which was very specifically about something which is a persistent feature of Black society – namely, the continuous presence of racism – and the question of race was not ducked [in the story about] the security man. Well, there, of course, [was] the racial factor, but also the class factor, which is very classically British. You don't get one without the other in Britain.[64]

In recent years, the BBC has featured programmes featuring relationships that have fared better, within reason. The television BBC programme *Hustle* (BBC, 2004) featured Adrian Lester's and Jaime Murray's characters, who shared an uneasy interracial attraction. As well as the narrative tool of sexual tension, the relationship carried concerns of a past relationship, which had obviously failed somehow. As other television programming features similar circumstances, race may become a secondary social construct when compared to class differences. However, the choice of which character is of which class becomes disconcerting. Within the narratives of *Rainbow City*, *Holding On* or others, cultural differences – with foundations within racial difference – abound. The five-part mini-series *Five Days* (BBC, 2007) featured David Oyelowo as a Black British father who, through a series of mysterious circumstances, loses his White partner and both their biracial children. As one character remarks about the disappearance of his family, despite all else, 'if he's Black and [his wife is] White, then it's a racial issue'.[65]

Further possibilities

Based upon previous research and interviews, the future of Black people in the media was a highly important issue as the new millennium approached. Opportunities for training and better representations were essential, as was a firmer control of cultural production and representations within the media. I asked each of the interviewees where they saw Blacks within British media in ten years. Oliver of the BBC said,

> Well, if I'm absolutely honest with you, probably not much further along than we are now. There might be the old one or two more Black faces, because broadcasters are fighting to keep their audiences. Although, having said that, it goes to show that in about fifteen years' time, there're going to be a hell of a lot more Black people in this country, and we are going to be an economic force to be reckoned with. I think that there is a serious feeling of frustration at the moment, because I have a lot of young friends who are out of work. A lot of my friends do want to work in this industry, but the 'old boys' network is still at work, and it is still a matter of who you know and being in the right place at the right time.[66]

Stuart Hall expressed his desires:

> Well, what I would like, particularly, to see is more Black directors, and people working, I mean, in the production side of television, at a senior level. I mean, there're now, some Black technicians, so you find television crews that would include a Black person who has had training, and so on. [However] there're not enough opportunities. A lot of Black kids would be interested in going into the media and they would be good at it. What I want to see is the creative talent that we know that exists in the cinema, in video work. [This] translates into giving people an opportunity to make really serious, you know, serious television work. I want to see some Black independent companies like that being much more used in British television. But ... you know, I also think that that strategy must go directly hand in hand with an increasingly multiculturalisation of the technical and production force, integrated within White companies that mix Black and White people on the technical and production side.[67]

The best strategy for the future of Black projects and marketability is, according to Etienne, financial independence coupled with artistic freedom. However, Etienne's concerns over the appropriation of Black culture by eager production companies attempting to compete were evident in his development of a variety programme *Club Class* (Crown 10, 1996). Etienne had developed the fast-paced variety show for sale to a British network for regional broadcast, with London as the target market. The videotaped programme took place in a fictitious local club where the viewing audience was invited in despite a line of hopeful patrons that awaited approval from a 'bouncer' to enter. The studio band consisted of an all-female jazz quartet that inundated the programme with jazz-fusion and funk tunes, much to the audience's delight. Much like *Playboy after Dark* (Playboy, 1969–70), the patron's point of view would see guests attending the event; in the case of *Club Class*, a very mixed multicultural audience. The pilot also featured a Black stand-up comedian as host, singers, and comedy skits that generated excitement and laughter throughout the all-Black 15-minute segment.[68]

According to Etienne, the taped pilot had been submitted to the Paramount Channel with the approval of Etienne's then partner, Black British producer Beverly Randall. As Etienne explains, Randall's boss, White Executive Producer Phil Chilvers, promptly dismissed his creative input and hired Randall to oversee pre-production. The show was recorded with a White comic, the point of view of a patron was eliminated, and most other aspects of the programme were duplicated, including the band. Etienne's production experience allowed him to create the programme in a manner that would appeal to Black British and multiethnic audiences. However, it had been transformed into cultural capital by Chilvers for a primarily White, urban demographic. In this case, Chilvers and Randall recontextualised Etienne's endeavour through a sinister form of bricolage, as the cultural importance of the project became mere commodity. Further, the newer version of the pilot was not picked up as a regular programme.[69] The intrinsic notion of authorship for Etienne was lost, as was his potential agency. He had attempted to initiate his own television programme in which he as producer determined the authenticity and behaviour of the characters. Despite this circumstance, Etienne still felt the best solution toward diversi-fication of imagery was to have financial independence and creative control:

> We can all become artists, and I think that we will all be in a very strong position in the next twenty-five years because that's what we need to do. We need to become banks, and then we don't fall prey to putting a lot of energy into a creative idea and then having to go to a broadcaster, or to a moneylender or to film financiers. As artists, as, administrators, as producers, we need to become the banks, so that we are administrating that money and allocating it to other bankable people or bankable projects.[70]

When Brenda Emmanus discussed the need for autonomy when working within television, she was concerned about White producers having the last word in programming decisions. Despite good, marketable ideas for programming developed by Black Britons, the authority of white cultural production stood fast:

> It's probably a wake-up call which was necessary, and a number of Black brothers and sisters who work in the media have identified that and are trying to do their own thing. But the reality of the situation is we may come up with some brilliant ideas where we have first-class programmes, which you want to

make; we're still at the mercy of getting a commission from White males, predominantly.[71]

When asked about the future of Black people in British media, Sesay stated somewhat pessimistically that

> Five years from now, I don't think we're going to be much further from where we are, because it's going to be the same generation of people. They need to change their attitude and their mindset. They need to think more global. But, my personal opinion is, to be honest with you, I don't really think we should see ourselves as being [in the UK] permanently anyway. At the end of the day, I see us living in a host society, a host culture. When you're a guest in somebody's house, when they're ready to kick you out, they will kick you out. We should be here learning and taking whatever we can, and learn as much as we can just to be prepared, and we should be making our bases outside of this country, to make our old home places stronger. It's crazy, because we're never going to own anything, [and] even if we do own anything here, it's always gonna be threatened. I think people's attitudes reflect that.[72]

'Identity' television

As a catalyst for efforts of independence in programming and subsequent representations, Sesay had great hopes for Identity Television. The channel, also known as IDTV, was to target Black Britons with programming written and produced by Blacks. Registered in July 1992, the company later formed a partnership with America's Black Entertainment Television (BET) International, and premiered in June 1993. By July, articles in the minority press heralded 'Britain's first-ever Black TV channel'. Identity TV had originally hoped to provide programming for primarily African-Caribbean viewers in the London market. It was estimated that approximately 500,000 Black households in the city would tune in to the cable channel.[73] A short time after the channel premiered, Sesay became involved with IDTV in a public relations capacity.

Petra Bernard served as the channel's managing director, and wanted to eventually 'bring the Black programming from all over the country' to London viewers. Bernard, a Black British woman with ten years' worth of television experience, had previously worked for BET president and founder Bob Johnson in the USA. The company had become highly popular among young and middle-aged urban viewers with its mix of rap, hip-hop, and rhythm and blues videos. By 1993, BET had amassed a subscription audience of 33 million, and Bernard felt a similar success story could follow IDTV into the homes of London's Black population. She also felt the channel would, via original programming, 'show that Blacks have huge contributions to make on the television and we need to project that as much as we possibly can'.[74] As part of a basic cable package, IDTV reached 150,000 households on its first broadcasting day. Bernard wanted very much to reach out to all Black audiences, and her best hope was that the station would be watched at least a half-hour to an hour a day by viewers.[75] After a month of broadcasting via cable, IDTV, according to journalists, 'made a strident mark within its medium', and 'industry pundits and customers alike' were singing its praises.[76] Predictions at the time for the year 2000 suggested that nearly 6.8 million homes would be able to receive cable or satellite, boasting the potential audience of over 1.3 million.[77]

However, it was three years later when IDTV reached its early demise. It was believed that the advent of cable would offer the Black British viewer more diverse choices of programming. However, BET International had continued to offer a diet of videos and ultimately switched to an all-jazz format. This, by proxy, caused IDTV to offer much of the same and limit the choices for Black British audiences even more. The failure was also thought to be a lack of advertising, which was one of the main reasons behind the sudden switch to a jazz-formatted station by BET. It was also written that many in the media business felt that IDTV's venture into Black programmes was inevitably doomed to failure from the start due to lack of proper resources.[78] Sesay felt that a lack of proper training might have led to improper decision-making within IDTV. Despite enormous possibilities, she soon concluded that many of the staff members were not ready to embark on such an endeavour. She was also disappointed at the degree of unprofessional practices that existed within the young firm:

> I think one of the things that's wrong, not just with the media, but in terms of Black things overall, is that once people get a little in, they're so scared of letting it go, or letting anybody else in. It would have been nice, for example, if IDTV or cable had helped with production training. That was essential. But, even from the outset, that was not going to happen very well, because I don't think they had enough confidence in themselves, that they [could] make it big. So they started off thinking small. We found out from the people who handle advertising that [IDTV's] business plan was that they didn't expect to raise any money in their first twelve months of operation. Tell me; don't you think that is strange?[79]

Sesay was also involved with a more prominent show in IDTV's line-up, *African Scene*, a programme she called 'their flashy, hour of arts kind of programme'. Her input came as a person potentially selling advertising time on *Black Arts Here* and *Africa 2*. Sesay was concerned over selling ad time for Black-themed programming because

> [IDTV] wanted to charge advertisers to help develop the show or to put the thing on. But then, I heard they were commissioning White production

companies, and buying stuff off them. You see what I'm saying? They didn't
tell us this, but you know, England is so small. We heard this on the grapevine.
You know, rubbish like that was not going to help the situation, really. That's
why I keep reiterating that even if it's Black-orientated [programming], it has
to be so good that anybody will want to watch it. But if it's just 'tacky Black',
there's only some Black people [that] are going to watch it because they just at
least want to see some representation.[80]

'Newer' programming and representations

As a means of targeting contemporary urban audiences, both BBC and
Channel 4 created programming that highlighted Black culture. In 1996, the
BBC created a two-and-a-half-hour Friday-night slot that featured *The A-
Force*, a mixed bag of variety programming that incorporated humour,
interviews, game shows, music, and reports on the urban lifestyle. The
segment also offered 'the first Black drama series' on UK television. *Brothers
and Sisters* was to follow the lives of members of a northern Pentecostal
church. Then BBC2 controller Michael Jackson felt that this 'zone' was the
'best chance of the BBC serving its Afro-Caribbean audience better'. *Black
Britain* was also part of this strategy.[81]

The programmes offered were similar to the controversial programme
Baadasss TV from Channel 4 in 1995, in which segments covered cultural
issues in an obviously campy fashion. African-American rapper Ice-T,
dressed in a brightly coloured pimp outfit complete with a wide-brimmed
hat, was co-host along with Black British presenter Andrea Oliver. The
premiere episode featured stories such as an expose on the 20-inch pros-
thetic penis of porn star Long Dong Silver. An additional segment detailed a
day in the life of 'a British artist who used elephant faeces as a medium'. Also
covered was American rapper and hip-hop artist Sir Mixalot, noted as a
'champion purveyor of tits' in a playful bit of self-critique.[82]

In an article written by veteran television producer Trevor Phillips and
cultural critic Duran Adebayo, the programme was critiqued from two
perspectives. Phillips maintained that the show diminished the importance
of Black cultural contributions while exuding harmful stereotypes. When
considering the seamy approach, Phillips noted that he did not 'have a
problem with the wild side of black culture', citing a programme segment he
had produced for London Weekend Television (LWT) some years earlier.
The *Devil's Advocate* programme (1992–93) was 'the first to devote a whole
segment (tx. 8 March 1993) to reggae artistes who "chat slackness" i.e., use
lewd lyrics'.[83] He continued his attack on the programme as showing
'nothing but contempt for ordinary black Britons; and the days when most
of us would stand by and allow ourselves to be insulted by white boys are
long gone'.[84] Adebayo wrote of appreciation for the range of issues discussed,

despite the seemingly bizarre approaches. He hailed segments on rappers Vicious and Method Man as intriguing and 'infinitely less patronizing' than audiences being warned of 'the evil of music promos packed with "video hos"'. As a means of breaking away from traditional problematic readings of 'gansta rappers', Adebayo praised the show's producers for not relying on the 'Snoop Doggy Dog has two heads and cloven feet' type headlines for its window on the hip-hop nation. The emphasis on Black American culture was obvious within the programme's content.[85]

Kambona considered whether Black British representations had improved via shows like the *A Force* or *Baadasss TV*. As she addressed both programmes, she stated that

> [Black representations have] probably stayed the same. There was quite a bit of Black programming five years ago, but that has been withdrawn, for whatever reason, and we're still not part of the mainstream. In fact, there's still ghettoised programming. Something like the *A Force*, or *Baadasss* TV they put it on at eleven or twelve at night, when everyone's falling asleep or out and about. In terms of the images I wouldn't say it's so much the stereotyping of the Black criminal or drug addict; you might get the family man. But, if it's within a drama programme, then it's only one Black family, or Black man, so it still seems very tokenistic. And that won't change until we have more of our own production teams.[86]

Sesay's perceptions about recent programming were similar. She addressed themed-programming and their time slots:

> Lots of [the] stuff that's going on, like the *Get Up, Stand Up* [comedy segment] is appalling, absolutely appalling. It's not even funny to Black people, let alone everybody else. I know the woman who's one of the show's editors. She's a great friend, but I think some of [the segments on the show are] kind of weird. Personally, I don't feel [programmes are] saying very much. You know, I like good TV, no matter who's depicted in it.[87]

Kambona felt that many representations had not changed,

> They tried to do a Black sitcom, which was just so poor. I don't know how it got commissioned. It was called *Us Girls* [BBC, 1992–93] or something like that. The standards were very low and the scripts were hopeless. The characters were completely two-dimensional. I think the premise was a grandmother, and then a mother and a daughter all living in one house, which is fine. But the grandmother was such a stereotypical West Indian – an overpowering, bossy type, and it just didn't work. I'm not saying that we don't have those characters. We do, but she wasn't three-dimensional. Another example was *Brothers and Sisters*; it was just appalling. They had a West Indian girl who's just coming over from Jamaica and she was supposed to be

this vulgar dancehall queen. She couldn't speak English properly and I hardly watched it because I couldn't bear it; it was so embarrassing. That was BBC2, and was part of the *A-Force*.[88]

When Hall and I discussed the harmful aspects of sitcoms and Black representations, he again felt that the stand-up comic was quite different. These comics are free to express a sense of their identity,

And that's quite recent. It's grown largely out in the stand-up comedy halls outside of television. Those shows are very often self-referential, where classic Black situations are examined, et cetera, and they make comic situations out of them without becoming complicit with a racist attitude. The regular situation comedies, with either Black families or Black and White families, are patronising to Blacks, on the whole. The stand-up comedians, themselves, are more in charge of their own situation. They can have established their own relationship with their audiences, whereas the situation comedies tend, on the whole, to feature Black characters run the other way around.[89]

Hall noted Lenny Henry's pirate-radio disc jockey character, Delbert Wilkins, who broadcasts ska, drum and bass, and Black British hip-hop music illegally. The police and local broadcast authorities are constantly seeking to shut him down. However, the character is constantly moving about, keeping his equipment at the ready for immediate transportation to a new location where is able to resume programming.[90] This type of humour and Hall's appreciation of it, seems metaphorical for the kind of humour Black stand-up allows. Since Henry had control over the depiction of his character on BBC's *Lenny Henry Show*, he was able to highlight personal aspects of the Black British experience he deemed appropriate, despite the overseers at BBC television.

Another highly important site in which stand-up allowed for culture reaffirmation and creative freedom was a play performed in London in 1992 by a group of seasoned Black British actors. Once a consensus was nearly met, the men decided to call themselves the 'Posse'. They consisted of Brian Bovell, Michael Buffong, Victor Romero Evans, Robbie Gee, Roger Griffiths, Gary MacDonald, Eddie Nestor, and Sylvester Williams. Among the men, they had multiple television credits that included *Desmond's*, *EastEnders* (BBC1, 1985–), *Casualty*, *South of the Border* (BBC1, 1990) and Charlie Hanson's *The Real McCoy* (BBC1, 1991) variety show. One of the first of many comedic and dramatic sketches they created was based upon an actual meeting the eight-man company held in 1991. Frustrated by the lack of portrayals available to Black British actors within British media, they elected to form a production company. The first task was to write the humorous, yet poignant, play *Armed and Dangerous* (1992), which consisted of brief sketches that highlighted the Black British experience in a comedic fashion with serious undertones. The writers for this very reason had considered the show 'seriously funny'. Sketches included pieces about inter-island rivalry among African-Caribbeans, Black fairy tales, homosexuality, failed relationships, and a tragicomic tale of physical abuse and a lack of opportunities for Blacks on British television.[91]

The show was originally supposed to be a one-night performance, but sold out before it had opened. It delighted Black, White, and Asian audiences, and was a hit with critics. *Armed and Dangerous* then extended its run due to its huge success. Part of the play's appeal was the following of fans actors had from working with the National Theatre, the Black Theatre Company, and in the West End. Of additional appeal were depictions of Black British life in Britain for people of colour. According to interviewer Malcolm Hay, 'they didn't call themselves the Posse simply because of its Western associations, [they] had another meaning in mind too': the term also has the meaning within Black American slang of a 'group of people who work together, rely on each other, trust each other, and move together'. One of the members felt as though the changes that the company had brought to their working lives allowed them to become a 'concentrated force'.[92] Through adversity, this concentrated force superseded differences. The posse was then better able to experience and exercise their authority of ethnic depictions and highlight cultural similarities and differences. Their combined efforts, as with those of stand-up comedians, were self-referential, yet hailed many. Despite working outside of television, these men were able to self-produce multiple images of their culture as second-generation Black British. The normative Whiteness that may have altered their stories to entertain a multicultural audience was not present. This self-definition then avoided pluralism that could have eroded their messages to audiences, as the material was coming clearly from Black British hearts and souls. These comics represented their experiences within the cultural milieu of England, often given sentimental homage to family and friends. Even within certain skits written and performed by Black comics there is intrinsic recognition where multigenerational Black British find their own hailing, often with multiple meanings. In the case of these actors, they were seemingly able to express their own authorship within the White cultural production of Black Britons.

Assessments and future challenges

Years later, when I again interviewed some of my subjects, I was interested in their current perceptions of British television and whether substantial progress had been made for Black Britons. In one of the first recaps, Etienne suggested the film *Secrets and Lies* (Channel 4 Films, 1996) had been an example of progress because the Black British lead had received Oscar nominations. I questioned him further:

> I see it as an improvement, simply because there are more visible ethnic faces on the screens, and there's been quite a large input over the last five years of more images in commercials, presenters in factual programmes, newsreaders, journalists, and footballers. I mean, in April of '97, there was a black actress nominated for a BAFTA [British Academy of Film and Television Arts award], Marianne Jean-Baptiste for her part in *Secrets and Lies*. That was a huge achievement and a huge statement for us as Black actors here. Unfortunately, she didn't win. And, unfortunately, the British media didn't really promote or support her bid for a BAFTA award. They were concentrating very much on the likes of Ralph Fiennes and Kristin Scott Thomas, who were also being nominated for *The English Patient*. Unfortunately, [Jean-Baptiste] got marginalised and she wasn't really talked about. The British tend to emulate whatever America approves of. And, they had the approval – *English Patient* had all the Oscar nominations, whereas *Secrets and Lies* only had, I think, about four or five. I don't think that the British media – or the Black British media – really picked up on the achievement that this girl had made. I think that's a tragedy.[93]

The appreciation of *The English Patient* (Miramax, 1996) by both countries signals a reinforcement of Whiteness via classic British stories. The nature of *Secrets and Lies* as a cult film signals a coding of this story as exotic. Within the film, we are not aware of the Black women's history or ethnic roots, a disconnection from her British roots or historical culture, reinforcing British nationalism as White. Whereas a story that addresses the classic British romance is framed as normative, a story of an estranged Black daughter within a White family was framed as disconcerting and unlikely.

As to the biggest challenge facing Blacks in British television at the time of the interview and in the future, Oliver again stated that more Black people in upper management would help considerably. She didn't express concern over whether they would fight for diversity in Black images shown on the BBC. Her assertion and belief were clear:

> I think it goes back to my point about the decision-making process. We're not involved in this at all. There's nobody out there fighting in our corner. There's nobody out there to remind them that, you know, 'we should have … a Black person in that role'. Or, 'why can't a Black person play [that role] whatever [it is]?' Nobody has that kind of power, and that's our challenge; to move up in organisations like the BBC, where we are involved and we can say, 'well, this is what want to see and want to see it now'.[94]

When asked about television in the 2004 season, Sesay expressed a lack of enthusiasm for the diversity of images on British television. She noted that she felt

Then what I do now. I just don't rush home to watch anything they put on. Once in a while, there is a one-off programme, although they are usually touted for being controversial. Like the recent *Shoot the Messenger* – which I will watch at a later time, when people have stopped talking about it so that I can watch it with a more unbiased eye. Although I know the writer – we used to go to the same school so I'm not surprised that she wrote something like that. And then stupid programmes like *Black like Beckham* (Channel 4, 2003) which interviewed people – including men in a Black barbershop –who basically said – yes, Beckham is one of us! And gave all these very ignorant reasons for saying so. It culminated with the EMMAs [Ethnic Minority Media Awards] which honour media multicultural personalities, and gave the joint award to David Beckham and black footballer Thierry Henry, as the Best Sporting Personality of the Year 2004. How stupid are we – really. The same year, the media personality of the year was Greg Dyke! Funny isn't it?

I keep on holding out in hope for the Beeb. They do have more Black and Asian presenters, although, mainly for children's and youth TV, which is a good sign, but their programme content is lacking. Dramatising the book *White Teeth* (Company, 2002) was also a good move. I really can't remember, Black books being televised in series before – for radio, yes; not for TV. The BBC has [its] diversity department with plenty of Black faces in it, but I'm not sure how much difference they can make. For example, BBC is getting in on the act of finding new talent, both in front of the camera and at the writing end. It's almost like they have just discovered that people love writing! They had a great idea, a competition ... to finish the ending of a story written by a well-known writer. There were about ten writers. The problem for me was that none of them were Black. Did someone really have to put a finger in their face to point it out to them or is it that they just don't care?[95]

When considering recent BBC programmes that addressed race and Black culture, such as *Babyfather*, *Shoot the Messenger*, or *Small Island*, opinions, depending upon the programme, were mixed. Peter Ansorge addressed each, and noted that

All were worthwhile projects but, apart from *Messenger*, these have been adaptations of well-known books. Since *Empire Road*, no Black writer has been employed by the BBC to write an original contemporary drama series for television. Younger Blacks remember watching the show with their parents. They all say there's been nothing like it since, and [there is] not much parents and children can watch together. This may also have to do with the changed role of media in young people's lives.[96]

As for what the future holds for representations of Black culture on British television, Ansorge discussed the channel with the best approach to diversity and the most balanced presentations:

Channel 4 began broadcasting in 1982, and its first Chief Executive Jeremy Isaacs had watched and liked our work at Pebble Mill. Jeremy gave Channel 4 a specific brief to cater to ethnic minorities, [and] created a post for a multi-cultural commissioning editor. David Rose created the *Film On 4* slot, and among his first major successes was *My Beautiful Laundrette*, written by a young Asian writer and directed by Stephen Frears. When I commissioned *Traffik* (Carnival, 1989), a major element was the sequences shot in Pakistan, and I chose Alastair Reid who had directed *Gangsters* for us in Birmingham. Farrukh Dhondy, the multicultural editor, commissioned Norman Beaton for *Desmond's* in a role that echoed Everton Bennett in *Empire Road*. The third Chief Executive, Michael Jackson, announced that there was no need to continue the policy since multicultural was now mainstream. This proved wrong, and I understand there is a re-think taking place at present. Even so, Channel 4's biggest drama success in recent years has been its investment in its *Film on 4*, *Slumdog Millionaire*, proving that the story is not yet over.[97]

I suggested to Ansorge that some Black Britons were sorely disappointed with the marketing of *Babyfather* and with the content of *Shoot the Messenger*, while *Small Island* (BBC, 2009), despite its scheduling, was well received. I was concerned over what the future held for these kinds of Black-themed programmes.

> The first thing to say is that the culture for new writing has changed at the BBC. At the time of *Empire Road*, the single play was at the heart of the enter-prise. So it was possible for Michael to write his first original BBC film *Black Christmas* and then follow it with an original series, having won his spurs. There are hardly any single plays on primetime BBC television today. The current policy is for new writers to win credibility by first writing episodes for long-running soaps like *EastEnders* and *Casualty*. As a result, BBC drama has become far more formulaic. The kind of opportunity that gave rise to *Empire Road* or *Play for Today* is no longer there – either for Black or White writers. The likelihood is that there will be further adaptations of well-known novels like *Small Island*, adapted by White writers with an established track record, and there is also more integrated casting than in the past. Black and Asian actors [are] cast, largely colour-blind, in police and crime series. This situation is unlikely to change until a commissioning editor sympathetic to real diversity in drama is appointed. Interestingly two UK Black actors – Idris Elba and Clark Peters – recently won acclaim here for a television drama – but it was *The Wire*. As a result Elba has been cast in a new BBC cop show written by a team of White writers with strong soap connections. It all feels more derivative.[98]

Separate interviews on these and related matters conducted with African-Caribbean/Black British working within or analysing British television determined that, despite differences in socio-economic lifestyles, life histories, and post-structural identities, highly similar beliefs about the challenges confronting Black British media professionals existed. Analogous concerns regarding television representations, limited opportunities within

British media, and the influence of American television programming often arose in these discussions. There also existed a consensus of cause and effect, and potential solutions. Some media professionals of colour may have altered the previous encoding of their television imagery, yet BBC as author made this transition highly difficult. Examined in Chapter 5 will be the importance of multiethnic coalitions as bases for resistance power, particularly within the time of BBC's last great White hope, Greg Dyke. Also discussed are recent attempts by the BBC to incorporate Black programming, and themes, but often with disconcerting effects.

Notes

 1 Neema Kambona, personal interview, 23 August 1993.
 2 Jan Oliver, personal interview, 7 June 2007.
 3 Anonymous, 'Babyfather author furious with BBC', *BBC News World Edition*, 28 October 2002, http://news.bbc.co.uk/2/hi/entertainment/2367643.stm (accessed on 21 April 2010).
 4 Kadija (George) Sesay, personal interview, 18 August 1997.
 5 Vahimagi, *British Television*, 316.
 6 'Holding On, part 2–6', Dir. Adrian Shergold, BBC Television, 15 September 1997.
 7 'The Last Train, part 1–7', Dir. Alex Pillai, Granada Television, 1999.
 8 Dan Slater, 'Exclusive: flaming row as TV stars quit', *News of the World*, 27 January 1991: 16; Treva Etienne, personal interview, 11 August 1998.
 9 Kambona, 23 August 1993.
10 Brenda Emmanus, telephone interview, 22 August 1993.
11 Stephen Bourne, *Black in the British Frame: The Black Experience in British Film and Television*. London: Continuum, 2001.
12 Geoff Small, 'Who's behind the camera?', *The Guardian*, 27 October 1997: 12.
13 Sesay, 18 August 1997.
14 *Ibid.*
15 Kadija Sesay, e-mail interview, 1 October 2006.
16 Jan Oliver, personal interview, 14 August 1998.
17 *Ibid.*
18 Stuart Hall, telephone interview, 11 October 1997.
19 Michael McMillan, e-mail interview, 16 June 2007.
20 *Ibid.*
21 Pines, *Black and White in Colour.* 204–5.
22 Treva Etienne, personal interview, 22 August 1993.
23 Oliver, 14 August 1998.
24 Simon Banner, 'That's all we ever are: prostitutes or princesses from Africa', *The Guardian*, 9 March 1986: 12.
25 bell hooks, 'Buffoons. Gangsters. Whores. Is this what filmmakers mean by meaty roles for Blacks?', *The Guardian*, 29 June 1997: sec. 2, 6–7.

26 *Ibid.*

27 Brenda Emmanus, telephone interview, 14 August 1997.

28 Hall, 11 October 1997.

29 Etienne, 22 August 1993.

30 Patrick Stoddart, 'A crucial step for black comedy', *Sunday Times*, 28 October 1989: 15.

31 *Ibid.*, 14.

32 Steve Clarke, 'TV Lenny looks for "wicked" new talent', *Evening Standard*, 23 October 1989: 1.

33 Joe Knowsley, 'Now BBC reserves trainee jobs for non-whites', *Sunday Telegraph*, 12 June 1994: 2.

34 Patrick Stoddart, 'A crucial step for Black comedy', *Sunday Times*, 29 October 1989: 14.

35 Margaret Hussey, 'BBC criticized', *Daily Express*, 13 June 1994: 3.

36 Anonymous, 'Beeb in race bias storm', *The Sun*, 13 June 1994: 3.

37 Anonymous, 'Ethic scheme dropped by BBC', *The Guardian*, 1 October 1994: 4.

38 Anonymous, 'Is it allowed to be our BBC?', *Weekly Journal*, 1 December 1992: 2.

39 *Ibid.*

40 Deborah Ward, 'Anger as BBC closes Black unit', *The Voice*, 24 November 1992: 4.

41 Anonymous, 'Not on your telly! New BBC snub to Black programming', *The Voice*, 9 March 1995: 3.

42 Anonymous, 'BBC-wide plan to boost ethnic programming', *Ariel*, 9 May 1995: 2.

43 *Ibid.*

44 The *Times, Guardian, Express,* and *Mirror* were chosen as topics for study by Paul Hartmann and Charles Husband, *Racism and the Mass Media: A Study of the Role of the Mass Media in the Formation of White Beliefs and Attitudes in Britain.* London: Davis-Poynter, 1974: 136–7.

45 Kambona, 23 August 1993.

46 Etienne, 22 August 1993.

47 Oliver, 14 August 1998.

48 Decca Aitkenhead, 'BBC tries to vault the ghetto walls with Black news', *Independent on Sunday*, 7 July 1996: 3.

49 Donu Kobaru, 'Paint it Black – and right', *Evening Standard*, 10 July 1996: 3.

50 Oliver, 14 August 1998.

51 Brenda Emmanus, telephone interview, 22 August 1993.

52 Treva Etienne, personal interview, 11 August 1998.

53 Anonymous, 'Better than the theatre', *Daily Worker*, 13 July 1953: 5.

54 Pines, *Black and White in Colour*, 80–1.

55 Norman Beaton, 'A taste of nothing much', *The Guardian*, 9 February 1979: 13–14.

56 Etienne, 11 August 1998.

57 Oliver, 14 August 1998.

58 *Ibid.*

59 Hall, 11 October 1997.
60 Susan Young, 'Battle over BBC series role offers hope for end to Black typecast-ing', *The Observer*, 9 February 1992: 3.
61 Jenny Diski, 'Skeletons and corpses', *Sight and Sound*, 3 and 1 January 1993: 15.
62 Hall, 11 October 1997.
63 'Holding On, part 5', Dir. Adrian Shergold, BBC, 13 October 1997.
64 Hall, 11 October 1997.
65 'Five Days', Dir. Simon Curtis, BBC/HBO, 2007.
66 Oliver, 14 August 1998.
67 Hall, 11 October 1997.
68 'Club Class', Dir. Treva Etienne, Prod. Treva Etienne for Crown 10 Productions, 1996.
69 'Club Class', Dir. Phil Chilvers, Prod. Beverly Randall for the Paramount Channel, 1996.
70 Etienne, 11 August 1998.
71 Emmanus, 22 August 1993.
72 Sesay, 18 August 1997.
73 Anonymous, 'Black cable TV launched', *The Voice*, 20 July 1993: 3.
74 *Ibid.*
75 *Ibid.*
76 Dionne St Hill, 'Identity television', *Artrage*, July 1993: 12–13.
77 *Ibid.*
78 Cumberbatch, Sylvan. 'Pulling the Plug on All That Jazz', *The Voice*, 25 June 1996: 3.
79 Sesay, 18 August 1997.
80 *Ibid.*
81 Anonymous, 'Programming notes', *Sight and Sound*, 6:10 (October 1996): 33.
82 Trevor Phillips and Diran Adebayo, 'The right thing?', *The Guardian*, 7 April 1995: 26.
83 *Ibid.*
84 *Ibid.*
85 *Ibid.*
86 Neema Kambona, personal interview, 18 August 1997.
87 Sesay, 18 August 1997.
88 Kambona, 18 August 1997.
89 Hall, 11 October 1997.
90 Pines, *Black and White in Colour*, 214.
91 Malcolm Hay, 'Posse galore', *Time Out*, 13–20 May 1992: 54.
92 *Ibid.*
93 Etienne, 19 November 2000.
94 Jan Oliver, personal interview, 8 July 2004.
95 Sesay, 1 October 2006.
96 Peter Ansorge, e-mail interview, 4–12 February 2010.
97 *Ibid.*
98 *Ibid.*

5

Contemporary voices from within

Let's put multicultural programming and diversity at the heart of our promises. If Channel 4 can do it, we can do it better, and we must enforce these principles in all our sister companies which carry the BBC name. My friends, this is the route we must take if we are to be at the forefront of change in 21-Century multicultural Britain.

(BBC Accountant Valerie Johnson Crooks, BBC Black Forum, question and answer session, 21 June 2001)

As the BBC attempted to create opportunities for Black and Asian people to participate in television production, a series of published reports criticised the organisation and others not only for negative representations of ethnic minorities, but also for an absence of them in most popular programming. In 1991, Channel 4 in conjunction with the Centre for Mass Communication Research at the University of Leicester held a conference on minorities in television. The conference resulted in a document written by Professor James Halloran and others, *Ethnic Minorities and Television: A Study of Use, Reactions, and Preferences – A Report for Channel 4*. The eighty-three-page report included an evaluation of programming on Channel 4 and BBC2 as it related to ethnic minorities and was widely disseminated to the press and television media.[1]

Professor Karen Ross examined soap operas, drama series, and race. She considered the programmes to be prejudiced toward ethnic minorities, in that only 5 per cent of characters were Black or Asian. When featured, ethnic minorities were usually portrayed as criminals or drug abusers. Ross was highly critical of negative stereotyping in BBC programmes such as *Neighbours* (BBC 1985–2008; Five 2008–), hospital drama *Casualty* (1986–), the soap opera *EastEnders* (1985–), and the hard-hitting crime drama *The Paradise Club* (1989–90). Ross cited that in *EastEnders*, as with other programmes, families or people of colour were usually depicted as negative and highly problematic. She gave an example of an Asian family who ran a successful grocery in the neighbourhood, but left the area after an adultery scandal. Also featured were a Turkish character who lost all his money gambling and a Black West Indian character who was dealing in stolen property.[2] The images shown and promoted primarily served to reinforce the notion of immigrant life as culturally incongruent to Britishness.

There were common findings among the reports and findings discussed:

1 ethnic minorities desperately needed more diverse representations on British television;
2 Black British audiences, much like Black American audiences, were now realising that there were alternatives to the disappointing programmes being offered on regular or terrestrial channels; and
3 if White production and programming staff could not rise to the challenge of diversity in programming and opportunities, then ethnic minorities should be given autonomy through funding.

In February of 1996, another report called *Ethnic Minorities on Television* was released, authored by researchers Guy Cumberbatch and Samantha Woods of the Communications Research Group at Aston University in Birmingham. The report surveyed spending habits, advertisements, and ethnic audiences for BBC1, BBC2, ITV, and Channel 4.[3]

In the same year, the highly influential Commission for Racial Equality, in conjunction with the Independent Television Commission (ITC) and the BBC, released a report called *Race and Television in Britain: Channels of Diversity*. This report, based upon a seminar that took place on 14 March 1996, examined two major issues, the first of which was an examination of implications based upon previous research into the representations of ethnic minorities on British television. The seminar was to assemble senior producers and management from the BBC and Independent Television (ITV) along with independent programme producers, actors, and researchers to analyse the problems and their potential solutions. This report also included the findings of a qualitative survey of ethnic minority opinions regarding television output.[4] The second, perhaps most important, issue analysed at the seminar was a determination of what future action was required to ensure that television contributed to the development of an egalitarian society that reflected the true cultural diversity of Britain.

Carlton Television released an additional publication in 1997, written by filmmaker and television producer Parminder Vir: *The Opportunities of Diversity: A Report for Carlton Television on the American Experience*. This report was based upon a trip Vir made to New York to speak with producers at two major networks, the United Paramount Network (UPN) and Warner Brothers Television Network. Vir also travelled to Los Angeles and Washington DC to speak with television executives responsible for programming and talent development. Her research also included the major cable channels Home Box Office (HBO), Bravo, Showtime, and BET. The unfortunate aspect of this report is that Vir summarised the belief that American television offered the best opportunity for television diversity. The most prominent genre she reported upon was comedy, so when this information was reported to the management of Carlton, the belief was that sitcoms were the best avenues for balanced ethnic representations on British television; a highly damaging premise.

The future of television audiences was also an issue for discussion when market studies from LWT (London Weekend Television) found that, by the year 2000, 20 per cent of viewers between the ages of 18 and 45 would be non-White.[5] Meanwhile, Conservative Party member and journalist Thomas Quinn accused the BBC of trying to increase the number of people from racial minorities seen on television by building up a list of 'Black and Asian experts for journalists to contact', prompted by the BBC's plan to ensure that more Black people and women take part in news and current affairs broadcasts.[6]

However, the BBC again made headway when producing and transmitting the series *Black and White in Colour* (BBC, 1992). The retrospective examined West Indians on the BBC and other channels, from 1936 until the present. The programme criticised depictions of race and suggested that negative depictions of Black people in British television existed, including on the BBC. The programme featured portions of historic programmes such as the aforementioned *A Man from the Sun* and *Fable*. Also featured in the programme was the documentary *Has Britain a Colour Bar?*, described in Chapter 2. *Emergency Ward Ten* (ITV, 1957–67) and *Z Cars* were featured as well, particularly stories about miscegenation and immigration issues. Ironically, BBC1 also broadcast a historic look at the creation of BBC television, *Auntie: The Inside Story of the BBC* (1997), which ran in four parts, yet featured no Black involvement.

The most important aspect of *Black and White in Colour* was the controversial discourse that surrounded stories about race. Though the net effect of the programme was not to 'focus on the anguish but on the achievements and the huge contribution of black writers, directors and performers', issues of skewed representations and distressing television practices were obvious. Historian Stephen Bourne, whose work chronicles Black actors throughout Britain's history, felt that Blacks and Whites in the UK did not fully appreciate the efforts and talents of Black Britons in television.[7] When discussing the special, he told the *Observer* that the average Briton 'could easily name ten Black American stars, but you'd be hard-pressed to name many British ones'. In the USA he felt that there had been 'a gradual progression from shows like *Beulah* [ABC, 1950–53] a fifties comedy about a black cook, towards integration in series like *Star Trek* [NBC, 1966–69] through to major series like *Roots* [ABC, 1977] and top-rating shows like *The Cosby Show* [NBC, 1984–92]. In Britain, the story has been six steps forward and three steps back.'[8]

As the 1990s came to a close, as cities increased their populations of colour, the BBC and other broadcasters had to begin considering ways to reach more ethnic audiences. In 1991, the *Voice* entered into an agreement with Rupert Murdoch's Star Television to create a television channel aimed at Black audiences, much as IDTV had done with the support of BET in 1993. The cable channel, then owned by African-American Robert L. Johnson, was later sold to mega-conglomerate Viacom in 2003. Programming was to consist largely of music videos and imported US shows aimed at Black British audiences. The venture was Voice Communication's first foray into broadcasting, offering shows for British cable operators looking for a source of Black programming.[9] There was to be a strong emphasis on music – 'everything from hard core rap through to Whitney Houston', said *Voice* company chairman Val McCalla, although he anxiously dispelled ideas that Star TV would be a Black version of music channel MTV, promising a 'commitment to the new generation of black artists and programme-makers'. *Voice* newspaper editor Winsome Cornish said the issue proved that the Black market was 'growing in importance. The tie-up with Star TV is fantastic news for our quarter-million readers and the whole of the black community.'[10] In a possible avoidance of Americanisation, Star hoped to set up a production company to make a small number of British programmes.

Additional competition for Black audiences began with a 'Black cable TV' that became part of north London's cable packages. The Afro-Caribbean Channel (ACC) had planned to bring not videos, but Black programming from Britain, Africa, the Caribbean, and America to the homes of north Londoners. Viewers of the channel would be able to watch documentaries, news, music, and light entertainment in 20,000 homes, broadcasting six hours a day, from 6 p.m. to midnight. Black Briton and ex-politician Vernon King felt that 'both viewers and programme-makers have been crying out for a Black channel. We all want to see something better about our people on TV and think it's important for us to come together and do something for ourselves', he told the *Voice* in 1992.[11]

Efforts to utilise cable television and other forms of newer media were seemingly necessary for a degree of Black self-definition. The *Voice* criticised the BBC, as it had before, for lacking in service to Black viewers and personnel. Internal sources recommended radical changes, yet the *Voice* reminded its readers 'we have heard all this before. Two years ago the Beeb initiated Project 2000 to ensure that it employed a higher percentage of

Black staff. Well, it completely missed the target.' During this same time the BBC had suggested an increase in its licence fees for diversification of content and additional channels. However, the paper suggested that until the BBC 'reached its target figures for Black staff and is producing well-made intelligent Black programmes, we will unwillingly pay our TV licences'.[12] As a counter-measure to the BBC's inability to effect these changes, more collaborative efforts between Black British within media became a means to an end. More importantly to many, it was the only means to improve representations of Blacks on British television. It was felt that this would only be achieved if Black actors, writers, producers, and directors formed their own independent production companies, as suggested by Treva Etienne in the interviews outlined in Chapter 4. Speaking at a prestigious Royal Television Society workshop on ethnic representation, Alby James, artistic director of a Black theatre company who had also worked on television, said 'real change could only be implemented through the independent sector'.[13] He reminded actors and media professionals of colour that change and autonomy would only occur when 'more of us who have experience in working in television … can move to that stage of forming independent production companies'. He spoke of Asian acting troupes that did 'the work, training actors, directors, and writers' and that this effort helped 'them move further into the mainstream'. Alby stated that 'screaming at the BBC or Channel 4 or anybody else' would not help.[14]

In 1998, the possibility for further opportunities to create film and programming began with the launch of a cable and satellite TV channel targeted specifically at the African-Caribbean community. The ITC had granted the African Broadcasting Corporation a licence to launch the African Broadcasting Corporation (ABC TV), a channel dedicated to African-Caribbean culture and the contributions made within the UK. Director of the channel, A. Soyode, said that ABC TV eventually hoped to provide a platform for British African-Caribbean programme-makers, and that it was the channel's intention to show the more positive side of African people and 'break down the barriers' created by the negative representations currently shown on TV. The new channel had predicted that 90 per cent of viewers would be of African-Caribbean descent, with the other 10 per cent represented by those with an interest in Africa.[15]

Dyke and diversity: the last great white hope?

In April 1999, Greg Dyke accepted the position as the new director general of the BBC. Previously he had served as chief executive of Pearson Television, and would now replace Sir John Birt. Dyke's new position would earn him a salary estimated at £400,000, but also hostile coverage in the rest of the media. BBC News stated that his new position would allow him to head one of the greatest broadcast institutions in the world, but arguably the most important cultural institution in Britain. His primary tasks would include the challenges of maintaining the BBC's prominence in the face of a massive expansion of digital channels and international competition.[16]

Upon his appointment, Greg Dyke unveiled the BBC's new management structure (which did not include an African-Caribbean person), and he announced that the BBC would be spending at least £100 million more on BBC programming and services in the coming year. As Dyke made the transition to his new post, the television industry came under more criticism, accused of lagging behind society and failing to reflect the multicultural nature of the country. In a 1999 report from the Broadcasting Standards Commission, ethnic minority groups expressed concerns that 'programmes were [still] guilty of presenting characters from ethnic minorities as two-dimensional and without a role in society as a whole'.[17] Negative stereotyping had been evident, the report found, for season after season with several respondents mentioning a particular episode of *Coronation Street* (1960) in which a Black character was introduced, only to become involved immediately in a crime. Lord Holmes, the chairman of the Commission told the *Guardian*:

> Despite a growing understanding of what a multicultural Britain means, pockets of institutionalized racism persist in our society. Broadcasters have an important role in overcoming prejudice; because of the educative role television can play. There are challenges here which must not be ignored.[18]

On Friday, 7 April 1999, the Race in Media Awards ceremony was held in London. The event, co-sponsored by the Commission for Racial Equality, chose Dyke to serve as keynote speaker. The presentation, entitled 'The BBC: leading cultural change for a rich and diverse UK' addressed Dyke's new structure for the BBC and his 'aim of creating a new culture'. The primary issue he planned to address was 'the BBC and its role' in a '21st century Britain, a multi-channel, multi-cultural Britain'.[19] He planned to head up 'a BBC where diversity is seen as an asset not an issue or a problem'; one open to talent from various cultures; 'a BBC which reflects the world in which we live today not the world of yesterday'.[20] He had also expressed concern that younger Britons recognised a need for change even before the organisation had. He told the audience that British culture was already 'multi-ethnic, multi-everything', and for younger people 'multi-culturalism is not about political correctness but is simply a part of the furniture of their everyday lives'. Dyke expressed the importance of the BBC having a special role because it was 'the UK's most important cultural institution', although he doubted if younger age groups recognised this issue.

Another major responsibility of this new BBC was to 'explore and articulate the meaning of Britishness in a multi-cultural devolving Britain'. Dyke believed that the BBC had, 'in recent years, made genuine and well-intentioned efforts to respond to multi-cultural Britain by opening up the organization to talented people from ethnic minorities'. He congratulated the BBC on promoting more women to higher posts but pointed out that if the BBC had made progress with issues of gender they could 'do it with race'. Dyke stated that had he wandered around the BBC a decade earlier, he would have found it 'disproportionately male and white; today it just seems disproportionately white'. Although the organisation had met the 8 per cent target for all staff, people of colour made up less than 2 per cent of management. Dyke acknowledged that many creative people from ethnic minorities still preferred 'to go to work for independents or other channels rather than the BBC', and he professed himself sure that 'glass ceilings and obstructive bureaucratic practices' existed, but he did not consider these to be the biggest problems. Dyke announced the appointment of Black Briton Linda Mitchell as Head of Diversity, describing his plan for her as helping the service achieve a new target for the BBC staff overall: '10 per cent by 2003 and to at least double the number of managers from diverse backgrounds in the same time'. Dyke closed by telling the audience of media professional and community leaders that 'getting this right' would be a 'benchmark for [his] time at the BBC'. His position was that the BBC 'must change and embrace multi-culturalism – because this is Britain in the 21st century, and 21st century Britain is diverse.'[21]

Within months, Dyke's presence as a harbinger of change was reinforced by many newspapers. Highlighted was an effort by all channels to launch a new drive to increase the number of ethnic minority faces on screen and behind the cameras. A joint initiative was launched called the Cultural Diversity Network, involving the BBC, ITV, Carlton Television, Granada Media, Good Morning Television (GMTV), Independent Television News (ITN), Channel 4, Channel 5, and Rupert Murdoch's British Sky Broadcasting (BskyB). According to the *Guardian*, 'TV chiefs' were 'concerned that black and Asian viewers are deserting them quicker than others', and admitted that not enough had been done to reflect the changing culture of Britain. These men and a few women all promised to stop endless meetings and to 'take action to promote talent from ethnic minority backgrounds'. The project's first chairman was Carlton TV's chief executive Clive Jones. Jones reminded broadcasters that they would 'lose even more viewers' if changes did not occur. Britain was rapidly facing a change in demographics, described by Jones as a revolution, which clearly signalled a need for rapid change. 'Either [they] adapt', stated Jones, 'or what we do will become increasingly irrelevant for a vital part of the audience.' Years of attending meetings and commissioning reports were no longer adequate, as 'the time had come to act. The status quo simply cannot be allowed to continue.' Via a mandate from Jones' office, each company produced an action plan, with employment targets and commitments to increase the number of Black and Asian screen actors and broadcasters. The BBC, Channel 4, and Channel 5 set specific targets for increasing staff diversity. Chris Smith, the Culture Secretary for the Labour government was to monitor progress.

Dyke repeated his commitment to increase the number of ethnic minority staff at the corporation from 8 per cent to 10 per cent in 2003. Although the BBC was not driven by advertising revenue, its licence fee obligations meant 'it must produce programmes of wide appeal'. ITV said it would order programme makers to consider how they portray cultural diversity in their programmes. In its revived soap, the popular *Crossroads* (ATV 1964–81; Central 1981–88; Carlton 2001–03), would now have a strong multicultural theme. Channel 4 said it would increase its ethnic minority staff from 9 per cent of its payroll to 11 per cent by 2003, and Channel 5 said it aimed to reach 13 per cent. BskyB pledged to introduce a mentoring system. Chairman of the Equal Opportunities Commission Sir Herman Ouseley said he detected a change in mood and was hopeful that the initiative was a 'watershed because the high-level executives have come here and pledged themselves to commitments, along with the secretary of state'.

Meanwhile research conducted by each channel had shown that Black (and Asian) people were 'abandoning terrestrial television channels quicker than any other section of the community', and that it was projected that ethnic minorities would constitute 7 per cent of the UK population within a year; in London alone, the level was expected to reach 30 per cent. Culture Secretary Smith reminded the press that the action was not an initiative based upon 'political correctness, but about the plain realities of life'.[22] Despite the initiative by these channels, critics from within questioned the lack of progress at the upper rungs of management. Asian news presenter Krishnan Guru-Murthy remarked that at the launch of the Cultural Diversity Network each of the 'middle-class, middle-aged, white men who run British television promised better portrayal and new targets for minority representations'. Yet only one 'non-white face in a position of power' was there; Waheed Ali of Carlton Television. The reporter called this lack of effort 'embarrassing – no, appalling' that no one from an ethnic minority was in top-level management at the BBC, ITV, BSkyB, Channel 4, or the new network, Channel 5. At Channel 4 the two most senior Black people remained segregated to multicultural programmes. Guru-Murthy reminded readers that it was not because there were no suitably qualified people from ethnic minorities. Having begun working for the channel in

1988, he had noticed some improvement and there were many more people of colour working there. But getting Black and Asian staff into production and on the television screen was not enough; they needed 'to be in the boardrooms and chief executives' offices if British television was to achieve the 'step change the men at the top say they want'. Guru-Murthy felt it was 'fashionable' for those in power to have seminars, but now it had become 'fashionable to say: "We're fed up with seminars, let's do things"'. He was highly optimistic because he felt that these chiefs were 'actually scared of what will happen if they do not stop talking and start doing something'. They had set 'targets we can all judge them by, and they know that if they fail, huge parts of the TV audience will simply desert them'.[23]

At the start of 2001, Dyke had begun to settle into his new responsibilities at the BBC. However, he shocked the press and public by stating in interview that he again considered the BBC to be sorely lacking in diversity, calling the organisation 'hideously white' and accusing it of having gross problems with race relations. Though not admitting that the corporation was racist, he did note the management structure at the BBC was more than 98 per cent White. And he also mentioned that the organisation was unable to retain ethnic minorities working at Television Centre and elsewhere because he doubted 'if they were made to feel welcome'. He felt that failure of the corporation's equal opportunities policies was most noticeable at the highest levels. He, as Guru-Murthy and many others had stated, found that the most noticeable absence was at management level. Dyke told an interviewer that he 'had a management Christmas lunch and as I looked around I thought: "We've got a real problem here." There were 80-odd people there and only one person who wasn't white'.[24] Soon after this admittance, the BBC's senior most 'non-white news presenter' criticised Dyke. Presenter George Alagiah felt that 'many journalists will be saying that it is no longer good enough to identify a problem if he can't come up with solutions'. He supported Dyke's desire to address the problem, but warned the BBC against playing the 'numbers game'. He reminded the press that staff should be promoted on merit, not simply because of their ethnic origin.[25]

By April of 2001, media correspondents were still criticising the lack of ethnic minorities on popular television programmes. The additional concern with these articles was that, despite promises to the contrary from television managers, Black and Asian people were still almost non-existent on many popular television shows. In one week on BBC2, the only ethnic minority faces in the channel's top ten programmes – with combined viewing figures of 33 million viewers of various cultures – were cartoon characters in *The Simpsons*. With drama programming there was now another concern: many production teams were guilty of colour-blind casting. Characters from minority communities with supposedly rich cultural histories could just as easily have been White, because they displayed no evidence of their ethnic background. The appearance of ethnic minority characters in the popular evening soaps *EastEnders* (BBC1) and *Coronation Street* (Granada TV) were occasional even though the programmes are set in highly diverse London and Manchester, cities with large ethnic minority populations. Only Channel 4's *Brookside* soap, which was set in Liverpool, was 'consistent'. By examining 204 programmes between 20 November and 17 December 2000 (considered the 'heart of the most competitive autumn season between the broadcasters for years'), researchers for the networks found that ethnic minority representation did not compare equally with the 'real world'. These results came nearly one year after the formation of the Cultural Diversity Network.

To ensure the plans and promises made by Dyke's administration, the BBC appointed Peter Salmon, a White Briton, to serve as 'diversity champion for race', an appointment to oversee diversity efforts. Joy Francis, a former editor of the Black-themed *Pride* magazine and founder of the Creative Collective (a consortium of journalists whose aim was to boost recruitment from ethnic minorities) welcomed the initiative, but criticised the BBC for leaving itself open to further accusations of racism. Francis said that the Collective didn't object to the 'race adviser being white', but suggested that Dyke's office could always have delayed the announcement until they found the 'appropriate person'. She also told the *Guardian* that after Dyke's 'outburst about the lack of ethnic minority staff in management roles, it seems at odds with this to appoint a champion of diversity who is a senior, white male manager'. An unknown BBC source told the press that that the diversity champion for race needed to come from the executive committee and there was no Black or Asian executive at this level. Noted producer and broadcaster Trevor Phillips felt that Salmon was 'a good choice', because it wouldn't matter if he was White as long as he's 'got the guns to make things happen', but added 'we'll have to see whether he really does make things happen'.[26]

As part of the diversity initiative under Dyke, the BBC's Senior Communication Adviser Chantal Benjamin supervised the development of a booklet and CD-ROM that provided an overview of the corporation's efforts. Included were rosters of programmes featuring portrayals and characters of colour. This included BBC1, BBC2, BBC Choice, BBC Knowledge, BBC Radio 4 and BBC Radio Five Live. Radio programming for all the regions was also included, as were their emphases and target audiences. Under the heading 'Connecting with Audiences', efforts to share information with publicists, marketing personnel, and press officers were explained, as the corporation attempted to convince these professionals of the potential of marketing to diverse audiences. To further help achieve this goal,

Benjamin and others conducted workshops aimed at emphasising the growing ethnic minority community, and the campaigns needed to reach these consumers. This included sharing information about Black and Asian media sources and community activities. In April 2001 the organisation began actively working toward a marked improvement in representations of ethnic minority communities, many of whom, according to surveys, believed the BBC to have improved. Benjamin noted that her 'main aim as the communications person responsible for diversity was to show that the BBC had lots to be proud of but that we had a tendency to hide our light under a bushel when it came to our multicultural programmes'. Also important was a 'better understanding' among marketing staff that diversity was a good business resource, particularly when considering the future of the UK. However, impressions of the BBC among the demographic noted as Black Caribbeans were less than favourable. They did not feel positively about the programme offerings on BBC1, or 2, and were more likely to watch ITV and Sky One. The group expressed even more of a preference to programming on Channel 4 and Channel 5. Yet 20 per cent of those polled felt the BBC had 'improved recently', which was higher than the average for the UK population.

Dyke and the BBC Black Forum

Dyke's commitment to efforts at the BBC were literally questioned when Jan Oliver and the BBC Black Forum (BBF) held an open question and answer session on 21 June 2001 with Greg Dyke and the diversity champion Peter Salmon. Those who addressed specific concerns by Black and Asian staff members were Valerie Johnson Crooks, Senior Manager; Elonka Sorrosl Diversity Editor for BBC English Regions; Chantal Benjamin, Marketing and Communications; Peter Salmon, Director of Sport and also BBC Race Champion. Linda Mitchell, the new Director of Diversity sat in for listening purposes. Besides a live audience of BBF members, there was a teleconference hook-up established with the BBC's Manchester office. According to a transcript of the meeting e-mailed to me by Oliver, the attendance was 'tremendous'.

Chibs Ifeanyi, a steering group member of BBF (later called the BBC Black and Asian Forum or BBAF) commented at the start of the question and answer session that 'lots and lots of e-mails' had come from people who wanted to attend. He reminded the audience that what was needed was for members to actually involve themselves in more than just 'parties and B-B-Qs', but become active members. An additional issue was the need for more representation across departments of the BBC. Linda Mitchell reminded the group 'there are black people in Scotland, Wales and Northern

Ireland' though she was 'sitting here in a listening capacity, you know'. Ifeanyi then introduced Mitchell as 'Head of the Diversity Centre'. She again remarked that she was there to listen and take notes 'unless somebody specifically wants me to answer'.

Jan Oliver, Chair of the BBC Black Forum, then officially began the meeting. She introduced herself, then welcomed and thanked Dyke and Salmon for 'taking time out of their diaries to join us'. She then told Dyke that since he had spoken so much about those staff members of colour, he should actually meet them, hence the meeting. She explained fifteen years previously, a small group of Black production staff had got together and formed the Forum, known 'more fondly as the BBF': 'a forum where ethnic minority staff can support and network each other as well as campaign and lobby for change to improve opportunities at the BBC', through organising meetings that addressed challenges like improving representation, and promoting interactions from ethnic staff across nations and regions. Oliver stated that their membership stood at approximately 400 members of staff, which represented about 20 per cent of Black and Asian staff in the BBC.

One of the first issues mentioned came by telephone from a BBC office in Manchester. The caller stated that the feeling among Black and Asian staff across the north was that there were many opportunities, but that management did not consult Black and Asian staff on issues of diversity or opportunities. She stated that the BBC seemed to be 'bending over backwards now trying to attract Black talent but, you know, what about the talent that exists within the BBC?' She noted that among her and colleagues sitting there, they had nearly 40 years of service, but management did very little to support their desires to move upward in the organisation. Neither Dyke nor Salmon responded.

After establishing the conference connection with the northern offices, Oliver reminded the audience that they were there to 'give Greg and Peter an opportunity to hear a view from the front line: how the BBC's diversity politics …' (amid laughter, she corrected the perhaps Freudian slip to say) 'sorry, how the BBC's diversity *policies* are affecting Black and Asian staff'. Oliver noted that the first presentation was by Valerie Johnson Crooks, who highlighted the current working environment in the BBC from the perspective of ethnic minorities. Elonka Sorros called for a review of the racial harassment policy at the BBC, and Chantal Benjamin offered 'suggestions for change in the culture'.

Crooks, who called herself a BBC ambassador, felt good about the organisation's possibilities yet expressed that she felt her success 'came in spite of, not because of, our policies and practices'. She had the 'dubious honour of being the only and possibly first Black female BBC employee to achieve a specific lower management grade'. At the time of her presentation, there were finally new ethnic minority faces at the higher grades and she was 'happy to relinquish [her] record'. She then strongly suggested that the BBC had not made sufficient progress in the area of ethnic minority representation. Ethnic minorities at the BBC stood at 8 per cent of its workforce at the beginning of 2001. She admitted that this statistic compared favourably with the national statistic (in 2001 ethnic minorities made up 7.9 per cent of the total UK population), but that only some 2 per cent occupied higher-grade positions. The BBC was also yet to celebrate the appointment of its first ethnic minority Director, while a 'large number of ethnic minority employees [are] stuck in the same lower grade jobs for a number of years'. Their White counterparts received training and career support, sometimes resulting in their promotion, 'even though they may be less qualified or skilled'. Crooks then addressed the issue of policies and procedures, telling Dyke and Salmon that when inequality of treatment or discrimination occurred, they were unsure of whom to turn to within the organisation. She asked

> Who can we turn to in the BBC for swift and fair justice? The perpetrators? Human Resources? And what sanctions do perpetrators face? If we challenge these unfair practices, we face character assassination, relegation, or even reprisal. We are dubbed troublemakers, rabble-rousers, unable to fit in, difficult, even incompetent. Judgements are then made about our careers based on these comments rather than fact even if we have impeccable credentials.

She then reminded the two men of the vast contributions ethnic minorities had made to British society. Similar ambitions for careers and their children's future were shared with White Britons, as were 'anxieties over education, health, and transport'. She expressed the vast similarities that minorities had with White Britons, 'yet [they] appear most visibly on our screens as participants in sports, domestic activities, or in one-dimensional subordinate roles'. News and documentary discussions referred to their concerns as ethnic issues, yet there were no 'ethnic minority commissioners and senior programme makers to ensure that Black and Asian talent are cast in lead or major roles in mainstream programmes'. In 'today's BBC', Crooks stated that 'old man inequality' was 'on his deathbed' and that they must be 'vigilant and guard against those who want to keep the old order alive'. Yet she advised the audience that the old guard were clearly not 'all male, and they are not all White'. She expressed a need to implement accurate tracking of applications, hirings, promotions, attachments, and salaries detailing ethnicity but also gender, disability, and age for these held clues as to potential areas of concern which would need to be addressed. As for plans, Crooks stated eloquently:

Let's strengthen our policies to promote zero tolerance on discrimination, bullying, and harassment with severe penalties for perpetrators. Let's start defending the rights and liberties of all our employees who fall victim to the system and turn our might against the offenders. Let's get tough on our Managers who fail to engage in division but choose to perpetuate the old order. And our suppliers? Let's invoke disqualification procedures where they fail to comply with contractual requirements on diversity. Let's put multicultural programming and diversity at the heart of our promises. If Channel 4 can do it, we can do it better and we must enforce these principals in all our sister companies which carry the BBC name. My friends, this is the route we must take if we are to be at the forefront of change in twenty-first-century multicultural Britain. So we are the British Broadcasting Corporation, the UK's most important cultural institution, and when we do I for one will believe that my BBC is truly committed to equal opportunities for all irrespective of race, colour, creed, ethnic or national origins, gender, marital status, sexuality, disability, or age and I know you will too. Thank you.

Elonka Sorros, Diversity Editor for BBC English Regions, spoke next. She told the audience, Dyke, and Salmon that her role on the BBF Steering Group was to help widen the network of support offered by the forum to minority ethnic staff working in the regions. As suggested by Crooks, racism 'goes right across the Organisation; no matter which petal or directorate you work in, there may be times when you feel bullied or harassed and you may feel that the bullying or harassment is because of your ethnicity'. She criticised the Manager's Guidelines and the BBC's Statement of Intent regarding equal opportunities for not providing a clear, effective policy for dealing with racial harassment. According to Sorros, the BBC should ask itself what could be done to get more minority ethnic talent, but also what could be done about the 'perceived or real racism' in the organisation.

The perception was growing that the BBC did not embrace legislation intended to protect Black and Asian staff working in the public sector. The BBF recommended that as an organisation the BBC 'develop and implement a clear policy and procedure to deal with racial harassment and bullying; it must be accessible, visible and effective'. This action would then include mediation services staffed by Black, Asian, and other minority ethnic specialists. This 'objective ear' would allow one somewhere to discuss concerns, without being 'labelled as a trouble maker or having a chip on your shoulder', and, more importantly, where employees could speak confidentially about the issues, and receive 'independent and impartial advice' on how to proceed.

The final presentation came from Chantal Benjamin in Marketing and Communications. Benjamin had been with the BBC for ten years, and also served as the Press and Events Manager for BBC Black Forum. She considered herself as 'light relief' but that her intention was to address the changing culture. Benjamin discussed the 'little cultural things that go on in an organisation that actually breed the seeds of resentment'. She then told everyone a poignant example of how a White person may meet a

> British Indian or British African or British Caribbean person or British Pakistani, Bangladeshi, whatever, for the first time and neither of them is quite sure what to do [or] what to call ... the person with the difficult name, [so] they end up not being called anything at all or they have to call themselves by some sort of short version which is acceptable. So for example, I have a wonderful Sierra Leonean friend in Resources whose name is Taminu; a beautiful name but he calls himself Tom because it's easier for the English people in his office. My name is Chantal but ... you wouldn't know that walking around the BBC because I'm always called Shantelle, Shontle, Chantel, Chantle, all kinds of things, you know. Now it may not seem a big deal but it's these tiny things that resentment like a cancer grows in people's hearts and then they end up thinking, 'I hate this White person' you know, and it becomes a race thing where it needn't have been from the start.

Another issue discussed by Benjamin was pride and confidence to wear their national dress. She suggested that she '[looks] around the BBC and I see many people from different ethnic minorities who don't feel confident to wear their national clothes'. She told of a story in which her friend who works as a news reporter wanted so much to go on air 'with her sari but feels that the news editors would not take her seriously' if she did. Another friend of Benjamin's wanted to wear a chemise to work, but felt as though 'she would not be taken as a professional senior member of staff if she did this'. Benjamin felt that it was highly important that culture be appreciated and that racism

> isn't just about overt stuff. Actually generally in the BBC I think there is very little overt racism, it's the covert stuff, it's the body language, it's the subtle things – those are the things that make you go home and ... Ooooh! And you stir all night thinking 'I'll get them one day', you know? Three years later, you've got a race case on your hands. It could have been sorted from the start ... I've been in the BBC ten years; I've never been invited to a focus group to talk about how I feel as a Black person at the BBC [or] establishing an ongoing ethnic minority network for employees. And the way that we can help is we can share our experiences. Now not everyone in this room, just because you're Black or Asian, [is] an expert on diversity. [But] let's get real; we are experts on being Black and Asian in the BBC.

Benjamin suggested that a database of ethnicities be established at the BBC to provide other levels of expertise. She told of a time she watched a presenter misstate issues about Sierra Leone. She, having an ethnic connection to Sierra Leone, would hear things said that were often inaccurate, and, cringing, would ask, 'Why didn't [someone at the BBC] call me before you put this report out?' She noted that no diversity database of experts in the BBC existed in house. Benjamin told Dyke and Salmon that 'culture shock' could also educate White managers about specific issues. She also mentioned that there were people of colour on staff that could provide talent, thereby avoiding the notion of 'oh we would have a Black actor, but can't find any, or there's no one out there'.

Benjamin then told Dyke that she and other ethnic staff weren't concerned about their commitment; their concern was regarding the middle management, or supervisory level. She felt that blockages existed there. Middle management needed to know 'how [they as ethnic minorities] feel and this is how we can make things better for you at the BBC because we are experienced too'. They wanted to assist with diversity in the BBC, they didn't 'just want to be recipients of it, we want to give stuff back and help this Organisation [and] we're all here because we want to be at the BBC, that's why we're here and we want to do a good job'.

Oliver then advised Dyke that the issues expressed had been 'stored up for a long, long time in the BBC'. As Chair, Oliver stated that she had committed herself to taking the BBF 'onto the next level' by having a dialogue directly with him and Salmon. It was important she said that they both 'know how we're feeling … but I think hopefully you've got a lot from it and if you'd like to respond please feel free to do so at this point'.

Dyke thanked the group for the presentations, which made 'a lot of sense'. He then began to recount his first days at the BBC and his analysis of statistics regarding women. He mentioned that if someone 'looked around the place' they might say, 'that this was a place where women didn't do too well ten years ago. That's been broken.' The obvious importance of this improvement was worth noting, yet the issues raised were indeed of ethnic consideration. The early portion of his response was similar to affirmative action policies in America, in which White men of power gladly discuss the advance of women, usually White, to managerial roles.

Dyke acknowledged that when he made the famous, or infamous, 'hideously White' comment, people suggested later that he apologise for it, which he had not, reminding the audience, somewhat defensively, of his concern. He explained that his answer actually had made 'an impact'. The impact Dyke referred to was a series of letters, mainly critical, that had been sent to the *Daily Telegraph* within that week, which Dyke called 'quite wonderful'. Yet he noted that they mostly responded, 'of course it's White, it's a White society', prompting him to wonder where these writers lived, and where they came from. Had they not come to notice the increasing diversity of the country?

Dyke then referenced criticism such as those levelled by his senior news anchor, George Alagiah, who warned Dyke 'that his words must soon be matched by actions'.[27] Dyke recalled how somebody had said to him, '"are you saying we should appoint Black people just because they're Black?" and I said "no, but don't tell me there aren't talented Black people who could do most of these jobs". Our problem is we've got to find them.' The immediate concern here was that the BBF had clearly identified the amount of talented people already within the ranks of the organisation. Furthermore, as suggested by Benjamin, these ethnic minorities were excellent resources for gaining information otherwise overlooked by their White counterparts; perhaps even qualified minorities.

Dyke then admitted that an organisation could have 'all the Management Policies you like in the world but if in the end you've got a gatekeeper who doesn't let Black people through the gate you're not going to get anywhere', an acknowledgement to a comment made by Elonka Sorros. Dyke suggested that he and Salmon 'go away and have a look at that because I think if we haven't got [an] effective policy and effective means' to handle complaints 'and people saying "I feel racially discriminated against", or even "I feel racially insecure" then we ought to have. So let me take that away and we'll come back with some ideas and then throw them around.'

Dyke then discussed the issues that had seemingly grasped the attention of the television managers with the Cultural Diversity Network: 'statistics of what places like London are going to be, you know, of non-Anglo-Saxon-White population' within 'ten years, fifteen years' time'. Again came the warning that 'if the BBC doesn't reflect that sort of diversity, we're going to be as an Organisation irrelevant, it's as simple as that'. More statistics were quoted along with the reminder that the BBC was 'absolutely committed but … being committed isn't enough unless you can do it. … it is important that more people from ethnic minorities get into management because then it will change and until that happens I don't think it will change.'

He then deferred to questions from the audience, saying that the BBC had to change 'attitudes at every level [to] make the place much more attractive'. As a reference again to statistics, Salmon reminded the audience and himself that it was 'very, very important for us to keep monitoring the figures' while it was also 'very, very important for us to keep listening' to the BBF and its constituency. Salmon said that he planned to continue 'listening to the group, in lots of different ways, whether it's in training or representation or editorial issues or employment issues or whatever because you're a fantastic resource for us'. He projected that in the next year and beyond they could come back and 'talk at these meetings'. At that point, 'these rooms will be fuller and fuller of people who feel more and more engaged with the process that Greg and I are involved in'. It would seem that if progress were being made, perhaps the meetings Salmon referred to would be unneeded. After a round of applause, Oliver took question and answers.

The first came from BBC employee Devon Daley from the East Midlands and West Midlands who wanted to stress that there was life outside London 'first of all'. Daley began by congratulating the BBC on a jazz documentary (which he felt ran too late at night, much like other ethnically themed programmes) and having a Black presenter on *The Holiday Show*, which was obviously an achievement for the BBC. He cited that there was a need for an African-Caribbean network of employees, and how on election night, he stayed up all night, even knowing the result was going to be a Labour win and 'didn't see any Black people apart from one person serving coffee in this very elaborate studio that was set up'. The audience responded with applause. On one of the newer digital channels, BBC Knowledge, Daley saw an entire season of programmes on Black history (whether it was American or British wasn't made clear) 'that would have been excellent on mainstream BBC' and asked why the organisation didn't use them in this fashion.

Another question asked of Dyke and Salmon came from a programme maker who had previously worked with the BBC's now defunct African Caribbean Unit. He asked how the two of them felt about the shut-down of the unit. He also stated that the Community Programme Unit, which had made lots of Black programming, had effectively closed down and it seemed from his perspective as if, even though things were changing, 'things [weren't] really improving'. Similar issues that were 'seeds being planted years' ago hadn't 'given fruit'.

At this point Linda Mitchell chimed in to remind everyone that because the African Caribbean Unit was shutting down did not mean the 'end of Black programming'. She suggested that Commissioning Editor Maxine Watson (also a Black female) had 'a great deal of autonomy and she has the enhanced budget' and another woman who had worked in the African Caribbean Unit was now working in drama. Mitchell also suggested that progress was being made and that 'an awful lot of work [was] being done, but [that] a huge amount of things that we're doing at the moment won't actually come to fruition'. She explained that she was investing in a Development Editor whose responsibility would be to go out and get Black writers who could be moved into working on the show *Doctors* (BBC1) and then on to *EastEnders*. She described to the audience how Kate Roland of Drama went out to all of the main educational institutions for drama looking for minority ethnic talent and there was one minority ethnic acting student out of 800. However, she did tell Dyke and Salmon that production departments were telling her that 'Commissioning Editors and Channel Controllers are not willing to take a risk', and that she therefore encouraged them to

> Embrace risk and if somebody tries something new with a new face or a new
> location or a new scene whatever, it may not work, it may not attract the big

ratings that we say we're chasing. But, we've got to do that because unless we start doing the same things differently and different things, we're only going to end up having the same frustrating painful arguments.

From the Manchester office, a British Indian employee named Paresh suggested that Dyke pay a visit to the area. Dyke had mentioned that there was a distinct need for more ethnic minorities in managerial roles, but Paresh suggested that, to allow this to happen, 'you've got to get them through the front door as we all know, and there are various reasons why this is not happening in the regions'. She suggested that if he truly championed this cause of race employment, he should go to every region, and 'maybe spend half a day and just bring this home to some of the management'. She advised Dyke to a room full of laughter that he would surely 'rattle a lot of cages out in the regions'. Via telephone, also from Manchester, an unidentified male acknowledged how poor the opportunities were for ethnic minorities there. He explained that there were various reasons for this, but he felt that one of the obsessions of television news in the regions was 'this thing about the target audience wanting supposedly pretty White females as opposed to Black journalists'. Dyke suggested that the office in Manchester had been downsizing at the time, but not any longer, and therefore he would look into the issues raised.

As one of the most important final questions, a woman named Jackie asked about a regulation already imposed upon Channel 4 by the ITC. According to her comments, the directive would 'assure that certain kinds of 'programmes [are] targeted … at peak times'. She stated that it was all very well having Black programmes, 'but if they're going out at 11.15 at night' then audiences perceive them as unimportant or unpopular.

Dyke responded that 'to change the perceptions of Black people in White society it's about putting Black people in mainstream television'. He understood that she was 'talking about … programming aimed at specific audiences', but that the proposed new digital channel BBC3, if started, 'should help a lot because it's aimed at 15- to 25-year-olds. Well if you miss out the ethnic minority populations in 15- to 25-year- olds you're wasting your time, you know, you just are.' Since BBC3 was to be a digital channel, Dyke imagined comparatively small audiences to start, but 'it doesn't mean that we shouldn't also be looking at doing that on BBC1 and BBC2'.

Jan Oliver then thanked Dyke and Salmon, reminding them that summaries of the presentations would be forwarded and that the organisation would 'wait to hear from [them] to continue the dialogue'. She thanked everyone for coming and sharing concerns, issues, and questions, and she hoped that they 'got as much from it' as she did.[28] Within days after the conference, the BBC prepared a list of issues and recommendations for Dyke and Salmon, particularly as they addressed EMs (ethnic minorities):

KEY ISSUES	RECOMMENDATIONS
1. The BBC does not have an effective policy and procedure for dealing with racial harassment and bullying.	• Develop and implement a clear policy and procedure. • Establish an independent mediation service staffed by Black and Asian specialists but not excluding BBC staff.
2. The portrayal and representation of EMs on our screens still don't adequately reflect the contribution made by EMs to British culture.	• Like C4, BBC to commit to at least three hours per week of multicultural programming (some to transmit in peak time). • Set up a taskforce to look at how the BBC can attract the best EM talent.
3. There are not enough EM role models as only 2 per cent of EM at the BBC are in grades 10 and above and there is no EM Director.	• BBC is already actively progressing this issue.
4. A large number of EM employees are stuck in the same grade for a number of years. Promotion opportunities are rarely forthcoming. Although *ASCEND* will partially address this there is still an issue with the way managers perceive their EM staff in terms of career advancement.	• There needs to be meaningful and effective monitoring of all applications, appraisals, recruitment, promotions, and attachments detailing salary, ethnicity, gender, disability, and age. • Effective feedback for EMs if unsuccessful at interviews • Training and development modules to include sessions that encourage managers to think about the workforce they already have in new ways.
5. It is believed that in some areas salaries paid to EMs for doing the same job as White colleagues are less favourable.	• Audit to assess the extent to which this is happening, if at all. • On-going monitoring.
6. Suppliers of services like catering, cleaning, and security seem to perpetuate the stereotypes of EMs.	• All major suppliers of goods and services to be pre-qualified and must satisfy the BBC's diversity requirements. • On-going monitoring for compliance. • Procurement procedures to be amended to include disqualification for failure to comply.
7. Lack of tolerance and understanding of non-White cultures remains an issue.	• EM staff to run informal workshops for managers.

Some of the most promising issues in the meeting revolved around Black and Asian representations within programming. Oliver noted that 'the BBF does influence on-screen representation' and had been working hard to 'ensure that commissioning editors within the service are made aware of new emerging talent'. An example was a young Black comedienne, Gina Yashere, who had her own show on BBC Choice. According to Oliver, this was a first.[29]

Three years later, in 2004, Oliver expressed some concerns over the lack of change within the BBC. Many BBF members no longer found time for meetings, and very little follow-up had been done. In a personal interview, Oliver felt that the BBF made 'the best of what we had when we had it', yet she had great concern and curiosity over what the BBC would do about problems left unsolved. She explained that Mitchell, despite her efforts, had left the BBC within a matter of years. She 'wasn't around very long and could have had a different approach', Oliver said, 'to solving some of the BBF's concerns – particularly issues related to recent diversity efforts'. Since African-Caribbeans accounted for only 8 per cent of the population, Oliver expressed concerns for the future and for urban areas where many of these citizens lived, and certain programming was viewed.[30] When asked about new Black programming on the BBC, Oliver advised me that 'there is [still] very little' targeted programming specifically for Black people. The focus now seemed to be upon integration and 'ensuring that all programmes reflect different faces and voices' no matter what the ethnic background.[31] Oliver did suggest that the BBC had hired more people of colour, but they remained 'on the low grade'.[32]

African-Caribbean Cyril Husbands, one of five senior diversity mangers hired during the Dyke tenure, discussed issues related to diversity efforts at the BBC. He described how, in 2003, the Diversity Centre was attempting to provide strategic advice at the BBC and to add value to what the BBC did – by ensuring that 'adequate creative and consistent attention is paid to diversity issues as related to age, culture, faith, disability, sexuality, race, and other social constructs'.[33] Husbands described his position while still with the BBC (he has since left) as a regular liaison with senior resource people and mangers to maintain strategies around diversity issues. Husbands also spoke of a credibility gap that occurred since many of the Diversity Centre staff were not programme makers, and instead were seen as those who 'block the creative process rather than enhancing the process'.[34] As an example, he explained that executive and series producers of the sitcom *The Crouches* (BBC, 2003–05) were concerned with several issues raised about the programme's inaccuracies in its portrayal of Black life. 'Important concerns', as Husbands called them, 'were raised with the programme's White writer [Ian Patterson] and director [Nick Wood], but there was an issue taken with the production team's judgement over content'. However, Black members of the programme's production team also raised concerns over these skewed representations.[35] African-Caribbeans working at the BBC saw rushes of the show prior to its premiere, and were also highly displeased. Their sentiments were echoed in the minority and majority press. The BBC considered the programme, called the first Black BBC sitcom, an experiment, originally received by over three million viewers. The programme was widely panned and considered a clumsy attempt to be funny through shallow stereotypes by the reviewers, who compared it unfavourably with the *Windrush* special (BBC, 1998) shown on BBC years earlier.[36] In addition, the minority-themed *New Nation* and Ally Ross, TV critic of the mainstream paper *The Sun*, found the show 'paralysingly unfunny', and also 'deeply patronising'. The BBC gave the show a second chance and used new writers for series two, but it was still considered to be inconsistent in its humour.[37]

Another major *faux pas* discussed was the marketing plan for BBC's *Babyfather* (2001–02). Despite some critical acclaim for the diverse representations of Black British maledom, featured were posters and billboards of four naked Black men (the show's main characters) in a communal shower. The caption provided read 'men just want to be boys', reinforcing African-Caribbean males as child-like and as sex objects, and thereby trivialising their experiences within the programmes' narratives. Husbands remarked how the image harkened to notions of slaves headed toward the auction block. Most disappointing to him was that 'many Blacks at the BBC could have been polled about this marketing scheme' (developed by two White women), and since they weren't it 'provided a deeply disappointing experience'.[38] The marketing failed, says Husband, 'and had I not worked for the BBC at the time, I wouldn't have bothered to watch the new *Babyfather* either'. Husbands remained hopeful about the future of the BBC, thanks to the efforts of Dyke before his departure. He insisted that, five years on, the BBC would be more culturally diverse, and even if 'we got a card-carrying fascist as our new Director General, the cultural changes that occurred under Dyke made the BBC more accessible – and someplace young people aspire to work'. He added,

> Our children's programming was, and is, the most culturally diverse programming worldwide, which is nothing to sniff at. The concern is these young Black people who've grown up here will ask, 'When I was younger I saw programmes that featured people like me. Now that I'm 25, why can't I see myself? Why should I pay a licence fee when you keep doing this?' The recruitment of more, younger writers of colour will help change this.

What remained as a major concern for many was the BBC's inability to alter cultural practices with consideration to images of race, and subsequently involve those of colour in attempts to promote progressive representations. When addressing concerns by the BBF, Dyke listened (it would seem) to their issues, but added, 'in the end the change only comes about if there are enough people in enough parts of the BBC who come from different backgrounds'. The immediate concern here was that the BBF had clearly identified the amount of talented people already within the ranks of the organisation. Furthermore, as suggested by Benjamin, these ethnic minorities were excellent resources for gaining information otherwise overlooked by their White counterparts. Positive results did occur under the directives established by Dyke, yet problematic constructs still remained, as evidenced in recent programming.

Ethnic audiences have gained a degree of economic and social clout, and senior managers in television have acknowledged that the multiethnic audience as a commodity represents millions of pounds per year in spending capital. However, should the BBC continue efforts toward diversification of programming and hiring practices, ethnic minorities within the service must have the freedom and the fluidity to actively effect change, not merely serve as figureheads or tokens.

When faced with racist practices that link essentialism with social structures of domination, exclusion, or discrimination, those Black Britons interviewed within this study acknowledged a need for a subaltern authorship of cultural stories. They defend their interests as media professionals through allying their efforts or banding together while attempting to launch media-related projects. This combination of heterogeneous elements allows for the seizing of opportunities as a means to continue a struggle for ideological survival. These same considerations continue to explode myths of any singular Black identity, celebrate the access of representations by Black cultural workers (e.g., actors and writers), and further contest stereotyping and fetishisation by BBC producers and writers. Tactics such as the formation of television and cinematic production groups, letters and petitions of protest over representations and minor opportunities for Black people in television, theatre troupes that develop Black talent and allow for creative outlets, grassroots community-based organisations that allow for financing of minority media projects, and the like demonstrate how these efforts have indeed been progressive. Furthermore, historically their presence further linked these new citizens to postcolonial Blacks in the West Indies via radio broadcasts and newsreels, further illuminating struggles that characterised historical issues of colonisation and imperialism. An assessment of these African-Caribbeans and their impact upon British broadcasting and BBC policies is thus shown to be a highly important historical concern within studies of British television.

Conclusion

The history of Blacks in the BBC has been well-chronicled by Stephen Bourne, while the frustrations of African-Caribbeans on British television are discussed in a multitude of media, particularly within the work of Jim Pines. Sarita Malik's analyses of Black and Asian representations in British television speak volumes about the discourses surrounding the authorship process in the UK media. It would be impossible to discuss each and every issue directly related to race and BBC, and this was not my intent. This study hopefully allowed the reader an examination of documents discovered during this research study, decisions made within the ranks of the BBC, and their subsequent effects. Other aspects can't be emphasised enough, such as the visual impact of African-Caribbeans on television screens in the 1950s, and the wrangling with racial representations. The BBC until 1956, a mid-point of the highly nationalistic post-war 1950s, did not produce programmes and documentaries that addressed the West Indian as a potential citizen (or threat). As determined by BBC viewer research panels, the images of these hopeful citizens had a very meaningful effect. Though many Britons had yet to acknowledge a colour bar in the UK, there had been criticism levelled at the USA and against South Africa for patterns of insti-tutionalised racism and colour prejudice. After immigration had begun to increase, Britons had to acknowledge that race prejudice was an issue worth examining. The BBC's onus to educate audiences included the task of examining the West Indian presence via television.

There had been Africans that attended Oxford and Cambridge, and African-Americans serving in the war and stationed in the UK, some of whom married British women. However, as West Indians streamed into post-war Britain from Jamaica and the British West Indies on word that employment was plentiful, Britain's African-Caribbean Black population increased to over 50,000 within a five-year period. The reaction of many White Britons was apparent. Within years, these matters would surge to the forefront as racial rioting broke out in the country. Disturbances occurred in the Camden Town area of London's flea market district, sparked off by an argument between a Jamaican and a White British girl, and lasted for two days, four years before the riots of Nottingham and Notting Hill.[39] Subsequently, the means by which BBC television cautiously structured the television persona of the West Indian immigrant/African-Caribbean as a new neighbour helped to maintain directives that would successfully integrate West Indians into popular British culture. The televised images and representations of these new citizens reflected a stridently liberal position as compared to other popular responses by White Britons to the Black presence in the UK. Yet the BBC's desire to please viewers was still being held hostage by the very public they had chosen to educate.

If popular culture disapproved of the exposure of these West Indians, producers politely surrendered to avoid negative publicity or sentiment. Television voiceovers reminded audiences that these immigrants should be 'welcomed as citizens of the Empire sailing to the Mother country with good intent'. Yet, despite an affirmation of liberalism and citizenship, the service linked these citizens to what was termed the 'Jamaican problem', a condition allegedly brought about by the continued influx of immigrants from the Caribbean and the reactions of Whites to their increasing numbers. Yet, in one particular case, racial jokes heard on international radio programming directly instigated a change of policy in the Television Service. The BBC Variety Programmes Policy Guide for Writers and Producers, released in 1948, covered vulgarity, the mention of charitable organisations, the usage of British and English, popular music, special considerations for overseas broadcasting, and miscellaneous points which addressed references to racial groups.[40]

Vacillation over a commitment to dismantle the taboo of race continued. As far as the relationship between White Britons at the BBC and their West Indian counterparts in early broadcasting was concerned, there existed a respect for participants of colour; one that allowed cultural values to flourish within the educational onus that was the corporation's intent. However, there was a need for the autonomous self-expression of these hopeful citizens, allowing African-Caribbean people to self-define their experiences, despite constructs of British nationalism and cultural supremacy through public education and entertainment. The West Indian constantly had to adjust to governmental regulations and social practices, yet the more established these West Indians became within British society, the more White Britons, and the BBC, had to reimagine nationalism. The re-release of Paul Gilroy's *There Ain't No Black in the Union Jack* in 2002 (originally published in 1987), reminds us even now, ten years after its second edition, of how topical the on-going struggle for self-definition is among Black Britons within the fictitious boundaries of Englishness and the national culture, which still includes xenophobic and racist attitudes.

Again, from the very moment that Whiteness engages with these others, the influence of Black Britons upon Britishness becomes inescapable, yet culturally enriching. Surely, the repression of these hopeful voices of citizens could not continue, as demonstrated by the Black Power movement, and criticisms of British television during the 1970s, 1980s, and beyond. There were attempts to address racialism by the BBC that helped to deconstruct assumptions about race, yet frustrated audiences because of the lack of resolution or guidance when it came to the social implications of postcolonial immigration. However, these questions and discussions helped to demonstrate the social issues that continue to envelop Britain and affect the conditions under which the service attempts to address a multiethnic nation. As noted when discussing representations of Blacks and race on the BBC, a report indicated that a major effort for race relations should be to reflect a social education for a positive acceptance of cultural diversity, not seen negatively as differences from present and superior norms, but seen as an enrichment of social and cultural lives, thereby defining a genuinely multiracial society. The report notes that the BBC had not 'risen to this challenge', or risen to it 'only inadequately', prompting their criticisms and suggestions.

When considering the topicality and pertinence of this perspective, the question becomes, when was this report written? Decades ago, or a matter of months? It is the uncertainty of the answer that continues to prompt more questions, and compel us toward meaningful changes in broadcast policies, racial relations, and televisual texts, particularly through a multitude of multiethnic voices.

Notes

1 James Halloran, Arvind Bhatt and Peggy Gray, *Ethnic Minorities and Television: A Study of Use, Reactions and Preferences – A Report for Channel Four*. University of Leicester, Centre for Mass Communication Research, April 1991.

2 Anonymous, 'EastEnders accused of racism', *Daily Mail*, 20 June 1992: 3.

3 Guy Cumberbatch, Samantha Woods et al., *Ethnic Minorities on Television: A Report for the ITC*. Aston University, Birmingham, The Communications Research Group, February 1996.

4 Herman Ouseley, ed., *Race and Television in Britain: Channels of Diversity – Seminar Report*. Commission for Racial Equality, March 1996.

5 Deltha McLeod, 'Taking it as read', *The Voice*, 15 November 1994: 12.

6 Thomas Quinn, 'Meanwhile BBC TV draws up a Blacklist if its own for a little more correctness', *Daily Express*, 14 June 1996: 8.

7 Stephen Bourne, *The Caribbean Presence on the BBC Television and Radio – A Chronology 1948–98*, Report produced for the BBC, June 1999: 12.

8 Jennifer Selway, 'Can you name ten Black British TV stars?', *The Observer*, 21 June 1992: 69.

9 Georgina Henry, 'Licence for first Black TV channel', *The Guardian*, 23 July 1991: 4.

10 Claire Hynes, 'Black TV channel OK to go!', *The Voice*, 23 July 1991: 1.

11 Anonymous, 'Black cable channel is set to be all the rage', *The Voice*, 28 January 1992: 5.

12 Anonymous, 'Beeb slaps its own wrists', *The Voice*, 21 April 1992: 6.

13 Angus Towler, 'Minorities told to organise', *Television Today*, 30 April 1992: 15.

14 *Ibid.*, 16.

15 Tim Dams, 'ABC to target Afro-Caribbeans', *Broadcast*, 7 March 1998: 8.

16 Anonymous, 'Dyke unveils moves to build "One BBC"', BBC news release, 26 June 1999, www.highbeam.com/doc/1G1–61244741.html (accessed on 3 March 2011).

17 Janine Gibson, 'TV failing to reflect multicultural society', *The Guardian*, 8

December 1999, www.guardian.co.uk/media/1999/dec/08/mondaymediasection.broadcasting (accessed on 3 March 2011).

18 *Ibid.*

19 Greg Dyke, 'The BBC: leading cultural change for a rich and diverse UK', Race in Media Awards 2000, Commission for Racial Equality, 7 April 2000, www.pearson-shoyama.ca/CDN/The%20BBC.htm (accessed on 3 March 2011).

20 *Ibid.*

21 *Ibid.*

22 Matt Wells, 'TV chiefs promise broader cultural picture', *The Guardian*, 13 October 2000, www.guardian.co.uk/media/2000/oct/13/raceintheuk?INTCMP =SRCH (accessed on 20 August 2001).

23 *Ibid.*

24 Anonymous, 'Dyke: BBC is "hideously white"', BBC website, 6 January 2001, http://news.bbc.co.uk/1/hi/scotland/1104305.stm (accessed on 3 March 2011).

25 Matt Wells, 'Dyke urged to act after calling BBC "hideously white"', *The Guardian*, 8 January 2001, www.guardian.co.uk/media/2001/jan/08/uknews1 (accessed on 15 September 2001).

26 Jessica Hodgson, 'BBC appoints Salmon to race job', *The Guardian*, 16 January 2001, www.guardian.co.uk/media/2001/jan/16/broadcasting.bbc (accessed on 3 March 2011).

27 Wells, 'Dyke urged to act'.

28 Jan Oliver, 'Re: Black British Forum Summary Points', e-mail correspondence, 20 August 2001.

29 Jan Oliver, 'Re: BBC Black Forum with Greg Dyke & Peter Salmon 6/21/01', e-mail correspondence, 18 August 2001.

30 *Ibid.*

31 Oliver, 20 August 2001.

32 Mitchell eventually left the BBC after reportedly feeling a great degree of frustration over a lack of progress by upper management to diversify. Jan Oliver, personal interview, 8 July 2004.

33 Cyril Husbands, personal interview, 7 January 2004.

34 *Ibid.*

35 Michael Eboda, 'Crouch! That hurts', *New Nation*, 10 September 2003; Ally Ross, 'The Ally Ross verdict', *The Sun*, 10 September 2003.

36 'Windrush', Series Prod. Trevor Phillips, Prod. and Dir. David Upshal of Pepper Productions for BBC Television, 1998.

37 From personal interviews with Cyril Husbands (7 January 2004) and cultural historian Stephen Bourne (2 April 2005), who considered the programme 'disgustingly distasteful'.

38 Husbands, 7 January 2004.

39 Anonymous, 'The color bar', *Time*, 27 December 1954: 1.

40 BBC, *The BBC Variety Programmes Policy Guide for Writers and Producers – 1948*. London: Her Majesty's Stationery Office: 4–15.

Appendix

BBC abbreviated titles – staff lists 1951

AAAD	Administrative Assistant, Administration Departments
AAChildren's Hour	Administrative Assistant, Children's Hour
AACPOps	Administrative Assistant, Central Programme Operations
AADrama	Administrative Assistant, Drama
AAF	Administrative Assistant, Finance
AAGram.	Administrative Assistant, Gramophone
AAOEur.S	Assistant Administrative Officer, European Services
AAOOS	Assistant Administrative Officer, Overseas Services
AApp.O	Assistant Appointments Officer
AAPublicity	Administrative Assistant, Publicity
AARB	Administrative Assistant, Religious Broadcasting
AASchool Broadcasting	Administrative Assistant, School Broadcasting
AAVariety	Administrative Assistant, Variety
ACAF	Assistant Chief Accountant, Finance
ACAS	Assistant Chief Accountant, Services
ACE	Assistant Chief Engineer
ACM	Assistant Circulation Manager
ACMExport	Assistant Circulation Manager, Export
ACOES	Assistant Controller, Overseas English Services
ACOS	Assistant Controller, Overseas Service
ACT	Assistant Controller, Talks
ADOS	Assistant Director Outside Broadcasts
ADT	Assistant Director of Talks
ADXB	Assistant to the Director of External Broadcasting
AEEO	Assistant Engineering Establishment Officer
AEOEnt.	Assistant Establishment Officer, Entertainment

Af.PO	Afrikaans Programme Organiser
AHAD	Assistant Head of Advertisement Department
AHAR	Assistant Head of Audience Research
AHCEO	Assistant Head of Central Establishment Office
AHCEur.S	Assistant Head of Central European Service
AHCH	Assistant Head of Children's Hour
AHCop.	Assistant Head of Copyright
AHCPOpsGen.	Assistant Head of Central Programme Operations, General
AHCPOpsRec.	Assistant Head of Central Programme Operations, Recording
AHCS	Assistant Head of Colonial Service
AHD	Assistant Head of Drama
AHDD	Assistant Head of Designs Department
AHEastS	Assistant Head of Eastern Services
AHEEur.S	Assistant Head of East European Service
AHES	Assistant Head of Engineering Secretariat
AHESG	Assistant Head of Engineering Services Group
AHETD	Assistant Head of Engineering Training Department
AHEur.POps	Assistant Head of European Programme Operations
AHEur.Prod.	Assistant Head of European Productions
AHF	Assistant Head of Features
AHFES	Assistant Head of Far Eastern Service
AHFSND	Assistant Head of Foreign Services News Department
AHGS	Assistant Head of German Service
AHLA	Assistant Head of London Area
AHLAS	Assistant Head of Latin American Service
AHM	Assistant Head of Music
AHMRP	Assistant Head of Midland Regional Programmes
AHMTel.	Assistant Head of Music, Television
AHNIP	Assistant Head of Northern Ireland Programmes
AHNRP	Assistant Head of North Regional Programmes
AHNT	Assistant Head of News Talks
AHOBSound	Assistant Head of Outside Broadcasts, Sound
AHOBTel.	Assistant Head of Outside Broadcasts, Television
AHOPOps	Assistant Head of Overseas Programme Operations

AHPC	Assistant Head of Programme Contracts
AHPH	Assistant Head of Publicity, Home
AHPID	Assistant Head of Planning and Installation Department
AHPO	Assistant Head of Publicity, Overseas
AHPS	Assistant Head of Premises and Stores
AHRB	Assistant Head of Religious Broadcasting
AHRD	Assistant Head of Research Department
AHSB	Assistant Head of School Broadcasting
AHSEur.S	Assistant Head of South European Service
AHSP	Assistant Head of Scottish Programmes
AHSS	Assistant Head of Scandinavian Service
AHTel.A	Assistant Head of Television Administration
AHTel.D	Assistant Head of Television Drama
AHTel.Des.	Assistant Head of Television Design
AHTel.T	Assistant Head of Television Talks
AHTGS	Assistant Head of Talks, General (Sound)
AHVMusic	Assistant Head of Variety, Music
AHVProductions	Assistant Head of Variety, Productions
AHWEur.S	Assistant Head of West European Service
AHWP	Assistant Head of Welsh Programmes
AHWRP	Assistant Head of West Regional Programmes
All.O	Allowances Officer
ALO	Agricultural Liaison Officer
AOEnt.	Administrative and Establishment Officer, Entertainment
AOEur.S	Administrative Officer, European Services
AOMS	Administrative Officer, Monitoring Service
AON	Administrative Officer, News
AOOS	Administrative Officer, Overseas Services
AOT	Administrative and Establishment Officer, Talks
APDM	Assistant Publications Distribution Manager
APO	Arabic Programme Organiser
App.O	Appointments Officer
ARTOC	Assistant Recruitment and Transfer Officer, Clerical
ASAO	Assistant Staff Administration Officer
ASD	African Service Director
ASEE	Assistant Senior Education Engineer
ASEL	Assistant Superintendent Engineer, Lines
ASEO	Assistant Senior Education Officer
ASER	Assistant Superintendent Engineer, Recording

ASES	Assistant Superintendent Engineer, Studios
ASET	Assistant Superintendent Engineer, Transmitters
ASETel.	Assistant Superintendent Engineer, Television
ASPD	Assistant Scottish Programme Director
ATel.PM	Assistant Television Productions Manager
CA	Chief Accountant
Cat.Man.	Catering Manager
CE	Chief Engineer
CEnt.	Controller, Entertainment
CEur.S	Controller, European Services
CF	Controller, Finance
CH	Controller, Home
CHS	Controller, Home Service
Civ.E	Civil Engineer
CLP	Controller, Light Programme
CM	Circulation Manager
CMR	Controller, Midland Region
CN	Controller, News
CNI	Controller, Northern Ireland
CNR	Controller, North Region
COO	Conductor of Opera Orchestra
COS	Controller, Overseas Services
CP	Controller of Programmes
CPP	Controller, Programme Planning (Sound)
CS	Controller, Scotland
CSA	Controller, Staff Administration
CSTA	Controller, Staff Training and Appointments
CT	Controller, Talks
CTel.P	Controller of Television Programmes
CTP	Controller, Third Programme
CW	Controller, Wales
CWR	Controller, West Region
DA	Director of Administration
DCE	Deputy Chief Engineer
DCS	Director of Colonial Service
DDES	Deputy Director Eastern Service
DDOS	Deputy Director of Overseas Services
DEN	Deputy Editor, News
DG	Director-General
DHB	Director of Home Broadcasting
DHV	Deputy Head of Variety
DOS	Director of Overseas Services

DSB	Director of Sounds Broadcasting
DSW	Director of the Spoken Word
DT	Director of Talks
DTel.	Director of Television
DTS	Director of Technical Services
EA	Engineering Accountant
EEO	Engineering Establishment Officer
EN	Editor, News
ENCA	Editor, News and Current Affairs
EOCat.	Establishment Officer, Catering
EOLA	Establishment Officer, London Area
Eur.AAGS	European Administrative Assistant, General Services
Eur.MS	European Music Supervisor
Eur.POpsMan.	European Programme Operations Manager
FEO	Further Education Officer
FO	Features Organiser
FS	Finance Secretary
GMP	General Manager, Publications
GOS	General Office Supervisor
GOSO	General Overseas Service Organiser
HAD	Head of Advertisement Department
HAR	Head of Audience Research
HBD	Head of Building Department
HBFEBS	Head of British Far Eastern Broadcasting Service
HCat.	Head of Catering
HCEO	Head of Central Establishment Office
HCEur.S	Head of Central European Service
HCH	Head of Children's Hour
HCPOps	Head of Central Programme Operations
HCop.	Head of Copyright
HCS	Head of Colonial Service
HD	Head of Drama
HDD	Head of Designs Department
HEast.S	Head of Eastern Services
HED	Head of Equipment Department
HEEur.S	Head of East European Service
HEPG	Head of Engineering Projects Group
HES	Head of Engineering Secretariat
HESG	Head of Engineering Services Group
HETD	Head of Engineering Training Department
HEur.POps	Head of European Programme Operations

HEur.Prod.	Head of European Productions
HEur.TED	Head of European Talks and English Department
HF	Head of Features
HFES	Head of Far Eastern Service
HFN	Head of Foreign News
HFSND	Head of Foreign Services News Department
HG	Head of Gramophone
HGS	Head of German Service
HLA	Head of London Area
HLAS	Head of Latin American Service
HLEG	Head of Light Entertainment Group (Television)
HM	Head of Music
HMRM	Head of Midland Regional Music
HMRP	Head of Midland Regional Programmes
HMS	Head of Monitoring Service
HNIP	Head of Northern Ireland Programmes
HNO	Head of News Output
HNRM	Head of North Regional Music
HNRP	Head of North Regional Programmes
HNT	Head of News Talks
HOB	Head of Outside Broadcasts
HOEID	Head of Overseas and Engineering Information Department
HOM	Head of Overseas Music
HOPOps	Head of Overseas Programme Operations
HOPS	Head of Overseas Programme Services
HOSA	Head of Overseas Services Administration
HP	Head of Publicity
HPC	Head of Programme Contracts
HPCS	Head of Programme Correspondence Section
HPID	Head of Planning and Installation Department
HPS	Head of Premises and Stores
HRB	Head of Religious Broadcasting
HRD	Head of Research Department
HS	Head of Secretariat
HSB	Head of School Broadcasting
HSEur.S	Head of South European Service
HSM	Head of Scottish Music
HSP	Head of Scottish Programmes
HSS	Head of Scandinavian Service

HSSB	Head of Scottish School Broadcasting
HST	Head of Staff Training
HSTS	Head of Secretarial Training School
HSupt	House Superintendent
HTCA	Head of Talks and Current Affairs
HTel.A	Head of Television, Administration
HTel.CP	Head of Television, Children's Programmes
HTel.Des.	Head of Television, Design
HTel.Doc.	Head of Television, Documentaries
HTel.F	Head of Television, Films
HTel.LE	Head of Television, Light Entertainment
HTel.T	Head of Television, Talks
HTS	Head of Transcription Service
HV	Head of Variety
HWEur.S	Head of West European Service
HWM	Head of Welsh Music
HWP	Head of Welsh Programmes
HWRM	Head of West Regional Music
HWRP	Head of West Regional Programmes
IA	Internal Auditor
Ins.Man.	Insurance Manager
IPO	Indian Programme Organiser
LAM	London Accommodation Manager
LOSM	London Office Services Manager
MER	Middle East Representative
MPO	Music Programme Organiser
MREx.	Midland Regional Executive
NAR	North American Representative
NASO	North American Service Organiser
News IO	News Information Officer
NIEx.	Northern Ireland Executive
NREx.	North Regional Executive
OBMan.	Outside Broadcasts Manager
OEIDM	Overseas and Engineering Information Department Manager
OLO	Overseas Liaison Officer
OPOpsMan.	Overseas Programme Operations Manager
OPP	Overseas Programme Planner
ORBO	Overseas Religious Broadcasting Organiser
OTM	Overseas Talks Manager
PDM	Publications Distribution Manager
PM	Production Manager

PPO	Pakistani Programme Organiser
Prog.Acct	Programme Accountant
PSASO	Pacific and South African Service Organiser
PubsEx.	Publications Executive
R & AA	Regions and Areas Accountant
Res.O	Resettlement Officer
RSEM	Regional Studio Engineer, Midland
RSEN	Regional Studio Engineer, North
RSENI	Regional Studio Engineer, Northern Ireland
RSES	Regional Studio Engineer, Scotland
RSEW	Regional Studio Engineer, West
RSEWales	Regional Studio Engineer, Wales
RTOC	Recruitment and Transfer Officer, Clerical
RTOHS	Recruitment and Transfer Officer, House Staff
SA	Salaries Accountant
SAAMusic	Senior Administrative Assistant, Music
SAAOS	Senior Administrative Assistant, Overseas Services
SAO	Staff Administration Officer
SATel.Fin.	Senior Assistant, Television Finance
SBM	School Broadcasting Manager
SCRE	Senior Control Room Engineer
SEAMS	Senior Establishment Assistant, Monitoring Service
SEE	Senior Education Engineer
SEL	Superintendent Engineer, Lines
SEO	Senior Education Officer
SER	Superintendent Engineer, Recording
SES	Superintendent Engineer, Studios
SET	Superintendent Engineer, Transmitters
SETel.	Superintendent Engineer, Television
SEx.	Scottish Executive
SOM	Studio Operations Manager
SSA	Senior Assistant Accountant/Southern Area Director
SSESound	Senior Superintendent Engineer, Sound
SSETel.	Senior Superintendent Engineer, Television
Tel.LO	Television Liaison Officer
Tel.PM	Television Productions Manager
Tel.PO	Television Programme Organiser
Tel.SPO	Television Special Projects Officer
TDM	Transcription Distribution Manager

TM   Traffic Manager
TO   Transcription Organiser
TPM   Transcription Production Manager
WEx.   Welsh Executive
WREx.   West Regional Executive

Selected bibliography

Allen, Theodore. *The Invention of the White Race: Volume One – Racial Oppression and Social Control.* London: Verso, 1994.

Amin, Samir. *Eurocentrism.* New York: Monthly Review Press, 1989.

Anderson, Benedict. *Imagined Communities: Reflections on the Origin and Spread of Nationalism.* London: Verso, 1983.

Arthur, John and Amy Shapiro. *Color, Class, Identity: The New Politics of Race.* Boulder, CO: Harper Collins, 1996.

Ashcroft, Bill, Gareth Griffiths, and Helen Tiffin. *Key Concepts in Post-Colonial Studies.* London: Routledge, 1998.

Athias, Floya and Nira Yuval-Davis. *Racialized Boundaries: Race, Nation, Gender, Colour, Class and the Anti-Racist Struggle.* London: Routledge, 1992.

Balibar, Etienne and Immanuel Wallerstein. *Race, Nation and Class.* London: Verso, 1993.

Ballantyne, James, ed. *Researcher's Guide to British Newsreels.* London: BUFVC, 1983.

Banton, Michael. *White and Coloured: The Behaviour of British People towards Coloured Immigrants.* Brunswick, NJ: Rutgers University Press, 1960.

Baucom, Ian. *Out of Place: Englishness, Empire and Locations of Identity.* Princeton, NJ: Princeton University Press, 1999.

Belson, William A. *The Impact of Television: Methods and Findings in Program Research.* London: Crosby Lockwood and Son, 1967.

Benson, Susan. *Ambiguous Ethnicity: Interracial Families in London.* Cambridge: Cambridge University Press, 1981.

Bernardi, Daniel, ed. *The Birth of Whiteness: Race and the Emergence of the US Cinema.* New Brunswick, NJ: Rutgers University Press, 1996.

Bhabha, Homi. *The Location of Culture.* London: Routledge, 1994.

Blackstone, Tessa, Bhikhu Parekh, and Peter Sanders, eds. *Race Relations in Britain: A Developing Agenda.* London: Routledge, 1998.

Bogle, Donald. *Toms, Coons, Mulattoes, Mammies and Bucks: An Interpretive*

History of Blacks in American Films. New York: Continuum, 1989.

Born, Georgina. *Uncertain Vision: Birt, Dyke and the Reinvention of the BBC.* London: Vintage, 2005.

Bourne, Stephen. *Black in the British Frame: Black People in British Film and Television 1896–1996.* London: Cassell, 1998.

Bourne, Stephen. *Elisabeth Welch: Soft Lights and Sweet Music.* Lanham, MD: Scarecrow, 2005.

Boyle, Andrew. *Only the Wind Will Listen: Reith of the BBC.* London: Hutchinson and Company, 1972.

Braithwaite, Lloyd. *Colonial West Indian Students in Britain.* Mona: University of the West Indies Press, 2001.

Brandt, George W., ed. *British Television Drama in the 1980s.* Cambridge: Cambridge University Press, 1993.

Briggs, Asa. *The History of Broadcasting in the United Kingdom, Volume 4: Sound and Vision.* Oxford: Oxford University Press, 1979.

Briggs, Asa. *The History of Broadcasting in the United Kingdom, Volume 5: Competition.* Oxford: Oxford University Press, 1995.

British Broadcasting Corporation. *The BBC Variety Programmes Policy Guide for Writers and Producers – 1948.* London: Her Majesty's Stationery Office, 1947.

British Broadcasting Corporation. *Colour in Britain.* London: British Broadcasting Corporation, 1965.

British Broadcasting Corporation. *Annual Reports and Accounts for 1968–69.* London: Her Majesty's Stationery Office, 1969.

British Broadcasting Corporation. 'Minister of posts and telecommunications', *Annual Report and the Accounts of the British Broadcasting Corporation, 1968–71.* London: HMSO, 1969.

British Broadcasting Corporation. *Annual Reports and Accounts for the Year 1970–71.* London: Her Majesty's Stationery Office, 1971.

British Caribbean Service. *Going to Britain?* London: British Broadcasting Corporation, 1957.

Brown, Maggie. *A Licence to be Different: The Story of Channel 4.* London: British Film Institute, 2007.

Bryon, Margaret. *Post-War Caribbean Migration to Britain: The Unfinished Cycle.* Aldershot: Avebury, 1994.

Carpenter, Humphrey. *The Envy of the World: Fifty Years of the BBC Third Programme and Radio Three.* London: Weidenfeld and Nicolson, 1996.

Centre for Contemporary Cultural Studies. *The Empire Strikes Back: Race and Racism in 70s Britain.* London: Hutchinson Publishing, 1982.

Chrisman, Laura. *Postcolonial Contraventions: Cultural Readings of Race, Imperialism, and Transnationalism.* Manchester: Manchester University Press, 2003.

Cooke, Lez. *British Television Drama: A History*. London: British Film Institute, 2003.

Corner, John, ed. *Popular Television in Britain: Studies in Cultural History*. London: British Film Institute, 1991.

Corner, John. *Critical Ideas in Television Studies*. Oxford: Oxford University Press, 1999.

Crisell, Andrew. *An Introductory History of British Broadcasting*. New York: Routledge, 1997.

Crossman, Richard. *The Diaries of a Cabinet Minister: Volume One: Minister of Housing 1964–1966*. London: Hamish Hamilton, 1975.

Curran, James and David Morely, eds. *Media and Cultural Theory*. New York: Routledge, 2006.

Dabydeen, David, John Gilmore, and Cecily Jones, eds. *The Oxford Companion to Black British History*. Oxford: Oxford University Press, 2007.

Daniels, Therese and Jane Gerson, eds. *The Colour Black*. London: British Film Institute, 1989.

Davidson, Robert Barry. *Black British: Immigrants to England*. London: Oxford University Press, 1966.

Dent, Gina. *Black Popular Culture*. Seattle, WA: Bay Press, 1992.

Donnell, Alison, ed. *Companion to Contemporary Black British Culture*. London: Routledge, 2002.

Dorte, P.H. 'The BBC television newsreel', *Yesterday's News: The British Cinema Newsreel Reader*. London: BUFVC, 2002.

Drucker, Henry et al., eds. *Developments in British Politics 2*. New York: St Martin's Press, 1986.

Fiske, John. *Power Plays, Power Works*. London: Verso, 1993.

Fiske, John. *Media Matters*. Minneapolis: University of Minnesota Press, 1994.

Foucault, Michel. *The Archaeology of Knowledge and the Discourse on Language*. New York: Pantheon, 1972.

Fox, Richard, ed. *Recapturing Anthology: Working in the Present*. Santa Fe, CA: School of American Research Press, 1991.

Franklin, Bob, ed. *British Television Policy: A Reader*. London: Routledge, 2001.

Freedman, Des. *Television Policies of the Labour Party: 1951–2001*. London: Frank Cass, 2003.

Friedman, Lester D. *Fires Were Started: British Cinema and Thatcherism*. London: Wallflower Press, 1993.

Fryer, Peter. *Staying Power: The History of Black People in Britain*. London: Pluto, 1984.

Geraghty, Christine and David Lusted, ed. *The Television Studies Book*.

London: Arnold, 1998.

Giddens, Anthony, ed. *Human Societies: An Introductory Reader in Sociology.* Cambridge: Polity, 1992.

Gillespie, Marie. *Television, Ethnicity and Cultural Change.* London: Routledge, 1995.

Gilroy, Paul. *The Black Atlantic: Modernity and Double Consciousness.* Cambridge, MA: Harvard University Press, 1993.

Goldie, Grace Wyndham. *Facing the Nation: Television and Politics, 1936–1976.* London: Bodley Head, 1977.

Goodwin, Peter. *Television under the Tories: Broadcasting Policy 1979–1997.* London: British Film Institute, 1998.

Goulbourne, Harry. *Race Relations in Britain Since 1945.* Basingstoke: Macmillan, 1998.

Goulbourne, Harry. *Caribbean Transnational Experience.* London: Pluto Press, 2002.

Greene, Sir Hugh. *The Third Floor Front: A View of Broadcasting in the Sixties.* London: The Bodley Head, 1969.

Gripsrud, Jostein, ed. *Television and Common Knowledge.* London: Routledge, 1999.

Hall, Stuart. 'The whites of their eyes: racist ideologies and the media', *The Media Reader.* London: British Film Institute, 1990.

Hall, Stuart. *Cultural Dialogues in Cultural Studies.* London: Routledge, 1996.

Hall, Stuart and Paul De Gay. *A Question of Cultural Identity.* London: Sage, 1996.

Halloran, James, ed. *The Effects of Television.* London: Panther Modern Society, 1970.

Hartmann, Paul and Charles Husband. *Racism and the Mass Media: A Study of the Role of the Mass Media in the Formation of White Beliefs and Attitudes in Britain.* London: Davis-Poynter, 1974.

Hawley, John C. and Emmanuel S. Nelson, eds. *Encyclopedia of Postcolonial Studies.* Westport, CT: Greenwood Press, 2001.

Hilmes, Michele. *The Television History Book.* London: British Film Institute, 2003.

Hiro, Dilip. *Black British, White British.* London: Eyre and Spottiswoode, 1971.

Hobson, Dorothy. *Channel 4: The Early Years and the Jeremy Issacs Legacy.* London: I.B. Tauris, 2008.

Holland, Patricia. *The Television Handbook.* London: Routledge, 2000.

Holmes, Colin, ed. *Immigrants and Minorities in British Society.* London: George Allen and Unwin, 1978.

Holmes, Su. *Entertaining Television: The BBC and Popular Television Culture in the 1950s*. Manchester: Manchester University Press, 2008.

Hood, Stuart, ed. *Behind the Scenes: The Structure of British Television in the Nineties*. London: Lawrence and Wishart, 1994.

Huggan, Graham. *The Postcolonial Exotic: Marketing the Margins*. New York: Routledge, 2001.

Husband, Charles, ed. *'Race' in Britain: Continuity and Change*. London: Hutchinson and Company, 1982.

Jackson, Peter, Philip Crang, and Claire Dwyer, eds. *Transnational Spaces*. New York: Routledge, 2004.

Jacobs, Jason. *The Intimate Screen: Early British Television Drama*. Oxford: Oxford University Press, 2000.

Jarrett-Macauley, Delia. *The Life of Una Marson, 1905–65*. Kingston: Ian Randle, 1998.

Jefferies, Sir Charles. *The Colonial Office*. London: Oxford University Press, 1956.

Jenkins, Clive. *Power behind the Screen: Ownership, Control and Motivation in British Commercial Television*. London: Macgibbon and Kee, 1961.

Jephcott, Pearl. *A Troubled Area: Notes on Notting Hill*. London: Faber and Faber, 1964.

Johnson, Catherine and Rob Turnock, eds. *ITV Cultures: Independent Television over Fifty Years*. Maidenhead: Open University Press, 2005.

Kennedy, Paul and Victor Roudometof, eds. *Communities across Borders: New Immigrants and Transnational Cultures*. London: Routledge, 2002.

Lambert, Stephen. *Channel Four: Television with a Difference?* London: British Film Institute, 1982.

MacCabe, Colin and Olivia Stewart. *The BBC and Public Service Broadcasting*. Manchester: Manchester University Press, 1986.

Madge, Tim. *Beyond the BBC: Broadcasting and the Public in the 1980s*. London: Macmillan, 1989.

Malik, Sarita. *Representing Black Britain: Black and Asian Images on Television*. London: Sage, 2002.

McKerman, Luke, ed. *Yesterday's News: The British Cinema Newsreel Reader*. London: BUFVC, 2002.

Meeks, Brian and Folke Lindahl. *New Caribbean Thought: A Reader*. Kingston: University of the West Indies Press, 2001.

Memmi, Albert. *The Colonizer and the Colonized*. Boston, MA: Beacon Press, 1967.

Morley, David. *Home Territories: Media, Mobility and Identity*. London: Routledge, 2000.

Morley, David and Kevin Robins. *Spaces of Identity: Global Media, Electronic Landscapes and Cultural Boundaries*. London: Routledge, 1995.

Morrison, Majbritt. *Jungle West 11*. London: Tandem: 1964.

Muggleton, David and Rupert Weinzierl. *The Post-Subcultures Reader*. New York: Berg, 2003.

Mullard, Chris. *Black Britain*. London: George Allen and Unwin, 1973.

Murphy, Patrick D. and Marwan M. Kraidy, eds. *Global Media Studies: Ethnographic Perspectives*. New York: Routledge, 2003.

Obelkevich, James and Peter Catterall, eds. *Understanding Post-war British Society*. London: Routledge, 1994.

Omi, Michael and Howard Winant. *Racial Formation in the United States: From the 1960s to the 1990s*. New York: Routledge, 1994.

Owusu, Kwesi, ed. *Black British Culture and Society*. London: Routledge, 2000.

Panayi, Pankos, ed. *Racial Violence in Britain in the Nineteenth and Twentieth Centuries*. Leicester: Leicester University Press, 1993.

Paul, Kathleen. *Whitewashing Britain: Race and Citizenship in the Post-war Era*. Ithaca, NY: Cornell University Press, 1997.

Paulu, Burton. *British Broadcasting: Radio and Television in the United Kingdom*. Minneapolis: University of Minnesota Press, 1956.

Paulu, Burton. *British Broadcasting in Transition*. Minneapolis: University of Minnesota Press, 1961.

Pearson, David. *Race, Class and Political Activism: A Study of West Indians in Britain*. Farnborough: Gower, 1981.

Phillips, Mike and Trevor Phillips. *Windrush: The Irresistible Rise of Multi-Racial Britain*. London: Harper Collins, 1998.

Pines, Jim, ed. *Black and White in Colour: Black People in British Television since 1936*. London: British Film Institute, 1992.

Pym, John. *Film on Four – 1982/1991: A Survey*. London: British Film Institute, 1992.

Reeves, Frank. *British Racial Discourse: A Study of British Political Discourse about Race and Race-related Matters*. Cambridge: Cambridge University Press, 1983.

Reith, John Charles Walsham. *Broadcast Over Britain*. London: Hodder and Stoughton, 1924.

Reith, John Charles Walsham. *Into the Wind*. London: Hodder and Stoughton, 1949.

Rich, Paul B. *Race and Empire in British Politics*. Cambridge: Cambridge University Press, 1986.

Richmond, Anthony. *Colour Prejudice in Britain: A Study of West Indian Workers in Liverpool*. London: Routledge, 1954.

Roediger, David. *Toward the Abolition of Whiteness*. London: Verso, 1994.

Rose, Eliot Joseph Benn. *Colour and Citizenship: A Report on British Race Relations*. London: Oxford University Press, 1969.

Sampson, Anthony. *The Changing Anatomy of Britain*. New York: Random

House, 1982.

Scannel, Paddy and David Cardiff. *A Social History of British Broadcasting: Volume One 1922–1939 Serving the Nation.* Oxford: Basil Blackwell, 1991.

Schaefer, Richard T. *The Extent and Content of Racial Prejudice in Great Britain.* San Francisco, CA: R and E Research, 1976.

Scott, Peter Graham. *British Television: An Insider's History.* London: McFarland and Company, 2000.

Sendall, Bernard. *Independent Television in Britain: Volume Two: Expansion and Change, 1958–68.* London: Macmillan, 1983.

Silvey, Robert. *Who's Listening? The Story of BBC Audience Research.* London: Ruskin House, 1974.

Smith, Anthony. *British Broadcasting.* Plymouth: David and Charles, 1974.

Smith, Prudence. *Africa in Transition.* London: Max Reinhardt, 1958.

Solomos, John. *Race and Racism in Contemporary Britain.* Basingstoke: Macmillan, 1989.

Spencer, Ian. *British Immigration Policy Since 1939: The Making of Multi-Racial Britain.* London: Routledge, 1997.

Sydney-Smith, Susan. *Beyond Dixon of Dock Green: Early British Police Series.* London: I.B. Tauris, 2002.

Thumim, Janet. *Inventing Television Culture: Men, Women and the Box.* London: Oxford, 2004.

Thurlow, Richard. *Fascism in Britain: A History, 1918–1985.* Oxford: Basil Blackwell, 1987.

Tomlinson, John. *Cultural Imperialism.* Baltimore, MD: Johns Hopkins Press, 1991.

Tracey, Michael. *The Decline and Fall of Public Service Broadcasting.* Oxford: Oxford University Press, 1998.

Tulloch, John. *Television Drama: Agency, Audience, and Myth.* London: Routledge, 1990.

Twitchin, John, ed. *The Black and White Media Show Book.* Stoke-on-Trent: Trentham, 1988.

Vahimagi, Tise. *British Television.* Oxford: Oxford University Press, 1994.

Webster, Wendy. *Imagining Home: Gender, Race and National Identity, 1945–64.* London: University College London Press, 1998.

Webster, Wendy. *Englishness and Empire 1939–1965.* Oxford: Oxford University Press, 2005.

Whitehouse, Mary. *Who Does She Think She Is?* London: New English Library, 1971.

Williams, Raymond. *Culture and Society: 1780–1950.* London: Chatto and Windus, 1958.

Williams, Raymond. *The Sociology of Culture.* Chicago, IL: University of Chicago Press, 1981.

Williams, Raymond. *Television: Technology and Cultural Form*. London: Routledge, 2003.

Young, Robert J.C. *Colonial Desire: Hybridity in Theory, Culture and Race*. London: Routledge, 1995.

Index